ASSAULT ON THE MEDIA

THE NIXON YEARS

William E. Porter

Ann Arbor   The University of Michigan Press

Grateful acknowledgment is made to the following publisher
for permission to reprint copyrighted material:

The New York Times for "Big-Time Pressures, Smalltown Press"
by Robert Boyle, March 24, 1973 Op-Ed. © 1973 by The New York Times
Company. Reprinted by permission.

For Lois

Preface

This book is an account of the wide-ranging efforts of governmental authority, over a period of five and one-half years, to intimidate, harass, regulate, and in other ways damage the news media in their functioning as part of the American political system. It is subtitled "The Nixon Years" because most of these initiatives came directly from the White House during Richard Nixon's administration, and the remainder derived, at least in part, from a spirit generated through those top-level attacks.

The reader should understand, therefore, that this does not purport to be a history of all aspects of the relationship between the Nixon administration and the press. It makes no serious attempt to evaluate the effects of the press response upon either Nixon or the presidency; nor does it deal with attitudes and actions of the administration which most journalists saw as favorable to the media and journalism as a profession. There was little of this at best, but there was, for example, a somewhat surprising, continuing concern for the protection of the individual reporter from the punitive use by judges and congressional committees of subpoenas and contempt judgments.

The full story, tangled and depressing and bizarre as it sometimes is, is in the process of emerging in other books. There will be much more of it. Meanwhile, this is an informal history of one facet of the Nixon-media relationship, the government's offensive.

The history is set out chronologically, with chapters divided roughly according to the years. This makes for a somewhat irregular arrangement. Much goes on during 1971 and 1972, but there is almost no activity after Nixon's public recognition of a Watergate scandal; the final sixteen months can be covered in a few pages. The alternative to chronology, however, was a thematic organization which, it seems to the writer, would inevitably distort the interplay of action in time which is a critical part of the account.

Chapter 7 consists of some discussion, much of it speculative, about possible effects of the offensive upon the media and American political journalism. It must be largely speculative because the most consequential effects will be long range, and our vision is too short for genuinely sound analysis.

Following chapter 7, the Documents of Significance give, as can no amount of retelling, something of the feel of the confrontation and the minds and spirit of the men central to carrying it on. It includes once-confidential White House memoranda, speeches, and excerpts from court decisions.

Acknowledgments

Many persons have provided assistance in collecting and verifying this material. The group includes the following journalists, editors, and other professionals in communications:

Ben Bagdikian
Burton Benjamin
Adam Clymer
Julius Duscha
Timothy Ferris
Philip Foisie
Robert Greene
James McCartney
Andrew Malcolm
Judith Martin
Cleve Matthews
Philip Meyer

R. Dean Mills
Christo Nizamoff
Christopher Porterfield
James Russell
Richard Salant
Jack Smith
Barry Sussman
Robert Thorpe
Sanford Unger
Thomas Winship
Les Whitten

For several years I have conducted a seminar dealing with government and the media in the University of Michigan Department of Journalism. The students in that seminar have contributed much since, like most college teachers, I have used it as a wind tunnel for testing. In addition, I cozened some of them into research projects which directly contributed to historical background or essential detail for this study. I made particular use of the work of Marianne Rzepka and Barbara Eisenstock; substantial contributions also were made by Ken Kerber, Beth Nissen, and Stanley Tickton.

Juanita Galle, Beth Nissen, and Joanne Kaufman were particularly helpful among the research assistants provided by the Department of Journalism; I am grateful to the department and to them.

Old friends and fellow academics Edward R. Barrett, William Rivers, Paul Jess, and John Stevens provided valuable help.

In addition, there are three earlier books to which I owe much, as even a casual reader will discern. Sanford Unger's *The Papers and the Papers* is a fine chronology and analysis of the Pentagon Papers case and much of the account of that episode is taken from it. William Small has been for several years a conscientious and insufficiently recognized student of the inter-action between media and government; his *Political Power and the Press* is a carefully documented history. Unger was formerly a member of the staff of the *Washington Post* and Small is a senior vice-president and director of news for CBS. Finally, David Wise's *The Politics of Lying* has been of great help. Wise, a former Washington bureau chief of the *New York Herald-Tribune,* is a stylish and thoughtful journalist who has, in my judgment, provided in several books—particularly his *The Invisible Government,* in addition to *The Politics of Lying*—the best journalism about the current federal establishment.

My wife, Lois, gave careful, detailed help in the editing and encouragement when it was needed most.

All of these people did work which I did not have to do. If I have reported their findings inaccurately, or have come to odd conclusions which their evidence does not justify, the fault is my own.

Contents

ONE

Background for the Nixon Attitude

As I leave you I want you to know—just think how much you're going to be missing. You won't have Nixon to kick around any more, because, ladies and gentlemen, this is my last press conference.

Richard Nixon
November 7, 1962

On the evening of April 30, 1973, Richard Nixon made his first major speech to his constituents about the Watergate affair. In describing his confidence in the strength of American democratic institutions, he said:

> It was the system that brought the facts to light and that will bring those guilty to justice—a system that in this case included a determined grand jury, honest prosecutors, a courageous judge, John Sirica—

He paused, swallowed, and went on:

> and a vigorous free press.

After the speech, he said something even more remarkable. This account is from the *Washington Post* (it would be almost unseemly to get it elsewhere):

While appearing in complete control of himself during the address, Mr. Nixon showed his emotions afterward by walking unexpectedly into the White House press room. Appearing gray and drawn, he said in a low voice:

"We've had our differences in the past, and just continue to give me hell when you think I'm wrong.

"I hope I'm worthy of your trust," he said as he shook hands with newsmen and photographers.[1]

While the action may have been more calculated than it then appeared, it still was a striking moment, a flicker of reconciliation sought, perhaps even a plea for help. It did not signal a real change in attitude, of course; within a few days the president was showing the old mustard again, making bitter remarks about the newspapers to some returned Vietnam veterans. But from the time Richard Nixon acknowledged the existence of the Watergate story, his administration's campaign against the media had to change. There was still enormous power in the United States presidency to affect their operations, but from that point forward the dynamics and the pressure points were different. His gravity that night may have reflected his foresight of the coming months when the credibility of the media would rise, his own credibility would all but disappear, and he would be forced from office.

The key staff officers of the old order were gone, too. Nixon had fired John Dean and accepted the resignations of H. R. Haldeman and John Ehrlichman that same day. As operational head of almost everything in the White House, Haldeman had inevitably been central to activities directed against the media, passing judgment on the proposals of inventive underlings such as Charles Colson and Jeb Stuart Magruder, both of whom by this time had already departed. And, although the president could hardly have known it in April, there would be no more of those alliterative castigations from the most popular media baiter of them all, the vice-president. Although the offensive might go on, it would never be the same.

Richard Nixon was not the first president to have trouble with the media; he was only the latest in an almost unbroken line that began with George Washington, who in his day grew choleric and cursed that rascal Philip Freneau and his *National Gazette.* There are certain elements in the relationships between the presidency and the media which inevitably cause tension and, sooner or later, personal bitterness. Almost every president of the United States has fought back in his own way. The administration of Richard Nixon differed in the speed with which it moved to attack the media at many levels and in the intensity and scope of its well-orchestrated activities. From the Nixon White House there emanated, for the first time, attacks intended to damage the credibility not of a single journalist but of whole classes of them; to intimidate publishers and broadcast ownerships; and, almost unthinkably, to establish in American jurisprudence the legality of censorship. Small government, and particularly the lower courts, hastened to follow the model at the top.

As a result, in the years since Richard Nixon became president both the mass media and the cause of free expression in this country have been damaged as in no other stretch of time. The damages may well be irreversible, although most of those in control of the media seem, through inattention or misperception, unconcerned.

There is a somewhat classic pattern of falling-out between modern presidents of the United States and the press. The new president comes into the job with a feeling that he can manage press relationships more effectively than his predecessor, who somehow managed to let things curdle. His past political experience has given him a relatively tough hide, his perspectives are rational (there's nothing personal in what the journalist writes, he's just doing his job), and some of his best friends are reporters. He appoints as his press secretary a former political reporter who probably has been on his personal staff for the last few years, makes a few friendly inviting noises toward the media, and then settles down to take hold of the really big problems. Media relationships are low on his list of concerns.

Things remain that way during the honeymoon period

allotted to the new man by all those institutions which later will bedevil him in one way or another—the Congress, the press, the permanent bureaucracy, public opinion. Then, after a few months, or sometimes only weeks, things begin to change.

That which is most changed is the new president himself. He has been seized, finally, by the position which he occupies; he has new perspectives and new sensitivities. The luxury of foreclosing the long-range view and focusing his attention on the linear, one thing at a time, is gone. However real his humility, he cannot avoid constantly seeing himself in history. There has been no such thing as a president of the United States who was thick-skinned about what the papers or the networks were saying about him; some simply have been better at not reading, not listening, and not watching.

In most cases his first quarrels with the media develop at a high level, because they center on two factors about which political leaders and journalists are constantly at war: salience and timing. The political leader feels he must handle the issues which seem to him most important, and handle them when he's ready to do so. The journalist insists upon his right to decide on relative importance and, once he's decided that the matter is important, to make the most of it immediately.

The president then feels himself somewhat tied to an agenda which someone else has set. He resents this profoundly, because these things are the substance of his presidency. His frustrations are intensified because his intentions are the best. When public opinion begins to swing away from him, he consoles himself that the people would agree with his position if they only understood the issue, whatever the issue, as he does, but the media undo his attempts to explain. Although it's like biting on an aching tooth, he pays more and more attention to what the media are saying so that he can more precisely circumvent them when he goes directly to the people in his speeches and formal statements. The more closely he looks, the more he becomes convinced that some of this is personal; he finds pettiness that can only grow out of a personal dislike for him or his family. He begins to reply in kind, exacting petty revenge in his own way. By the time his presidency ends, even his best relationships with the media are like those in a forced marriage grown old, held together by an accommodation to inescapable circumstances in which interaction consists largely of half-hearted bickering.

That, with variations, is the usual scenario. Herbert Hoover, darling of the press as the feeder of the Belgians and secretary of commerce, entered office with promising new schemes for better press relations. Within months he was convinced that he was being saddled with blame for economic collapse which he did not merit, was resentful of constant attempts to rupture his privacy, and ended his tenure by converting the few press conferences he still held to contemptuous monologues after which he answered no questions. Franklin Roosevelt, although treated with remarkable gentleness in personal terms, soon came to feel that the media were trying to defeat his plans for economic recovery and, later, his steering of foreign policy toward closer ties with England and France. He talked frequently with newsmen, but always under a comprehensive set of rules which reduced every session to what is now called "deep background." He expressed his personal feelings with public tongue-lashings and awarded an Iron Cross to a reporter he particularly detested. Harry Truman tried to dismiss the obviously political charges of an ignorant senator from Wisconsin as a "red herring" and then watched with growing anger as the media and the senator made Communist hunting a dominant story for years. This anger was intensified by what he felt was abuse of his family. His resentment of questioning led him into a gaffe at a press conference which profoundly affected international relations, and thus ironically became perhaps the most important thing ever said at a presidential press conference.* He wrote letters of complaint and was said to

---

*On December 3, 1950, Chinese troops had been rolling across the Yalu River for several days; Truman was asked if the use of atomic weapons, then a United States monopoly, was under consideration. His answer, although probably an attempt to waffle, was generally interpreted as confirmation that it was.

swear a great deal. He told a new president how to handle
"those damned columnists and editorial writers; you meet 'em,
cuss 'em and give 'em hell, and you'll win in 1964."[2] The most
significant thing about that advice is the unstated assumption
that it is the journalists' right to do what they do; coping with
the problems they create is like coping with flood waters that
inundate the basement; one sweeps up, fights back, gets ready
for the next round.

And one remembers John Kennedy, pathetically mouse-
trapped by the inherited folly of the Bay of Pigs. He pleaded
with newspaper executives to redefine news in such a way that
the long-range purposes of the United States in foreign policy
would overpower the traditional values of detachment and
objectivity. When they failed to do so, he summoned the
publisher of the *New York Times* to request that he fire a
reporter named David Halberstam who was reporting the wrong
things about the Vietnam war: the publisher refused. Kennedy's
problem with the media was classic; he wanted them to ignore
the war in Southeast Asia and concentrate on those matters
which made his administration look good. When they failed to
follow his lead, he resorted to such petty devices as ordering all
White House subscriptions to the *New York Herald Tribune*
cancelled.

Lyndon Johnson came to the presidency remembering the
cozy informality of dealings between the press and his idol,
Franklin Roosevelt. He began his tenure with attempts to recre-
ate it, popping down the hall to the press room for spontaneous
talks with whomever seemed to be around (which brought a
glut of traffic to those premises, normally occupied only by a
skeleton force of wire service types who hold the fort against
the unexpected), leading brisk walks around the White House
grounds, and generally making energetic use of the combination
of charm and personal muscle which by this time he knew he
possessed to a remarkable degree. None of these worked. Increasingly, the media refused to handle the open wound of
Vietnam as if it were a 1940s crusade for universal freedom.
Reporters he considered good old boys set the dog lovers of the
country in full cry by solemnly making some Texas folklore

about beagles and long ears into cruelty to animals. Others whom he considered bound by the good manners of all guests published gaudy accounts of his driving across the Texas plains at something approaching Indianapolis speeds. Most hurtful to him of all, one suspects, the media somehow converted his daughters and his strong, brilliant wife into shopworn jokes. He expressed his anger through his favorite communication device, the personal phone call, jawboning Reston and Clifton Daniel and Ben Bradlee and changing one of the most capable people ever to serve in the White House, Bill Moyers, into a hector of the second level of journalists.

Only Eisenhower among modern presidents escaped this pattern. His relations with the media were detached and coolly rigid throughout his eight years. Several factors contributed to this. The journalists of the time saw him as the American hero of the era and treated him gently. The closest thing to a personal attack was the circulation from hand to hand of typed copies of "If Eisenhower had given the Gettysburg Address," a stinging parody of his bumbling syntax. He was, in all probability, less attentive to the media than any other modern president. Outside of an occasional glance at the *New York Herald Tribune,* he did not read newspapers, and the books around the family quarters and Air Force One were said to be largely western novels. His place in history he had every reason to assume already was secure, which made him less sensitive. He had a first-rate press secretary in James Hagerty to whom he gave both freedom and authority to speak in his behalf. And the times, of course, were placid.

Eisenhower's media relations were not in the standard pattern of the presidency. Neither were Richard Nixon's, although the similarity ends there.

Of Nixon's media relations Arthur Krock, who for years headed the Washington bureau of the *New York Times,* once said, "It's a congenital battle. They were born to fight each other like some warring tribes in Africa."

Richard Nixon himself was very open in his dislike and distrust of journalists, and marked some places in his career which helped produce those attitudes. His first campaign was for a seat in the House of Representatives held by Jerry Voorhis, a liberal Democrat, in 1946. Ralph de Toledano, an early biographer, says that defeating Voorhis immediately made the new representative suspect in the eyes of the *New York Times* and the *Washington Post,* but an inspection of those papers for that period shows little evidence of it.[3] The *Post* simply included his name in a long list of winners; perhaps the *Times* offended him by referring to him as "Richard W. Nixon,"* but that seems improbable. He did not come to either publication's careful attention until the time of the Mundt-Nixon bill.

Both papers were against that legislation, on what now seems the timid line that, while the nation needed to be protected against Communist subversion, this legislation would only make Communists martyrs, drive them underground, and conceivably threaten the right of innocents. Nixon barely appeared in the *Times*'s accounts, but a *Post* editorial singled him out for what they called a "Freudian slip" during the debate in which he appeared unconcerned about civil rights. It was the first criticial observation made by the newspaper which was to become his most relentless and effective pursuer as well as the target of his most bitter private remarks.

In the fall of the same year, 1948, the Chambers-Hiss case began developing. With it Nixon became a major figure in the United States press for the first time. It also, judging by his own testimony, was the point at which his distrust and dislike for at least some elements of the press began. He was intensely aware of "the terrible attacks from the press, nasty cartoons, editorials. . . ."[4]

The idea that cartoons particularly affected him is made especially persuasive by the fact that the written coverage in the *Post* and *Times,* at least, was well balanced—far more so, one suspects, than the rankling memory indicated. December, 1948,

---

*Another New York institution was to have trouble with the middle initial under much more conspicuous circumstances. During the Republican convention of 1968, in his speech seconding Nixon's nomination, Nelson Rockefeller referred to "the next President of the United States, Richard E. Nixon."

was the month that Hiss brought suit against Chambers, the "pumpkin papers" were revealed, Truman made his spectacularly inept reference to the whole investigation as a "red herring," and Hiss was indicted for perjury by a New York grand jury. A rough content analysis of the two papers for that month indicates that the *Washington Post* gave Nixon far more favorable than unfavorable coverage (the ratio was about three to one); the great bulk of the coverage was neutral. The *Times* gave the young representative a good deal less coverage, with about the same kind of balance.[5]

Interestingly, a highly favorable piece about Nixon appeared in the *Post* the day after the "pumpkin papers" story broke. The regular "People in the News" feature for that day was headed:

NIXON CONSIDERED RESTRAINING INFLUENCE
ON OFTEN-SPECTACULAR HOUSE COMMITTEE

The accompanying photograph was captioned "Truth-seeker," and some of the text read:

> ... the tall, dark, and—yes—handsome freshman congressman who has been pressuring the House Un-American Activities committee to search out the truth in the Chambers-Hiss affair. ... He was unquestionably one of the outstanding first-termers in the Eightieth Congress.

And the piece closed on the edge of bathos:

> In February of '46, Representative Nixon broke his left arm and severely injured the other when he slipped on the ice while carrying 'Tricia in his arms. The child was unhurt.[6]

Not all the coverage was favorable. Both the *Post* and the *Times,* and particularly the former, were sometimes highly critical of the House committee, much more so than of any specific member. Herblock, the *Post*'s brilliant cartoonist, hit the committee frequently and hard. Editorials in both papers occasionally had an overtone which might have struck committee members as personally insulting, saying in effect that the committee's work was important (it must be remembered that the central issue, as they defined it at the time, was the ferreting out of Soviet spies, and no newspaper was likely to be against that with the Cold War at its worst), but that its methods were reprehensible and some of its members clumsy clowns. It must have been a recollection of the implication of headline-hunting incompetents that Nixon remembered when he wrote, several years later, "The *Post* had been consistently critical of me since the days of the Hiss case. . . ."[7] Perhaps he even had lodged somewhere in the back of his mind the fact that the *Post* referred in a headline on December 28, 1948, to "Mundt and Dixon." The evidence of any particular prejudice or calculated unfair treatment is not to be found in either paper. The explanation for this was probably not so much the attempt to be fair as the functional decision that Nixon was not yet big news.

This would seem to be the explanation, too, for the fact that Herblock did not once caricature him personally during the period. He drew the committee as figures with pumpkin heads and as Keystone cops shooting up the town. The devastating likeness was to come later, after Nixon's nomination as vice-president and at the time of the Checkers episode. Meanwhile, Nixon had won a Senate seat against Helen Gahagan Douglas in a campaign still remembered for its viciousness. Because it was essentially a California story, Eastern papers paid little attention to it, although both the *Times* and the *Post* carried an occasional brief feature. The *Post*'s coverage was pro-Douglas, but the most vigorous attacks against Nixon came not from its own newsroom but from Marquis Childs and Drew Pearson, syndicated columnists whose work the *Post* also carried. In any event, what Eastern papers said was of little moment, and Nixon had from the beginning the enthusiastic support of the Chandler family's *Los Angeles Times* and, by election time, that of the Hearst *Los Angeles Evening Herald and Express*. He won without difficulty.

By the time of his nomination as vice-presidential candidate in 1952, however, the *Post*'s direction was clearly anti-Nixon. It grumbled editorially:

> Inevitably the choice of Senator Richard M. Nixon as the Republican nominee for Vice President will be regarded with less enthusiasm than the selection of General Eisenhower himself.[8]

It nevertheless brought itself to endorse the ticket. The *New York Times* had endorsed it immediately, although its editorial writer pointed out that "we have disagreed with Mr. Nixon on certain issues."

For a little more than two months both papers cheered on the General while saying little about his running mate. Then in mid-September the story which is filed in the tribal memory under the word "Checkers" broke. The charge was that Nixon had received private gifts to take care of personal expenses without reporting them. The story appeared first in the *New York Post,* but according to the vice-presidential candidate, did not worry him much:

> "The [New York] *Post* was and still is the most partisan Democratic paper in the country. It had done an unusually neat smear job, but I did not expect anything to come of it.[9]

Something did. On September 19 the *Washington Post,* the *New York Times,* and the *New York Herald Tribune* all had the story (none of them credited the *New York Post*). The *Herald Tribune* suggested that Nixon offer his resignation to Eisenhower. It was an ominous portent, because the *Herald Tribune* was widely known as the paper closest to the "Eisenhower people," and Nixon frankly discussed in *Six Crises*—a more open and sensitive book than compulsive nonreaders might imagine—the agony it caused him and the cruelty with which he was left dangling.[10]

The *Washington Post* went even further than the *Herald*

Tribune and called for Nixon's immediate withdrawal from the ticket, although in what now seem curiously gentle terms:

> We do not doubt that Senator Nixon was free of any improper motives or immoral intentions in accepting $16,000 in private gifts and failing to report the sums in his tax returns. But this has nothing to do with the real issues involved. The Senator is, we believe, a man of basic decency with laudable aspirations for public service. But his transgression is a major one, however unconscious of this he may have been, and he has no decent course except to remove himself from the Republican ticket.[11]

Both political rhetoric and the sums of money involved in political scandals have been greatly inflated, obviously, since 1952.

The *New York Times* reported the *Washington Post*'s editorial, but in its own made a much more innocuous recommendation to the effect that the Republican leadership make up its mind immediately whether or not to ditch the man.

By the time of the "Checkers" speech on September 23, the situation was complicated by the fact that Adlai Stevenson, the Democratic candidate for president, had been accused (with good reason, apparently) of having a similar fund. The Stevenson element in the story generally has been neglected, but in the newspaper coverage at the time the two cases stood almost side by side.

Meanwhile, preparing to stake everything on a single public appearance, Nixon had developed a fundamental concept of media use which was to run throughout his career. It combined a commonsense insight into how mass communication works with a personal psychological set.

The Republican command had put him into a cruelly demanding situation: he had to bring in proof, in effect, that he would not harm the cause.

> My only hope to win rested with millions of people I would never meet, sitting in groups of two or three or four

in their living rooms, watching and listening to me on television. I determined as the plane took me to Los Angeles that I must do nothing which might reduce the size of that audience. And so I made up my mind that until after this broadcast, my only release to the press would be for the purpose of building up the audience which would be tuning in. Under no circumstances, therefore, could I tell the press in advance what I was going to say or what my decision would be.[12]

One of the standing convictions of any political leader is that the great mass of people would support him on any given issue if they only understood him; if he could only reach them directly, bring the force of his personality and his persuasiveness to bear, he could lead in the finest sense of the word. The chief barriers to that clear transmission from leader to willing follower are the journalists who write down and encapsulate and inevitably interpret inaccurately his ideas. A primary objective, therefore, becomes the finding of a way to bypass these interpreters. With this in mind, Woodrow Wilson had revived the then-dormant device of presenting the State of the Union Address in person to a joint session of the Congress. Although the summary accounts might be, in his judgment, distorted, he knew that a substantial part of what he had to say would be transmitted directly through straight news stories or publications of the text. Many years later, Lyndon Johnson felt the same thing, and sent out Bill Moyers to conduct a remarkable press conference in which the message was in effect that the president intended in the future to bypass paper-and-pencil reporters and use television much more because he could, in this way, reach the people directly. Long before he became president, Richard Nixon realized that television was the ultimate device for that kind of appeal, and he was to use it constantly.

An important distinction must be made here between television journalists and television as a medium of transmission. The very qualities of television make it an ultimately useful device to a political leader. The fact that it reaches almost everybody, in simple and direct terms, makes him especially sensitive to the unimpeded transmission of what he wishes to convey, not only his message but his personality, his sincerity, his devotion to the cause. A Dan Rather or a Marvin Kalb, in other words, is more dangerous than an Adam Clymer (of the *Baltimore Sun*) or James McCartney (of Knight Newspapers, Inc.). Appearing immediately after a presidential appearance on the same channel, the television analyst can color the message for the mass of people far more than any newspaper reporter. It was no accident that the first major, formally mounted blast of the Nixon administration against the media should have been, as we shall see, against television commentators and "instant analysis."

Something else appeared during the Checkers period of Richard Nixon's career which affected greatly his attitude toward the papers, and particularly toward the *Washington Post*. On September 20, 1952, there appeared on the editorial page of the *Post* a devastating Herblock caricature of Nixon. It was one of his most powerful cartoons, done with an artistry that would be commanding even if the viewer had never heard of the man or the scandal. The overline was "Death of a Salesman." The central figure was one which was very familiar to newspaper readers at the time: a bent, stocky shape, head down, a heavy bag in each hand, silhouetted against the horizon. The bag in the left hand overflowed with untidy personal oddments; the valise in the right was labelled "$16,000." The figure was that of Lee J. Cobb, at that time playing the role of Willy Loman in Arthur Miller's play. But the face was that of Richard Nixon, and it demonstrated not only Herblock's skill but Nixon's terrible vulnerability to caricature. The view was a one-quarter profile from the rear. Only a fragment of the face was visible, but it was unmistakeable—the sloping, pointed nose, the tacky unshaven cheeks and chin. (Herblock had by this time drawn many caricatures of Joe McCarthy, who also was always pictured as needing a shave.) Dozens of cartoons of the sort were to appear in the months to come, and they eventually were to touch Nixon so intensely that he forbade his young daughters to look at the *Post* at all because of the view of their father which they might see there.

The cartoon also, of course, was the first of several wildly inaccurate public pronouncements—including one by the man himself—of the political death of Richard Nixon.

There has been altogether too much psychologizing at a distance of recent presidents and candidates for the job, and there would be little point to adding to the oversupply in this study. At the same time, it is difficult to resist the temptation to speculate that the Checkers episode was the critical point in the fixing of Richard Nixon's attitudes toward the media. And those attitudes involve not just a continuing bitter skepticism and distrust (which most political leaders develop), but the determination, whether consciously framed or not, to strike back at the whole institution of political journalism. That decision is the key to a crisis in the ways the media function in this society. The dimensions of that crisis and its effect on the future of freedom of expression are as yet poorly perceived.

It is impossible to read the accounts of those few days between the breaking of the story of the $16,000 fund and the television speech which resolved the situation without feeling great empathy for its central figure. Politics is a notoriously cruel business, but never more cruel than when leadership abruptly suspends the principle upon which all else normally depends: group loyalty. There is within our system, the unarticulated contract goes, agreement that in return for never attacking the organization you will be protected, however great your incompetence or your ill fortune. A phrase of John Ehrlichman's from a much later day comes irresistibly to mind in contemplating Richard Nixon's travail in September, 1952. He was twisting, twisting slowly in the wind—and the Republican leadership was not about to cut him down.

And it was an agent of humiliation against which he could not conceivably, under any circumstances, strike back. Even if he had been as willing to violate the first principles of loyalty as the men who suspended him, even if he had broken with the party, any attack against the overpowering Eisenhower legend would simply have made him look foolish. It seems reasonable, therefore, that he should strike back at his more visible tormentors, the professional journalists. One suspects that it was not so much a matter of blaming them for his troubles as the feeling that they abused him when he was helpless.

Yet as vice-president during two Eisenhower terms he could do nothing effective to fight back. Even if the men around Eisenhower had been willing to unleash him to make Agnew-like speeches, he could not have done so. The putative point of the Agnew attacks was the defense of his boss, but Nixon's boss was treated with the greatest deference by the media; besides, thundering tides of nineteenth-century invective were not Nixon's style.

The basic inactivity imposed on him as vice-president kept him generally off the front pages of the papers and invisible on television except for two episodes. In both of these the possibility of his succeeding Eisenhower was sharply increased simply through their reporting events in which Nixon was the central, controlling figure. In May, 1958, while he was on a tour of Latin America, his car was stormed by mobs—generally identified as Communist students—in Lima, Quito, Bogota, and Caracas. He consistently showed personal courage in the face of flying rocks, and the media play was substantial and highly favorable. A wisecrack of the time referred to his being nominated for president in South America. In July, 1959, he went to Moscow to formally open the American National Exposition and fell into heated argument with Nikita Khrushchev in the kitchen of the model home which was a feature of the display. The rhetoric on both sides was remarkably forgettable, but many photographers were on hand. Again, the treatment was splashy and very favorable.

With his nomination for president in 1960, some of his old opponents on the editorial pages took after him again, but the memories of the Hiss case were long dead, and there was talk of a new Nixon. Like every Republican presidential candidate but one, he had the support of most of the newspapers in the country. The most conspicuous media role in the campaign, however, was that of television in the so-called "Great Debates." The extent to which Nixon "lost" in this series of joint appearances—and therefore possibly the election, since the final Kennedy margin was fantastically thin—is problematical; various researchers have come to differing conclusions. There is unanimous agreement, however, that even at best the debates did his cause no good, which has led to much speculation as to why he undertook them in the first place. Kennedy obviously had much to gain, Nixon very little.

Such is the clear vision of hindsight. But there were sound reasons for his judgment at the time. His past experience had led him to believe that television served him well; after all, it had saved his political career. He knew John Kennedy better than the public realized, and, although he liked him, he honestly felt he was Kennedy's intellectual superior. That meant he could beat him. He also must have realized that the joint sessions would give him access to an audience far larger than paid political time. The debates were on all the networks, which gave the viewer no place else to go, but paid one-shot appearances were generally on a single channel, with the result that the already converted made up most of the audience.

His personal difficulties with journalists during the campaign have been well set out by Theodore H. White in the first of his *Making of the President* series.[13] Press relations generally were botched, and Nixon was seldom available for questions. When he was, his manner tended to be aloof and suspicious. There seems to have been perpetual tension toward the end of the campaign, and when he contemplated the narrow margin of his defeat (a change of one vote per precinct in the United States would have elected Nixon), the influence of his old enemies must often have crossed his mind.

His deep feelings were to erupt two years later, after his loss to Edmund (Pat) Brown in the California governor's race. There is something more meaningful in that bitter outburst than anything conveyed by the famous "you won't have Nixon to kick around anymore." Beginning at that point, he was willing to think the unthinkable about the relationship between politics and the press. The conventional wisdom always had held it that concession speeches are attempts at a graceful exit, perhaps with a few barbs for the successful opponent, and a wry, in-group joke or two for the reporters. But no loser who had any thought of ever running again verbally assaulted the newsmen who might be covering another campaign in another day. Even if he was making the final political speech of his career (and Nixon intended it, at that moment, to be just that), the convention against unnecessary alienation of the press would have silenced most politicians. Nixon let it all spill out. It was the first in a series of actions in which he was willing to challenge the shibboleths which historically have guarded the media, like the walls of a fortress which hold out the barbarians, against the incursions of the gut-level demagogues.

There are many accounts of the outburst. William Small's is a good one:

> Reporters gathered in a hotel ballroom waiting for Nixon's concession remarks. A car was waiting at the rear exit of the hotel for the defeated candidate. Nixon advisors decided that his press spokesman, Herb Klein, would give the concession messages while a very tired Nixon could leave the hotel. As Nixon watched television he saw Klein enter the roomful of tired, surly reporters who shouted "Where's Nixon?" and implied the candidate was afraid to face them. Impulsively, Nixon stormed out of the room and headed for the press room. He interrupted Klein and snapped at the reporters, "Good morning, gentlemen. Now that Mr. Klein has made his statement, and now that all members of the press are so delighted that I have lost, I'd like to make a statement of my own."
>
> In a rambling monologue he went on for seventeen minutes, sometimes straying to national issues or to the race just finished, always returning to the press. He had never cancelled a subscription, "unlike some people." He wanted to read criticism. He never complained to an editor or a publisher.
>
> But he noted that the press was quick to pick up his flubs . . . and not those of his opponent. "I think it's time that our great newspapers have at least the same objectivity, the same fullness of coverage, that television has.

And I can only say thank God for television and radio for keeping the newspapers a little more honest."

Finally, he came to the end: "As I leave you I want you to know—just think how much you're going to be missing. You won't have Nixon to kick around any more, because, ladies and gentlemen, this is my last press conference."

On his way out, according to *Time* magazine, he turned to Herb Klein and said, "I know you don't agree. I gave it to them right in the behind. It had to be said, goddamit. It had to be said."[14]

It is important to note, perhaps, that this episode does not represent any further development of Nixon's attitudes toward the media; the attitudes were already there. But he was willing to speak from the bottom of his despair and his certainty that his political career was finished. At that point he could only speak. The time was coming when he would have power, and he would act upon it as freely as he spoke when powerless.

Before we set about the major business of this book—a summary history of government's war upon the media during the five and one-half years of the Nixon administration—it seems appropriate to the writer to explain his personal perceptions of, and beliefs about, the factors which have made Richard Nixon like no other president of this country in his actions toward the media. It would be more traditional to stay within a presumably scholarly third person, and, building upon the base of whatever evidence can be mustered, set out some conclusions as established truths. I am not competent to do that, and any implication of modesty in saying so is tempered by a feeling that neither is any other outside observer. If there is any justification for this personal excursion, it lies in providing assistance for the reader in judging my judgments.

My perceptions of Richard Nixon grow out of thousands of impressions, impressions gathered for the most part through the media. I met him personally only once, in the way hundreds of thousands of other Americans meet their presidents, in a

White House receiving line. Most of my perceptions of the man are based on careful attention to almost all his appearances on television, the reading of what must be, by this time, literally millions of words written about him. None of these are very good conduits of piercing insight. Personal chemistry and the flux of situations make responses vary widely; the Nixon speech in which I found him uncertain and obviously tense might be described as a masterful performance by a network analyst or somebody on the *Post*. Even at that, the secondhand image by way of the media is one of dubious fidelity.

The media must deal in essences, seeking the synthesized truth. The important things about Richard Nixon are the things he did and the identifiable pressures he successfully brought upon others to do certain things. The media generally report these accurately and, in time, thoroughly. But journalism has increasingly, over the past two decades, added to this genuine substance an overlay of personal detail and freestyle psychologizing, the focus of which is the analysis of intent.

Trying to explain Nixon's long punitive campaign against the media in terms of his personal characteristics would seem at best to be overreaching. It seems within the limits of prudence, however, to mention another element in the situation which has been widely noted. Nixon has, for whatever reasons, always been an outsider so far as the operational elite of public affairs in this society is concerned. This is not one observer's opinion, but many. The first major biography of Nixon in 1956 refers to it:

> Nixon had one strike against him. He had defeated Jerry Voorhis, who was popular with the predominantly liberal press corps. This was an unforgiveable sin in the eyes of many Washington correspondents whose Orwellian view of the two party system allowed them to suffer the Republican party only when it lost elections.[15]

The same theme was sounded by another strong Nixon partisan, James Keogh, more than a decade later,[16] and most impressively by one of the authentic insiders of the United States political establishment, Daniel Moynihan, in a famous article in *Commentary* in which he discusses, among other things, the tendency of the elite who man the most influential part of the press to impose "heavy expectations" on the presidency.[17] Moynihan is discussing the institution, not Nixon, but the context of the discussion is clear.

We very much need a taxonomy of that media-government-public-affairs elite and, more importantly, some synthesizing description of the dynamics through which it is formed. There seem to be a couple of identifiable elements in the state of In-ness: there is a clear touch of personal style, of "class," and a demonstration of willingness to sometimes run against the grain of the givens of normal allies.

Whatever being In is, one point needs to be made about it in terms of political leadership. It is not necessary to be In to be elected or to be a great leader. Harry Truman never made it. Although I have met many newsmen in recent years who hold Richard Nixon in contempt, I have met none whose contempt was stronger than that of some members of an earlier generation of reporters for Harry S (S for nothing, as *Time* always said) Truman.

The critical point is not if the political man is In or Out, but his sensitivity to his status. Truman, if he ever thought about it, didn't give a damn. Eisenhower always was Out, but in a curious covert way which would never come to his attention if he wasn't concerned, and he wasn't. (One can only wonder what he made of Emmet Hughes; a particularly quick staff sergeant, perhaps.) It is tempting to guess that much of Lyndon Johnson's bitterness in the later years of his administration grew out of his sensitive recognition of his own passage from In to Out. Kennedy, of course, always was the ultimate of In, a fact that increasingly hurts his presidential stature as the historical perspective lengthens. The Ins, of whatever persuasion, are never more wicked than when they realize that they have overestimated somebody.

Nixon seems to have realized early that he was not going to be accepted by that elite, to have accepted that fact, and—in many ways to his credit—broken the familiar pattern of politicians. He neither tried to gain acceptance, nor tried to ignore the snub, but chose instead to fight back.

There remains the interesting question of whether or not Richard Nixon has been treated unfairly by the media. I use the loose word "unfairly" deliberately. It might be quite possible to build a sound, demonstrated case, complete with tables and diagrams, that the media have been fair to him—particularly so during the early years of his career when his prejudices were forming—and still conclude, for reasons not easy to articulate, that in the larger sense he was treated unfairly. One of my graduate students went through something like that. After a long research project which demonstrated that media treatment at a particular stage had been evenhanded, she concluded with a rather bewildering switch considering the weight of her findings. She decided that "there was a basis of Nixon's dislike of the Eastern press."

I suspect that this will be the feeling of anyone who works at any length with the endless material touching on Nixon's relations with the media. Perhaps this is because of an inescapable feeling that for many years he was constantly overmatched. His opponents, politically and in the media, were always brighter, more imaginative, and God knows more attractive. The only weapons he could find were blunted lances—he was still running against the Communist conspiracy in California in 1962, promising California "the best Communist control of any state in the U. S." and asking rhetorical questions such as "what are our schools for if not for indoctrination against Communism?"—and he worked so incessantly, so fiercely hard at it. The bland and casual shifts in his position which early on tagged him with the name "Tricky Dick" seem, in retrospect, not so much deceit as making do. He was a man fighting always with the light in his eyes. Taking these aspects into consideration, it is easier perhaps, to give him a drop of understanding in his hatred of journalism and journalists.

All of which makes him sound like a loser. Instead he won the biggest prize of all and the power that went with it. He held it for more than five years, although not the eight to which he was elected. We turn now to what he did with this power.

On November 5, 1968, Richard Nixon was elected the thirty-seventh president of the United States. He was a minority winner, since there were three major candidates, and George Wallace drew almost ten million votes. Nixon's margin over Hubert Humphrey was about a half million votes out of some seventy million, not substantial but far more decisive than the margin by which he'd lost to John Kennedy, and his electoral college margin was a comfortable 301 to 191 over Humphrey.

It was a remarkable performance. He had demolished the "loser" image, to which he had in a burst of temper contributed himself. His comeback was a triumph of organization and attention to detail; it was the longest successful presidential campaign in modern history, beginning with the defeat of Barry Goldwater. For many months he had no public showcase. He was a lawyer whose international travels received casual coverage, but careful work was carried on within the Republican party. By the time he moved into the open drive for the nomination, the battle was already over. The formal campaign was equally well organized. He and his staff had learned much about the handling of the media in the 1960 campaign and the California disaster of 1962; this time press relations went smoothly. Efficient logistics made the journalists' job easier, and they responded, in the judgment of the campaign management, by providing a better shake for the candidate.

Planning for media relations during the first presidential term of Richard Nixon was underway before the election, and grew in part out of the analysis of campaign procedures. On November 25, 1968, a little less than three weeks after the voters decided, Herbert G. Klein was named director of communications for the executive branch. He was the first man to bear that title, and the announcement made it clear that his role was to be different from that of the traditional press secretary.

The office of press secretary had evolved from the obvious need for someone who understood the media and who could speak for the president. During his tenure as secretary of commerce, Herbert Hoover established a press office and hired George Akerson as his press spokesman. Hoover was a tremendously popular man at that time, very visible in the media, and Akerson helped him handle the demands of the media while, of course, stoking them further. When he moved to the White House, Hoover brought Akerson with him, and Akerson generally is considered to be the first presidential press secretary. It was he who instituted the device of twice-a-day press briefings, a practice generally followed until toward the end of Nixon's first term. Akerson proved inept eventually (Hoover wanted written questions at press conferences, and Akerson screened out those he thought below his boss's dignity, for example), and his replacement, Theodore Joslin, seems to have been even worse.[18]

Joslin, however, was a working Washington newsman before he was named to the White House job. During the next forty years, this became so standard a characteristic that it could be seen almost as a requirement. Franklin Roosevelt had Stephen Early, who as a young reporter covered the swearing in of Roosevelt as assistant secretary of the Navy; Harry Truman had Charles Ross of the *St. Louis Post Dispatch;* Eisenhower had James Hagerty, of an old newspaper family and the *New York Times* by way of Thomas E. Dewey; John Kennedy had a good California newsman in Pierre Salinger; Lyndon Johnson had Bill Moyers, who had studied journalism at the University of Texas and was to go into the news business after leaving the White House, and two fine professionals in George Reedy and George Christian.

There is great importance in the fact that all of these men had been not only working journalists, but political reporters. Although each had his own style, conditioned to a great extent by that of the president for whom he worked, each also had functioned as a part of the United States political system. There is a genuine symbiosis between the political man and the journalist who covers him. Each takes part of his identity from the other, as well as drawing his material from him. Between the two vocations there have grown up elaborate conventions, understandings, and unarticulated ground rules. Traditionally, for example, newsmen in this country have seldom reported personal scandal relating to politicians; drunks and womanizers and even homosexuals have been widely known as such within the press corps without ever being reported. Crime is reported, but incompetence is not until its implications are inescapable. This generally has meant that the political reporter has reported those in official positions of leadership as if they *were* competent, stretching the benefit of the doubt almost to the breaking point. The surrealistic combination of incompetence, personal problems, and brazen self-service of L. Mendel Rivers as chairman of the House Armed Services Committee, for example, was never really reported in the daily press; there were hints in the news magazines. Almost any capable state capitol reporter can dazzle his drinking companions with anecdotage about people who dominate his columns but who are reported there in neutral tones. There traditionally has been a commitment of the political journalist in this country to the belief that the system works; there may be occasional highly particularistic aberrations, but basically it works, and he feels a certain obligation to ignore many things which he feels are essentially irrelevant but might undermine public confidence. For his part, the political man traditionally refrained from attacking the media; on the uncommon occasions when he did so, he attacked particular reporters about particular stories. He did not attack the media as institutions or try to impugn the motives of a sizeable part of the profession. Perhaps the most common exception was that of the congressmen from the provinces who would boast in their campaigns about the way they were opposed by the powerful papers in the East. But this was for local consumption, campaign stuff from men of dubious standing.

The business of reporting the White House had been played by such rules for years by professionals with like backgrounds, and the same commitments held when the Nixon administration came into power. Within months it was to begin to change.

The beginning, however, was exemplary. Herbert Klein was very much an old professional, coming through the traditional newspaper beginnings to become head of the Copley newspapers' Washington bureau and then editor of the Copley's *San Diego Union.* The Copley papers tend to be blandly conservative and do not provide a framework for journalistic spectaculars. Klein was solidly competent and enough respected and liked to have been elected to the Board of Directors of the American Society of Newspaper Editors. ASNE is probably the highest-status organization in American journalism, and election to its board is never pro forma.

Klein thus was very much in the classic mold of the presidential press chief. Furthermore, he brought to media relations a relaxed, almost gentle personal manner that made many friends and few enemies among those who worked with him. Oddly, he appeared as a quite different figure to people who only saw photographs or television interviews. Nicholas von Hoffman of the *Washington Post* once referred to him as "looking like a Chicago hit man." Klein has heavy-lidded eyes which make him appear both threatening and shifty, a circumstance of physiognomy over which he has no more control than Clark Gable had over his extraordinary ears.

The members of the Washington press corps were not put off by the eyes. They knew him better than that, but they were a bit apprehensive about the new White House setup for media relations. What, exactly, was a director of communications for the executive branch? As Klein explained it at the time of the announcement of its creation, it would be, in effect, a line (rather than a staff) position which spoke for all the government other than the Congress, in contrast to the traditional press secretary who spoke only for the president. The director would informally coordinate activities of the information officers of the various executive departments and hoped to reduce the overall staff. To emphasize the difference between Klein's role and that of the traditional press secretary, a title which he was said to have refused, his office and modest staff were set up in the Executive Office Building. At the point of that first announcement, no one was designated as press secretary. Ronald Ziegler was called simply the "press spokesman," and his chief function was conducting the twice-a-day briefings.

Klein told reporters in his own first press conference as director that his primary commitment was to more open government, more and better communication. He said his job was "to eliminate any possibility of a credibility gap" (the student of the early Nixon presidency drowns in irony). He unquestionably meant it. Although both Klein and the incoming president were far too wise to anticipate any honeymoon with the media, Klein did feel that he could improve greatly upon the atmosphere of rancor which pervaded Lyndon Johnson's media relations during his last days in office.

Some other considerations Klein did not talk about seemed inherent in the new structure. It would be useful in the mechanics of politics, making liaison with the Republican party apparatus more efficient. It provided, through informal meetings under Klein's leadership, communication between departments which might otherwise speak in different voices to different objectives. Lateral communication in Washington always has been difficult. Even under the best of circumstances, the top levels of the permanent bureaucracy communicate among themselves primarily through what they read about each other's activities in the *Washington Post* and the *New York Times*, [19] and the new administration had the additional problem of dealing with many who were Democrats or had at least been appointed during a Democratic administration. The new structure was as much designed to expedite the movement of information within the government as to serve the media.

It also served another, personal purpose for Richard Nixon. It put a little more distance between him and the news business. He had been upset as vice-president at the amount of power which James Hagerty had accumulated as press secretary to Eisenhower. Insiders have reported how he was shocked when he took over the Oval Office as his own and found such evidences of Lyndon Johnson's preoccupation with the media as the famous triple-screen television set and the omnipresent news agency teleprinters (there was said to be one in a second floor White House men's room). He also had decided not to read the papers or watch television news broadcasts seriously, leaving to an aggressive young staffer named Patrick Buchanan and his assistants the job of preparing a private news summary for the beginning of each day. None of this, of course, helped much in preventing the development within a couple of years of an almost pathological preoccupation of his own with the media.

The undiscussed aspect of the new structure which disturbed the White House press corps most was the extent to which better coordination might mean tighter control. They questioned Klein about this promptly and reported his denials. Furthermore, he set about immediately to try to improve access for inquiring reporters. Two months after the inauguration, he was getting high marks from one of the best American newspapers. Writing in the *Wall Street Journal* in March of 1969, John Pierson began an admiring major story in this fashion:

> Herb Klein has clout.
>
> Not long ago, the Nixon Administration's Communications Director got a call from a reporter working on a story about "voluntarism"—President Nixon's program to enlist the help of private groups in solving social problems. The reporter hadn't been able to get in to see the man who's heading the effort, Secretary George Romney of the Department of Housing and Urban Development. Could Mr. Klein help him obtain an interview?
>
> Mr. Klein said he would try. A couple of days later, the reporter got to see Mr. Romney.

The substance of Pierson's overview was that the new scheme was working. Not only could Klein provide access which was otherwise impossible, he was indeed providing a useful coordination within the executive department.

Thus when the Post Office and the Pentagon were about to announce that troops were being dispatched to unload mail from strikebound ships, he discovered that neither department had checked with the Labor Department, which was trying to settle the longshoreman's walkout. If an agreement was imminent, Mr. Klein feared, the troop announcement might upset it. A check revealed that a settlement was several days off. So the Post Office and Defense Departments went ahead with their news release.

This was an example of what was seen at that point as a highly rational arrangement. One of the shabby aspects of the Johnson administration's later years was the handling of nuggets of upbeat news which made the administration look good. Johnson made it clear that all such items were to be routed first through the White House, which would announce them if the news seemed important enough. The Klein system generally left the satisfaction of announcing good news to the department responsible for it.

Klein's personal staff was small, with a total of five secretaries, four senior assistants, one junior assistant, and a researcher. The senior assistants were each assigned to a set of departments as liaison.

> Every day, an information man in each department tells the appropriate Klein assistant about the news releases he expects to issue that day and in the days ahead. . . . Mr. Klein keeps up with things by attending meetings of the Cabinet and Urban Affairs Council. He is also on hand when Mr. Nixon meets with Republican Congressional leaders. He's regularly in touch with all the top White House staffers and sees the President "two or three times a day and then maybe not for two or three days," supplementing these meetings with phone calls and memos.

The *Wall Street Journal*'s reporter had only one question about media relations in the Nixon administration:

> . . . Washington is wondering who really is the White House Press Secretary. The 29-year-old Mr. Ziegler, a former Los Angeles ad executive? Or the 50-year-old Mr. Klein, journalist and confidant of the President?[20]

For a few more months Klein was clearly in charge. In April his former colleagues in the American Society of Newspaper Editors passed a resolution praising his work on behalf of an open administration. In late December the *New York Times* carried an article much like the *Journal*'s in its tone of friendly admiration.[21] The office of the director of communication was sending out thousands of "fact kits" to media around the country. Klein continued to be a highly effective consultant on use of the media, particularly television, for other government officers. His office had taken over as well; Herbert Thompson, Agnew's press secretary, was a member of Klein's staff.

Klein served the media, but he also served his boss. According to the *New York Times*, he had a role in the Agnew attack on the networks in 1969 which was the first major thrust in the administration's war on the media; he suggested its basic direction. Afterward, he spent several hours "cooling the frayed nerves of his friends in the television business."[22] One of the things he told them was that he disagreed with the bitter rhetoric and overall tone of the speech, but did think that more rigorous self-examination by the networks was in order. A few days later he obtained an advance copy of the Agnew speech in which the vice-president dropped the other shoe and attacked the elite newspapers; only an hour or two before release he got some particularly vivid passages toned down.

There is an almost idyllic quality in the newspaper stories about White House activities as the first year of the new administration drew to a close, but sterner times were ahead. The incursion into Cambodia and the explosion on United States campuses came in April, and from that point forward the pressure of events upon the president and his staff was unremitting.

And the relative standing of Herbert Klein and Ronald Ziegler shifted. Columnists Evans and Novak insisted later that the papered-over fissure had been there all the time:

> . . . as Mr. Nixon's attitudes toward the press hardened, so did his attitude toward Klein. Even in 1960, he complained privately about Klein's "crybaby" recommenda-

tions for easier press access, grumbling that Herb wanted to make it easier on himself than help the candidate.

Mr. Nixon knew what he wanted for his second presidential try in 1968; a hard-nosed press secretary without friends in the press or unpleasant recommendations. H. R. Haldeman came up with a young advertising executive named Ron Ziegler. Klein was kept at arm's length, increasingly criticized by the imperious Haldeman.[23]

Klein finally left government in June of 1973, but rumors of his leaving had been endemic for months and his authority substantially eroded. Ziegler was named as his successor, which meant that from that point forward he had complete control of media relations, and his range was much wider than twice-a-day briefings—a chore which he cut in half, reducing the norm to one a day and increasingly handed off to such assistants as Gerald Warren.

It is important to note that the journalist who goes into the pay of the politician is not necessarily a martyred ideologue when he presses for openness and honesty in dealing with the media. If he is good at his trade, he realizes that these qualities eventually will work to his boss's advantage. Candor, combined with a plea for support of a higher cause, is very persuasive. This is something which people within the Kennedy organization, for example, knew or learned quickly. Typically in that era a high-ranking official invited a reporter to a quiet lunch, asked his advice on a vexatious problem or two, and asked for his help. All very inside and, of course, off the record. In the early sixties journalists such as Arthur Krock of the *New York Times* and Clark Mollenhof of the Cowles organization were fulminating against that kind of co-optation; Mollenhof toured with a speech entitled "Watchdogs or Lap Dogs?" and Krock wrote a stinging piece for *Fortune.*[24]

At worst, the media relations adviser who presses in such a direction is working in terms of enlightened self-interest. At best he may be convinced (and there is evidence that Klein was) that the best interests of democratic government are served by openness as complete as possible.

This is a totally different frame of reference from that of the corporate public relations man. That point is critical in the understanding of what happened to the Nixon administration's relations with the press as the major power passed from Klein to Ron Ziegler. The classic symbiotic relationship between political journalist and political leader was destroyed. A different kind of men had authority, and they saw themselves with the greatest and most powerful client in history.

To put the matter in those terms does not mean that it should be taken as a morality play. Corporate public relations men as a class are no more amoral—or venal—than ex-journalists turned information officers or, indeed, journalists. It is primarily a matter of the scope of vision. Quite properly, the corporate man is concerned only with the welfare of the company for which he works. It can be a disservice to be concerned with the larger issue. There is essentially a single client and a single motive—profit. The United States economic system is based upon the belief that such activities are fit and proper, and that in total a multitude of self-serving interests tend to cancel out each others excesses. But the executive branch of the United States government is not a single client, nor, heaven knows, does it have a single purpose or a simple cause.

There is another difference between the view from the office of the corporate public relations man and that of the government information officer. The issues with which the former has to deal are always, in the larger sense, trivial. Even in a matter as threatening as a chronic shortage of fossil fuels, no single corporation has an irreversibly central role. There are other corporations, an infinity of other possibilities for the solution of problems; the honest business leader, and his public relations people, seldom need to feel the awful weight of responsibility for the future of the republic.

The basic method of corporate public relations is as simple as the issues with which it normally has to deal. The most emphasis possible is given to that which makes the company look good. That which makes it look bad is hidden as much as possible. It is made not only easy, but downright pleasant, for journalists covering the corporation to report the good things. There are press releases, interviews are arranged, additional information of an appropriate sort developed at the journalist's request; there may even be personal favors (although there is much less of this than the cynical outsider thinks). The journalist who is seen as unfriendly gets few favors and, while business organizations seldom have enough clout to damage a newsman, they may on occasion find ways to make his work a great deal more difficult.

There is a kind of straightforward honesty in this kind of relationship. Both sides know the rules of the game and the system works well from the point of view of both the corporation and the media. The small-time business writer or financial editor who gets conned is generally a willing victim. At the highest level, such publications as the *Wall Street Journal* are heavily dependent upon information sources within the companies whose activities they report. Neither the *Journal*'s integrity nor the continued willingness of business to cooperate with it has ever come into serious question.

That serviceable but limited approach is what Haldeman and Ziegler brought with them. There were, and there continued to be after Klein's departure, professional journalists on the White House staff, including Gerald Warren and Kenneth W. Clawson, who eventually took over the director of communications title from Ziegler. Warren and Clawson were a long way from being insiders, however.

Ziegler was an insider, by the beginning of the second term second only to Haldeman, and after the Watergate purge second to none. His own view of his qualifications for the job of chief spokesman for the president and his administration came out one time in a starchy discussion with two representatives of the National News Council. This independent organization, financed by foundations, was set up in 1973 to analyze the performance of the media and investigate charges brought against them. When Nixon, in an angry outburst during a press conference on October 26, 1973, referred to "outrageous, vicious, and distorted reporting," the council set out to get a bill of particulars. The White House refused to provide it, although an unofficial list was leaked to some media critics. While explaining the refusal, Ziegler said impatiently to council staff members, "Look, I know about the way the media work. I bought advertising space for years."

That he did, as an executive in the Los Angeles office of the J. Walter Thompson advertising agency, where he was a subordinate of H. R. Haldeman and worked on such accounts as Seven-Up (interestingly, although probably inconsequentially, Nixon was once a lawyer for Pepsi-Cola). Whatever he learned about the media through placing advertisements for his clients did him little good in his personal relations with journalists. It is probably safe to say that no presidential spokesman within memory has been disliked so thoroughly by so many White House reporters.

Ziegler always made clear his distaste for the reporters for one thing. This led him to "jawbone" in briefings; on occasion he delivered bitter tongue-lashings, such as the one directed at the *Washington Post* as the Watergate story began to break.

Although personal style should not be a consideration in working relationships, there's no denying that it is, and the elite who work the White House have a strong sense of it. They did not like Ziegler's style and sometimes they even assisted in making it worse. His best-known grotesquerie was a word put in his mouth by a reporter who, after listening to an elaborate backtracking on some matters relating to Watergate, said: "Ron, does this mean your earlier statements are inoperative?" At first all Ziegler said was "yes," but he eventually picked up the word and used it himself later in the briefing.

The most pervasive reason for his unpopularity, however, rested in the continuing difficulty in getting information out of the administration. Zeigler stood at the head of the least informative group of information officers in many years, and he has been seen as the individual most responsible for suppressing what were once normal channels for the gossip and tips and off-the-record briefings from which news is developed. The centralized system set up by Herbert Klein—which some newsmen suspected from the beginning was a mechanism for tight control—became, whether or not Klein intended it, exactly that.

In addition to building an apparatus for control of outgoing information and the substitution of the corporate view of public relations for the traditional politician-journalist relationship, the White House staff also had an awesome monopoly of the presidential agenda. Through Patrick Buchanan, special consultant to the president, and his staff (more about them later), they apparently had control of what the president knew about the content of the media.

"I get my news from the news summary the staff prepares every day and it's great; it gives me all sides," he told Saul Pett of the Associated Press at the end of his first term. "I never watch TV commentators or the news shows when they are about me. That's because I don't want decisions influenced by personal emotional reactions."[25] Elsewhere in the same remarkable interview he made it clear that he also disregarded print columnists, speaking with amusement of Kissinger's trying to call his attention to something James Reston had said in the *New York Times*.

Patrick Buchanan and his staff, then, had the responsibility for choosing for the "briefing book" those items from the media which might reinforce the president or anger him. When angered, he was very specific about certain things which he wanted done in response, as we shall see. Beyond this, however, most of the White House offensive was planned by another set of aides of which Charles Colson and Jeb Stuart Magruder were the most active. From them came a wide range of proposals and initiatives, generally set out in memos to H. R. Haldeman. The tone of the memos is that of intimate and self-assured discourse among men who know the general thrust of their boss's mind. It seems likely that many of the minor hassles and hustles which are described in the pages which follow were never brought to Richard Nixon's attention and certainly were not submitted for his approval. At the same time, there is no evidence of any effort on his part to mitigate or redirect them.

A kind of analogy comes to mind. The situation as the Nixon administration moved against the media is somewhat comparable to a well-organized military force moving to occupy an area where there is suspicion and resentment but no organized resistance. The force has a commander who is clearly in charge. The orders he sends out are obeyed and carried out without question. But staff members and subcommanders all the way down the line, from brigadiers to sergeants, understand that they have a great deal of freedom to hit targets of opportunity in whatever fashion they choose. The essential frame of mind of the commanding officer is perfectly clear, and they know of no example of a zealous underling getting himself in trouble by overdoing. Furthermore, as they launch their offensive, they find they not only have friends in the countryside but imitators who will follow their example. Their target population, meanwhile, is fat, comfortable, and convinced that the whole business is transient.

That rather strained metaphor can usefully be kept in mind as we proceed.

TWO

Year 1969

We had private morality but not a sense of public morality. Instead of applying our private morality to public affairs, we accepted the President's standards of political behavior, and the results were tragic for him and for us.

Jeb Stuart Magruder

The new president settled quickly into routine after his inauguration on January 20 of 1969. His first press conference came a week later. He requested that questions be devoted to foreign affairs. The scheduling was interesting: 9:00 P.M. Such an hour is nerve-rackingly difficult for morning newspapers, such as the *Baltimore Sun,* the *Washington Post,* the *Detroit Free Press,* and the *New York Times*; their main editions normally are closing at about that time. Furthermore, in a press conference there is no advance text, no way to write a vague tentative account (the kind that generally uses the line "in a speech prepared for delivery tonight. . . ."); the lead story might well come with the last question. And even the fastest transcript comes too late for cross-checking.

It was, however, prime time television. Richard Nixon began his presidential relationship with the media by making clear he intended to go to the audience directly as much as possible.

That first press conference went well; Tom Wicker, along with a good many others, called it skillful. There was one touch of comic embarrassment in it which did not fully come out until a few days later.

There had been a good deal of preinaugural talk, led by the Secretary-designate of Defense Melvin Laird, about reestablishing United States weapons superiority over the USSR. During the January 27 press conference, Edward P. Morgan of ABC, a handsome, poised man who somehow always radiated sympathetic understanding, asked the president if this inflammatory talk of superiority wasn't somewhat contrary to the spirit of the word "sufficiency" which had been used in articles by his new special assistant, Henry Kissinger, in discussing these matters. The president looked surprised, hesitated a moment, and then picked up the word with obvious satisfaction. Well, yes, he said, perhaps "sufficiency" was a better word. He liked it so much, in fact, that before the press conference was over he worked in another reference to Kissinger's word "sufficiency."

As the reporters filed out, Herbert Klein casually remarked to Kissinger, who was present, that it was a good word indeed, and that Kissinger should be proud of himself. "I never used it," the professor said. "I never would. I think it's a stupid word."

Morgan's colleagues in the media didn't know about Kissinger's reply, but they did know that they couldn't find the word in their Kissinger clippings. Meanwhile, it had become big news; the press of United States allies in Europe, in particular, had picked it up with enthusiasm because of the overtone of decompression of a possible future arms race. The next morning, faced with insistent phone calls about his source, Morgan admitted cheerily that he *thought* Kissinger had said it, but that he could be wrong. He was, of course. Some reporters who had made a good deal of the use of the word in their stories were irritated, and a considerably larger group was amused. There is no record of what the president thought.

The international emphasis was heavy during the winter of 1969. The Vietnam war was not going well; the peace talks dragged, but the president began an eight-day tour of Europe on February 23 which went well. There were some protesters at airports, but he was well received officially, particularly by Charles de Gaulle. Back home, university campuses were blowing up, but there was still a tendency to take a kids-will-be-kids view of them. That attitude did nothing to diminish these activities, however. By April the situation was critical. There were genuinely bad scenes at Harvard and City College of New York. There also was a melancholy monument in Vietnam, when on April 3 the military announced that United States combat deaths in that war had surpassed those of the Korean war, with a total of 33,641. The prime lending rate went up, the beginning of what was to be a considerable jump, from 5½ percent to 6 percent. It then went to 7½ percent, and in early June went to 8½ percent. Inflation was roaring. June was better otherwise; Nixon met with Nguyen Van Thieu on the eighth, and the meeting concluded with the announcement of the first timetable for United States troop withdrawals. In late July the president made a round-the-world tour, beginning in the Philippines and ending with a visit to Rumania. In Bucharest, he gave the first public signal on the path to *detente* with China, although the troop of reporters which followed him did not recognize it. Chinese diplomatic representatives were present at the climactic banquet. During his turn at toast making Nixon used the term "People's Republic" in reference to China for the first time. There had been earlier indirect cues, but on the scale of diplomatic niceties, this almost was equivalent to turning on a neon sign. Within hours Chinese functionaries were in touch with their American equivalents. American newsmen who were present suspected nothing, to the great glee of Herb Klein, who later told the story with relish.[1]

Meanwhile, Klein had done a stalwart job of unblocking some channels plugged by Lyndon Johnson, and seemed to be a friend of the media at the court. On May 6 came the first sour note from a prestige source. Walter Cronkite spoke to the New York Chapter of the Association of Industrial Advertisers and denounced government attempts to control broadcast news. Despite Klein's help in particular cases, the news establishment

was becoming aware that the movement of information in and
out of this administration was more tightly controlled than in
the past. In late September, the White House press corps "quar-
reled politely," in the *New York Times*'s phrase,[2] over the fact
that the president had not held a press conference for three
months.

Frank Stanton, president of the Columbia Broadcasting
System, addressed the annual national convention of the Radio-
Television News Directors Association in Detroit on September
24 and warned against a "deeply troubling trend toward Government curbs on broadcast journalism." The next day Frank
Shakespeare, new director of the United States Information
Agency and a close adviser of the president, charged from the
same platform that many prominent journalists in broadcasting
had a strong and visible liberal bias which he found disturbing.

In October, with modest United States troop withdrawals
underway, the casualty rate in Vietnam began to drop sharply,
and October 9 was a magnificent day; for what seemed the first
time in memory, there were no United States combat deaths
over a twenty-four hour period. October 15 was something else,
Moratorium Day, with thousands of antiwar protesters taking
over Washington and the media giving them elaborate and
respectful coverage. The media recognition seems to have
grated more on the White House than the event itself. For
months afterward there were traces of resentment, as well as
pressure to give equal attention to occasional proadministration
rallies.

On October 17, Jeb Stuart Magruder wrote a remarkable
memorandum to the man who was, by this time, clearly established as the president's chief of staff, H. R. Haldeman. It was
entitled "The Shot-gun versus the Rifle," and it was remarkable
in two ways. First, it demonstrated the extent of Richard
Nixon's preoccupation with what the media said, and his personal role in trying to do something about it. Even Magruder
seemed surprised:

> I have enclosed from the log approximately 21 requests
> from the President in the last 30 days requesting specific

action relating to what could be considered unfair news coverage. This enclosure only includes actual memos sent out by Ken Cole's [Nixon's appointments secretary] office. In the short time I have been here, I would gather that there have been at least double or triple this many requests made through various other parties to accomplish the same objective.[3]

The enclosure is a log of twenty-one (one can only wonder what the phrase "approximately 21" meant to Magruder) requests from the president to a total of seven staff members. Klein got eleven of them, in whole or in part; others got one or two. Each individual is identified with a single initial and last name—"H. Klein"—except for "Dr. Kissinger," who was requested to look into critical stories by Jack Anderson and Walter Cronkite. (The complete text of the memorandum appears beginning on page 244.) With the president presumably reading only Patrick Buchanan's morning sampler, the mind reels a bit at the thought of what his concerns might have been if he were reading widely.

The second remarkable element in the Magruder memo is suggested by the shot-gun versus the rifle metaphor. Magruder felt that the attempts to handle complaints one at a time and person to person were futile. In the main body of his memo, he set out a series of proposals for attacks upon the media as institutions, including use of the Department of Justice to begin threatening antitrust actions, the Internal Revenue Service "as a method to look into the various organizations that we are most concerned about," indicating his confidence that just a threat would be enough to "turn their approach"; and use of the FCC as the basis of "an official monitoring system."

In retrospect, it was a naive and overeager document. There later was an attempt to use IRS investigations to intimidate individuals as well as companies, but with the possible exception of antitrust actions no other suggestions apparently were taken seriously.

It was an important memo, however, in the grimly punitive spirit which it reflected and the apparent confidence of its writer that Richard Nixon shared that spirit. Judging by the evidence he appended, Magruder was right.

Five weeks later Spiro Agnew addressed a Republican regional conference in Des Moines, Iowa. That was the crossing of the Rubicon in the new administration's assault upon the press. The vice-presidency of the United States is constitutionally so inconsequential that its tenants have been moved to grouse about it for almost two hundred years. John Adams, the first vice-president, said his job was "the most insignificant office that ever the invention of man contrived or his imagination conceived." About one hundred and forty years later, John Nance Garner of Texas, vice-president during the first and second terms of Franklin Roosevelt, was equally vivid in a different idiom: "the vice presidency isn't worth a pitcher of warm spit."

Spiro Agnew was to become the best known vice-president of all those who did not succeed to the presidency. The spectacular circumstances of his resignation in the fall of 1973 contributed most to that distinction, of course, but he was well on the way to it earlier and in great part on the basis of his attacks on the media.

Richard Nixon, like most modern presidents, announced his intention of giving his second a larger role than his predecessors had been given. (Eisenhower had said the same thing sixteen years earlier, and had made some gestures, but Nixon still had been a supernumerary, and he remembered it with resentment.) Nixon made Agnew a member of the National Security Council and vice-chairman of the newly-created Domestic Council. He also was head of a new Office of Intergovernmental Relations, an agency set up to make it easier for city and state governments to get help from Washington. But most of his visibility came out of his role as a partisan spokesman.

"Agnew's assignment," Herbert Klein explained at the time of the first attacks on the media, "is to explain in a missionary way what the administration's policies are and to seek support for them. He fills a basic need which a president can't do."[4]

Operationally, this meant Agnew's job was to attack in

hardline fashion the president's enemies, a job to which he took with joyous bombast. His first major target, it was decided, should be dissidents on the Vietnam war issue, the biggest issue of the day. Major antiwar rallies were scheduled for several cities, including Washington, during October of 1969. Agnew set out to the hustings with a message which reduced to three fundamentals: that the dissidents were intellectuals outside the American mainstream, which was made up of good, quiet patriotic citizens who backed the president; that the dissidents meant to destroy the American system and should take the blame for it; and that there was an overlap in the thinking of these dissidents and some of the leadership of the Democratic party.

Agnew and his staff felt—quite accurately—that he must be covered by first-rank reporters to get the attention the role required, and that he had to make it worth their while. Gaudy rhetoric was one of the ways: "You have to use strong language to get attention of the sort that lands on page one."[5]

The first of the anti–anti-Vietnam speeches was in New Orleans on October 19, 1969, shortly after Moratorium Day, and it contained a line which gained a kind of immortality. "A spirit of national masochism prevails," said the vice-president, "encouraged by an effete corps of impudent snobs. . . ." He was in Jackson, Mississippi, the next day; Harrisburg, Pennsylvania ten days later. The Harrisburg version of the speech was called "Impudence in the Streets." On November 10 he spoke to the National Municipal League. Then, on November 13, in Des Moines, Iowa, he spoke on national television about the sins of television.

The topic apparently originated with Herbert Klein, who was inspired by the telegrams and letters which came to the White House in response to a presidential speech of November 3, ten days earlier. Nixon's televised performance had been intended to be a major statement, a kind of progress report on our involvement in the Vietnam war and, at least inferentially, a palliative for the rising spirit of dissent. Although Agnew was to make a generic name of the phrase "instant analysis" in his references to network follow-ups of the Nixon speech, there was nothing instant about them. In no other Nixon speech did the administration make a greater effort to prepare network commentators for the reception of the message.

Five hours before the Nixon speech, the text had been released. This is more than ample time for a competent reporter to make a careful analysis. In case matters of importance were unclear, however, there had been a follow-up briefing session two hours later. Presidential adviser Henry Kissinger, among others, participated. Kissinger, always excellent with the press, with a sophisticated openness and candor more convincing than the bones of any particular message, had been in excellent form that night.

Unfortunately, the commentators for the networks—along with many others—had taken from a variety of cues, including the White House buildup, the impression that the speech would contain the announcement of a major, dramatic initiative toward a settlement. It did not. Its primary message might be summarized as "trust me; we're making progress."

Nevertheless the administration clearly felt that if this statement were properly understood, it would do much toward providing a greater acceptance of the presidential point of view. One might reasonably guess that Richard Nixon went before the cameras that night convinced, or at least greatly hopeful, that everybody of importance was on his side.

That had not turned out to be the case. Most of the network analysts took a critical tone; one of them, Marvin Kalb of CBS, came close to suggesting that the president was deliberately misspeaking in some of his contentions. There was no network commentary which could be regarded as heartily supportive. There was outrage and indignation in the White House.

November 4, the morning after the Nixon speech, there was a meeting of Haldeman, Ehrlichman, Ziegler, and Klein with the president. In going over the telegrams, Klein noticed that many of them referred bitterly to the follow-up commentary on the networks. The matter was discussed and the possibility of suggesting it as a speaking subject to the vice-president came up. Klein told *Newsweek* later that the Agnew speech "came as a result of a lot of discussion after the letters about November 3 came in."[6]

Another powerful arm of the administration came into play on November 5, two days after the Vietnam speech. On that morning Dean Burch, appointed October 31 as the new chairman of the Federal Communications Commission, telephoned the heads of the three networks and asked for transcripts of the remarks of their reporters and commentators.

This is another of those in-group actions the import of which is difficult to explain to outsiders. There would seem to be, from a detached perspective, nothing particularly untoward about such an action, given the putative role of the FCC in broadcasting. In fact, it was a breath taker. Chairmen of this country's regulatory agencies simply do not act that way. Their posture is more judicial, their involvement in day-to-day operations of the regulated industry is much more remote. Perhaps something of the impact of Burch's action might be conveyed by saying that it was rather like the average citizen's being summoned just after he's paid his income tax, not by the Internal Revenue Service, but by the judge who will preside over his trial for tax fraud. The act was simple harassment. There are easy ways for anybody to get transcripts from the networks, and if the FCC did not already have them they could have been obtained through a routine inquiry from one underling to another.

Burch had little choice, however. Later he openly told Frank Stanton, president of CBS, that he was calling on instructions from the White House.[7] And he must be credited with never doing anything like it again. In the judgment of most observers, he grew steadily in his job, showing himself judicious and straightforward, and eventually became a capable chairman before disappearing into the obscure role of special assistant to the president in early 1974.

Network executives had been unsettled earlier by the remarks of Frank Shakespeare at the annual meeting of the Radio-Television News Directors Association. The Burch request distinctly put them on edge. The speech of the vice-president eight days later increased the pressure.

The setting of the speech was conventional, if not pedestrian. The Midwest Republican Conference was scheduled to open in Des Moines the evening of November 13. The chief function of such meetings, regularly scheduled by both parties, is the tightening of organizational structure and the reinforcing of the convictions of the faithful. Featured performers normally are cabinet officers at best. Nobody expects news to be made or seeks it. McDill Boyd, Republican national committeeman from Kansas and chairman of the conference, therefore was somewhat surprised to receive a call from Agnew's office two days before the meeting suggesting that the vice-president might be available to speak at the opening session. It was easy enough to accommodate him; there was no program scheduled for the first evening other than registration and a reception by the governor of Iowa.

There is still some confusion about who wrote the Agnew speech. Up to that point Agnew's regular speechwriter had been Cynthia Rosenwald, a public relations professional who came from Maryland with him. William Small says that the speech was produced by a group headed by H. R. Haldeman, including members of James Keogh's White House speech writing team and Patrick Buchanan, with Rosenwald having responsibility before it was turned over to the vice-president for some touches of his own.[8] William Safire says flatly that it was the work of Buchanan, who denied having anything to do with the speech and insisted with a straight face that Agnew wrote it himself.[9] (The text of the Des Moines speech, slightly edited, begins on page 255.)

On the morning of the thirteenth, network bureau chiefs in Washington were called by Herbert Thompson, Agnew's chief press officer, and told that a copy of the speech was on the way and that it would be newsworthy. After reading it, they agreed. There were consultations with New York and eventually each network, acting independently, cleared the 7:00 P.M. time slot. It was the greatest break of the vice-president's career, and it gave enormous impetus to what had now become an overt campaign against the media.

Why did the networks choose to assist in the blackening of their own names and the effort to destroy their credibility? There was a mixture of motives. The speech clearly was newsworthy in the first place. Furthermore Agnew's text all but dared them to carry it: "Whether what I've said to you tonight will be seen or heard at all by the nation is not my decision, it's their decision." There was some feeling, certainly, that they might gain public stature through such a display of turning the other cheek. And, at bottom, they must have been seeking to placate an administration which could do them very great damage indeed.

It is a matter of clinical judgment to classify the Des Moines speech as pure demagoguery. Julian Goodman, president of NBC, called it "an appeal to prejudice," and he was right. It attempted to establish in the mind of the viewer the idea that newsmen are not his kind of people, that they represent a dangerously detached elite, representing not a real conspiracy but a shared contempt for plain people such as the viewer.

Using that characterization as a starting point, the speech went on to question the right of any such elite to try to impede the president of the United States in his efforts to govern. Although the vice-president was to refer several times in the next few weeks to his belief in the freedom of the press, the implications of a ludicrous comparison to an embattled Churchill in World War II could only be taken as implying that any criticism was close to treasonable. He pointed out to the viewer that American journalists continually gave a false impression of American life by choosing for attention the kind of people the viewer disliked: marchers in radical causes and disturbers of the peace.

And he warned the viewer that the network news departments have awesome potential for control—"a concentration of power over American public opinion unknown in history." Quiet usurpers, they had built up this power without the people's really being aware; the people were at the edge of thought control, and must awaken. "We would never trust such power over public opinion in the hands of an elected government—it is time we questioned it in the hands of a small and unelected elite," he concluded. "The great networks have dominated America's airwaves for decades; the people are entitled to a full account of their stewardship."

It was not a speech designed to stimulate more critical

analysis of broadcasting, although those who praised it said it was; looked at squarely, it was one more appeal to the great beast which is somewhere inside all popular governments. And it stirred. Calls, telegrams, and letters piled in; before they subsided, the three networks had received about 150,000 communications, and they were two-to-one in favor of Agnew. In addition, Agnew's own office received 74,000 letters—almost all, of course, favorable.[10]

Most of the network commentators and newspaper editorialists reacted with indigation, although Howard K. Smith, of ABC, indicated at least partial agreement with some of the vice-president's criticisms. Predictable Republicans supported him: Hugh Scott, Barry Goldwater, Robert Dole. Dean Burch of the FCC strongly supported Agnew's right to speak up and said of the networks "physician, heal thyself," but made it clear that he felt the FCC had no legitimate role in trying to evaluate and thus inferentially control news broadcasts (a point he was to repeat later when the Commerce committee of the House tried to cite CBS for contempt in another matter).

A few days later, CBS White House man Dan Rather pointed out that members of the president's staff had been calling television stations to check on comment following certain Nixon speeches. He quoted Richard Salant, president of the network's news division, as saying that White House callers had asked CBS stations in Minneapolis and Los Angeles not only if they planned editorial comment, but what they planned to say. Questioned at a briefing, Klein said it was indeed true, and that they did a good deal of that kind of checking on reaction to the president's activities, but that the practice had been encouraged by station executives and was not intended to intimidate anybody.

It nevertheless was a rather curious procedure. A variation extended to newspapers as well. Before most major Nixon speeches, Klein's office called a small group of editors of the country's major papers and asked for permission to call back for comment after the speech. This was another device to encourage careful attention to the speech, of course, and some editors may have found it flattering—but certainly not all. Thomas

Winship of the *Boston Globe,* for one, was regularly called, and regularly refused to participate.

The White House said* that it had nothing to do with the Agnew speech, that it was on his own initiative; there even was a halfhearted attempt to establish that no advance copy had been received. No one took that seriously, and it was generally accepted that the speech did represent a top-level consensus and a calculated ploy. Interestingly, the White House staff member who was most explicit to that effect was Clark Mollenhof, who had been a well-known muckraking reporter for Cowles publications and was at that time on the Nixon staff (he was to return to Cowles and by 1973 was one of the president's most embittered and noisy antagonists in press conferences).

Seven days after Des Moines, on November 20, 1969, in a speech to the Montgomery, Alabama, Chamber of Commerce, Agnew evened things up by attacking the *New York Times* and the *Washington Post.* His essential philosophical position was the same as that underlying the speech about the networks: these newspapers represent another small, self-appointed elite.

---

*It seems appropriate at this point to analyze the phrase which occurs so often in news reports and this book: "The White House said. . . ." It is vague and, on the face of it, a bit preposterous. Yet in a larger sense it is quite accurate and there frequently is no alternative to it. Things actually said by the president are contained in press releases and, of course, press conferences. Presidential attitudes on other matters are primarily conveyed through daily White House briefings; typically, the briefing staff member will say something like "The president feels that. . . ." Often, however, he reflects a kind of generalized administration view, one which has not come to presidential attention but about which the staff assumes there'll be no difficulty. Sometimes he speaks simply in terms of "we."

Therefore "The White House said. . . ." might represent, during the first term of Richard Nixon, the president's own statement, but not for attribution; a synthesis of opinion among his closest advisers; a personal interpretation or even an initiative by Ron Ziegler, based on his continuing intimate contact with his chief; or a careful attempt to convey an institutional point of view, in the case of Herbert Klein.

The attribution to the White House thus becomes a convenient shorthand with enough vagueness to encourage candor and enough specificity to assure responsibility.

Moving into specifics, he attacked the *Post* as part of an empire that had too much power through its ownership of radio and television stations and *Newsweek* magazine. As for the *Times*, although it may never have crossed Agnew's mind, Montgomery was a particularly appropriate place to attack it. It was a *Times* advertisement which resulted in what is commonly called the "Sullivan" decision of the United States Supreme Court.

L. B. Sullivan had been the commissioner of public affairs in Montgomery in 1963; he brought suit on the grounds that an advertisement in the *Times* placed by southern liberals libeled him by implying that the police, of whom he was in charge, had failed to carry out their obligations. He asked $500,000 in damages (the other commissioners of the Montgomery city government made it clear that each of them planned to file suit on the same grounds, one at a time). The *Times* lost in the first and second stages, but the United States Supreme Court not only reversed that judgment but used the case to set out a new, and from the point of view of the media, very liberal guideline on the libel of public officials. The *New York Times* was not a favorite publication in Montgomery.

Although he concentrated this time on two leading newspapers, the vice-president did not back down from his belligerent stance toward the networks.

> The day when the network commentators and even gentlemen of the *New York Times* enjoyed a form of diplomatic immunity from comment and criticism of what they said—that day is over.

It was indeed, and Spiro Agnew had summed up, even before it happened, the most important single effect of the Nixon administration's offensive against the media. Suddenly the media were fair game, and Washington was to set the style of the hunt.

Richard Nixon indicated, however, that he bore no grudges. In a press conference on December 9 he was asked questions about his attitude toward the Agnew speeches, and particularly the attack on the networks. He replied that the vice-president was his own man: "[he] does not clear his speeches with me, just as I did not clear my speeches with President Eisenhower," and went on to praise Agnew for a public service in talking "in a very dignified and courageous way" about the problem of unfair coverage.

In the same press conference there was an interesting contradiction of the impassioned remarks of 1962 when he had thanked television for keeping newspapers honest. " . . . perhaps this point should be well taken," he said, "that television stations might well follow the practice of newspapers of separating news from opinion. When opinion is expressed, label it so, but don't mix the opinion in with the reporting of the news." It was not a matter of being inconsistent, one suspects, so much as a matter of already feeling bedeviled.

THREE

Year 1970

... The people have a right to be informed, and the President has a duty to inform them, but the idea of the press playing the role of loyal opposition is a lot of malarkey.

Patrick J. Buchanan

The need probably is to concentrate on NBC and give some real thought as to how to handle the problem that they have created in their almost totally negative approach to everything the Administration does. I would like to see a plan from you; don't worry about fancy form, just some specific thinking on steps that can be taken to try to change this, and I should have this by Friday.

H. R. Haldeman
to J. S. Magruder

About six weeks after Vice-President Agnew's attack on communications empires in his Montgomery speech, a new Florida corporation took an action which suggested that they might have received his message. Greater Miami Telecasters, Inc., applied to the FCC to take over the license of Miami's Channel 10. Channel 10, WPLG-TV, was the property of the Post-Newsweek Stations, Inc., the broadcast arm of the corporation which owns those publications. Greater Miami Telecasters, Inc., was headed by a man named W. Sloan McCrea. McCrea was a business acquaintance of Richard Nixon and a partner of Bebe Rebozo.

The rhetoric of the application was reminiscent of that of minority groups which had contested other license renewals in other places. Local ownership, Greater Miami Telecasters argued, would be in the best interest of the local community because it would be more responsive to its needs; the general tone was that WPLG was a foreign outpost, representing an alien philosophy.

In the opinion of many people it also was the best television station in Florida, with the possible exception of WJXT-TV in Jacksonville, which also belonged to Post-Newsweek. Both stations provided aggressive coverage of community and Florida affairs and occasionally opposed major business interests. Nicholas Johnson, probably the FCC commissioner least easy to please in the history of the agency, later referred to WPLG-TV as the best station in the country in public affairs and news programming.

The challenge might have been motivated only by a sharp business sense, of course. A VHF television station in a major market is, as the biggest media baron of them all, Sir Roy Thomson, once said, "like a license to print money." Its license represents a franchise granted in the name of the people of the United States and renewed, presumably after careful reexamination, every three years. Furthermore, the general philosophy of both the Federal Radio Act of 1927 and the Federal Communications Act of 1934 is that applicants for broadcast licenses should be judged almost exclusively in terms of the service they give the public. Perhaps some student of business someday will explain why eager entrepreneurs have never lined up at license renewal time for profitable stations, trying to outbid each other with good works. Good enterprise-oriented capitalism would seem to require nothing else.

Nevertheless there have been few challenges on that basis, and the filing by Greater Miami Telecasters was generally seen as an attempt to intimidate the *Post*. To most it was unbelievable that the connection between the major figures in the new

Florida corporation and the president of the United States was coincidental.

Abruptly in mid-September, 1970, the challenge was dropped. The Post-Newsweek stations agreed to pay the legal costs of the action under an FCC rule which has since been rescinded, but they bought only a small respite. There would be more challenges by more people associated with Richard Nixon, and the next time, as shown by the tapes subpoenaed by the House Judiciary Committee in its impeachment hearings, the president himself was directly involved.

On February 4, 1970, H. R. Haldeman wrote a memo to J. S. Magruder. The word CONFIDENTIAL was typed on the left margin, at the top; the words HIGH PRIORITY were rubber-stamped alongside. It began:

> A couple of points I did not want to cover in the general meeting, but that you do need to move ahead on quickly. First, I'm sure you have studied that TV summary done by Buchanan, which is a devastating indictment of NBC, especially of David Brinkley.

We shall return to the substantive content of the memorandum later, but this is a good time to look briefly at Patrick Buchanan. Buchanan was the administration's resident expert on the media in general, and it was Buchanan who, by his involvement in the preparation of some of the vice-president's speeches, helped prime the biggest gun of all.

It was pointed out earlier that, as Herbert Klein's influence in the administration diminished, the essential job of media relations fell into the hands of staff members whose point of view was not that of the news business but of corporate public relations. Patrick Buchanan had had just enough involvement in the news business to understand it from the insider's point of view, but not enough to respect the good professional's commitments.

Buchanan was a graduate of the Columbia School of Journalism in 1962. Columbia generally is considered to have the
highest prestige of any journalism school in the country, a fact
not lost on those who gain admission to it. A year later they
come sailing out with a certain amount of *chutzpah*. Patrick
Buchanan came out with a hell of a lot, most of which he had
brought in with him. He was the most visible member of his
class, with almost stereotyped Irish aggressiveness. He did everything with great vigor, including knocking down a classmate in a
fight at a Christmas party. He was an announced conservative;
he also was one of the better students.

From Columbia he went to work on the *St. Louis Globe-
Democrat,* the publisher of which, Richard Amberg, was an old
friend of Richard Nixon. The *Globe-Democrat* has been for
more than half a century one of those newspapers which have
been edited against, or around, a more illustrious competitor. It
has drawn much of its identity from not being the *Post-
Dispatch*. It nevertheless has been a sound newspaper in its own
right. As a matter of fact, until the disappearance of the *St.
Louis Star-Times* in 1951, that relatively small city had two
very sound "other" newspapers. For most of this century,
nevertheless, the Pulitzer inheritance exemplified in the *Post-
Dispatch* has been overpowering. Its editorial page was always
well to the left, as newspaper politics go; its great long-time
cartoonist, Fitzpatrick, was a predecessor of Herblock in his
social commitments. The *Globe-Democrat* thus became—
perhaps more than its news columns indicated—a place where an
aggressive young conservative might land as an editorial writer.
Patrick Buchanan did just that shortly after he got his degree;
he never worked as a reporter. In 1966 he became assistant
editorial editor.

There was a shortage of Republican big names to work on
the Congressional campaign for 1966. Ronald Reagan, George
Romney, and Nelson Rockefeller all were caught up in their
own gubernatorial campaigns; Goldwater had been brutally discredited. The enterprise which called itself "Congress '66" began with a group of less than a dozen made up of Richard

Nixon's friends with Nixon as leader. One of them was Richard Amberg, who gave his young editorialist leave to go on Nixon's personal staff. Buchanan never returned to the *Globe-Democrat.*

There had been a close tie of personal friendship between Nixon and Buchanan from that beginning in 1966. When Buchanan married a White House receptionist in 1971, the Nixons attended; the occasion produced an appealing photograph, filled with mutual affection, which was widely published. Buchanan was to serve the president even after most of the other servitors were gone. In what must have seemed to the president the grim summer of 1973, he was the only witness before Senator Ervin's Watergate committee who defended his boss with flair and enthusiasm and who clearly scored some points in his behalf. Richard Nixon was heartened by the performance. That night the Nixons asked the Buchanans over for a drink and lifted a glass to better days. It was a fine, relaxed evening, Buchanan told acquaintances later.

As the Nixon administration moved into the second full year, Buchanan had been established in a key role in the relationship between the media and the administration. He had little direct contact with reporters or editors. That was Klein's, and increasingly Ziegler's, province. One of Buchanan's major tasks was the supervision of the preparation of the morning "briefing book." This mixture of summary and commentary at that stage normally ran between five and ten thousand words. Buchanan himself wrote the final five-hundred-word summary about an hour before the completed packet was placed on the president's desk. A staff of four or five worked on the report, monitoring the networks, the wire services, some magazines and a number of newspapers variously reported as ranging from thirty-five to fifty. EYES ONLY FOR THE PRESIDENT was stamped on the cover of the document. When Nixon was away from Washington, the material was transmitted by facsimile to wherever he might be. It was sent daily to both Peking and Moscow during the pioneering visits of February and May, 1972.

Although distribution was presumably tightly controlled,

many reporters saw a copy—Buchanan rather enjoyed showing
it off—and reported their impressions. William Small of CBS
said:

> This author saw one edition which was largely objective
> though it referred to NBC's David Brinkley as reporting
> "in his usual snide fashion" and in a report on Eric
> Sevareid, said he was "on our side for a change." The
> flavor of it was "us" versus "them."[1]

Julius Duscha, in a piece for the *New York Times Sunday
Magazine,* said:

> For the most part, the summary is a straight-forward
> bulletin version of what the networks, the wire services,
> the newspapers and magazines are reporting and analyzing.
> Most of the items noted are news about the Government,
> politics, or foreign policy. . . . But the summary does not
> ignore the lighter side of the news. "LA Times piece on
> Presidential humor gives RN positive treatment . . . notes
> such various quips as 'outhouse' question at news confer-
> ence. . . ."[2]

Duscha, writing before the explosion of the Watergate
matter, felt that Nixon was relying less on the daily briefing
book by the beginning of the second term, and there were
reports shortly before Nixon's resignation that he had abandoned it altogether. It is clear in any case that Patrick Buchanan
had from the beginning much to do with not only what Richard
Nixon knew, but what he felt, about the media. This makes
Buchanan's own feelings and attitudes of major importance in
the wide-ranging attacks upon the media and the inevitable
inferential thrusts at freedom of expression during the Nixon
years. He was the in-house philosopher. For purposes of analysis, it is fortunate that he has been willing to express his ideas
forcefully and publicly. They reduce to a very simple concept:
that the essential role of the media is to support and assist the

government in carrying out the purposes to which its leaders are pledged. He put it bluntly to Duscha in the summer of 1972.

> My primary concern is that the President have the right of untrammeled communication with the American people. When that communication is completed, what he has had to say should not be immediately torn apart or broken down even before the American people have had a chance to make their own judgment about what he said.
> The President is a unifying factor even if he is a politician as well as chief of state. The people have a right to be informed, and the President has the duty to inform them, but the idea of the press playing the role of loyal opposition is a lot of malarkey.[3]

Buchanan went on to make clear that he considered a broadcast system which permitted Eric Sevareid and David Brinkley, with antiadministration attitudes, to speak nightly to "20 million American homes" to be defective at best. He suggested at various times antitrust action and other procedures to challenge network ownership of broadcasting stations (the network-owned stations produce a significant share of those companies' profits). He suggested legislation, never very thoroughly described, to somehow break up what he read most of the time as hostility to the man he worked for.

Appearing on the "CBS Morning News" in October, 1973, shortly after a stormy Nixon press conference, Buchanan said it again:

> Every legal and constitutional means ought to be considered to break up that dominance, in order to spread it out so that you decentralize power in this area.[4]

It was to Buchanan's role as the administration's expert on the media that Haldeman referred in the memo of February 4, 1970, when he spoke of "that TV summary done by Buchanan,

which is a devastating indictment of NBC, especially of David
Brinkley."
    Brinkley was, at this relatively early stage of the regime, a
particular bête noire. This specific reference was to a commentary on the new budget; Haldeman said he was "completely off
base factually . . . and we need to get that one straightened
out." He wanted action, furthermore.

> The need probably is to concentrate on NBC and give
> some real thought as to how to handle the problem that
> they have created in their almost totally negative approach
> to everything the administration does. I would like to see a
> plan from you; don't worry about fancy form, just some
> specific thinking on steps that can be taken to try to
> change this, and I should have this by Friday.

    He then went on to suggest getting the Silent Majority (the
capitals are his) mobilized to write complaining letters to NBC,
Time, Newsweek, Life, the *New York Times,* and the *Washington Post.* The memo concludes with an exhortation to move
fast in preparing a mailing piece which would capitalize on
favorable editorial response to the State of the Union Address
of January 22. (The complete text of the memo begins on page
266.)
    The White House memoranda which were released through
the Watergate committee seem to be samples from what was
clearly a continuing flow, the full dimensions and content of
which probably never will be known. This particular one suggests the growing preoccupation with ways of hurting the networks badly enough to make them back off. It seems probable
that there must have been others like it.
    Troubles with the media notwithstanding, February of
1970 was a good month for the Nixon administration. Student
unrest was building up, but the corrosive numbers of wartime
casualties were declining. By the end of the month, United
States combat deaths in Vietnam were down 50 percent from
the comparable two-month period at the beginning of the
previous year. The Tet cease-fire turned out to be just that.

Bolstered, perhaps, by the thought that the opposition was weakening, the top United States command began planning a thrust which developed into a military farce and a domestic disaster.

Before that crisis, the president had to take an embarrassing failure, much of it due to the media. On April 8 the Senate refused to confirm G. Harrold Carswell as a justice of the United States Supreme Court. It was an astonishing second straight defeat for the president in trying to fill the vacancy left by Abe Fortas's forced resignation. The evidence that hurt most, it was generally agreed, was a 1948 Carswell speech praising segregation which was dug out by WJXT-TV in Jacksonville. The station belonged to the *Washington Post* group. Once serious questions about Carswell were raised, the media gave him a good deal of attention, and little of it was favorable.

Signs of serious unrest among young people multiplied during the late winter and early spring. Eminent universities such as Michigan and Yale were shut down by militant black students. A townhouse in Greenwich Village blew up, killing two people in their twenties who were affiliated with the Weatherman faction of the Students for a Democratic Society. The townhouse was a bomb factory. Within the next week there were six more bomb blasts in locales from Albuquerque to Manhattan.

On April 30 Richard Nixon addressed the nation on prime time television and announced that United States troops were, as he spoke, striking deep into Cambodia to wipe out "headquarters for the entire Communist military operation in South Vietnam" as well as major supply depots. He explained carefully that this was not an escalation of the war, and that United States troops would withdraw as soon as the operation was complete.

The matter of television technique was hardly consequential compared to the content of the message and the response which it provoked, but it is worth noting that Nixon moved beyond the familiar "talking head" arrangement and, picking up a pointer, showed the location of the strike on a map. In a second speech about the Cambodian action, a kind of progress report on May 8, he used films as supportive evidence of his assertion that the operation had been successful (media coverage had clearly indicated that it had not). The American audience thus had the new experience of hearing their president, like any newscaster, do voice-over narration for footage from the war zone.

In between the two prime time appearances explaining Cambodia the most severe civil disturbances of the Nixon presidency took place. There were furious attacks in Congress and the beginnings of activity to curb presidential power. A wave of boycotts and violent demonstrations rolled through American campuses; ROTC buildings and computer centers were attacked and burned, but any kind of building became a target of opportunity. Before it was over Stanford alone had more that $500,000 worth of broken glass.

And on May 4, Ohio National Guardsmen posted at a university most citizens had never heard of, Kent State, fired into a group of young people and killed four of them. Six days later troopers fired into a group of students at predominantly-black Jackson State. That time two died.

The death of students at the hands of the military or the police had been common enough in some of the rest of the world even in this century—but not in the United States. The shock was profound and the effect continuing. One of the immediate consequences was a series of events which made a one-time figure of suspicion into a minor martyr.

The appointment of Walter Hickel to the cabinet position of secretary of the interior at the beginning of the Nixon regime provoked cries of alarm from a wide range of Nixon opponents, particularly the groups interested in preservation of the environment. Hickel had been governor of Alaska, and his record was taken as indicating he was likely to do favors for oil and timber interests at the cost of the wilderness. He had been inconspicuous since the inauguration.

Then, on May 10, 1970, he sent a long, eloquent letter to the president (and his aides leaked it to the media) which called for more sympathetic attention to be paid to the voices—and the actions—of the young. He also suggested that a damper be put on the noisy rhetoric of the vice-president. The media suddenly found Hickel attractive, even a hero; friendly coverage burgeoned. It was the kind of thing, one suspects, which cuts more than the apparent depth of the blade might indicate. It is not clear precisely what it did to Richard Nixon, but it clearly did not go unnoticed. Six months later he fired Hickel.

In mid-summer some things which *Life* magazine stated Chet Huntley of NBC had said brought a flurry of White House brainstorming about further attacks on the media. Huntley was quoted in the magazine as saying that the thought of Nixon as president "frightens me" and that the man's "shallowness overwhelms me." Huntley immediately, and convincingly, denied it in letters to both *Life* and the president.[5] Since Huntley did not release a copy of the letter to Nixon to the press, the White House could not officially do so, but a staff member arranged to leak it.

The episode produced a CONFIDENTIAL/EYES ONLY memorandum to Haldeman and Klein from Jeb S. Magruder. This memo is extraordinarily useful because of the summary insight which it provides into the nature of the attack, which one White House staff member, at least, considered appropriate. Although he began by addressing himself to the presumed Huntley remark, Magruder dismissed that as something easily handled and got to the heart of the matter:

> Since the newscaster enjoys a very favorable public image and will apologize for his remarks, claiming to be misquoted, we should not attempt to discredit him personally. Also, since his remarks were expressed as an individual, we would have difficulty attacking his network directly. The focus of our effort should be to raise the larger question of objectivity and ethics in the media as an institution.

He spoke of his objective as "to generate a public reexamination of the role of the media in American life." He then set out a series of specific actions to achieve that purpose. There were eighteen of them, variegated. (Complete text of the memo begins on page 270.)

He suggested that Klein get Kevin Phillips, a conservative columnist, to write a piece about objectivity and ethics; that Lyn Nofziger, a former newsman who was then deputy assistant to the president for congressional relations, arrange for Dean Burch to express "concern" (the quotation marks are Magruder's) about press objectivity in response to a letter from a congressman; that Klein, through his contacts in the American Society of Newspaper Editors and the National Association of Broadcasters, bring up the question of a "fairness pledge" (his quotes) for their members. He suggested that Buchanan write a speech on the subject for the vice-president, that Nofziger "through independent Hill sources" stimulate nonpartisan congressional questioning of the issue, and then place such remarks in the *Congressional Record.* He proposed that through an "academic source" the dean of a leading graduate school of journalism be encouraged to acknowledge that press objectivity is a problem which needs discussion. (This one was proposed to Klein and Safire, who was regarded as the house intellectual at the time.) He even suggested that Nofziger arrange for a senator or congressman to write a public letter to the FCC suggesting the licensing of individual newsmen, in a kind of derivative analog of broadcast station licenses.

Some of the suggestions are close to preposterous, and the whole memorandum has about it the panting naiveté of the energetic underling trying to look good to his bosses. There is no available record of how Haldeman responded or how far any of the projects went; certainly none of them reached conspicuous fruition. More important than their content is the tone of gut attack on the whole institution and the evidence of what Magruder felt to be the temper of the men for whom he worked.

Not all the activities directed at the media during the summer and fall of 1970 were hostile. In large part because of Klein's sound insight into the news business and his still-considerable clout, some of the most persistent mechanical and bureaucratic annoyances of covering the government had been ironed out. The president's travels were announced well in advance and the logistics much improved over the Johnson and Kennedy days. Transcripts were quick and accurate. Access to people newsmen wanted to see—and whom the White House wanted them to see—was expedited. And in April of 1970, a suspicious White House press corps was moved from the west lobby into opulent new quarters which had been built over the old swimming pool in the west wing. The new facility was designated the West Terrace Press Center, and it was done expensively in what was described at the time by various veteran correspondents as "motel modern" and "fake Elizabethan steakhouse." There was much carpeting, potted plants, early American prints. And there was a discreet public address system through which announcements were made, although most of the time it purveyed the bland syrup of uninterrupted music. One old White House reporter is supposed to have said upon his first sight of the place, "well—all right, I'll have one drink, but I won't go upstairs."

In terms of the elemental creature comforts and communications facilities the new accommodations were much better than the old. The reason reporters grumbled suspiciously was that they now had no access to the west lobby. David Wise quotes Hugh Sidey, chief of *Time*'s Washington bureau:

> You are prevented from going in the old West Wing entrance. So you cannot see who is coming and going to see the President. The whole purpose is to cut the press off from the flow of visitors to the White House. You are barred from going out on the driveway. If you loiter by the West Wing, the guards tell you to go back.[6]

From the earliest days of systematic coverage of the White House, on-the-wing interviews with presidential visitors had been an important source of news stories. The process of making that more difficult began under the Eisenhower administration and with Nixon disappeared altogether. It was no longer possible to have any idea of movement in and around the president's working quarters.

In 1970 much emphasis also was put upon better briefing. The briefing process always has been fundamental, but Nixon— for a time—did far more with it than any of his predecessors. On June 25, for example, he invited executives from forty newspapers and broadcasting operations to San Clemente for a "private" briefing which lasted almost six hours. The *Washington Post* and the *New York Times* pointedly were not invited. The occasion was one of the earlier flowerings of what was by late summer a comprehensive plan to pay more attention to the press in the rest of the country and bypass the media in the Washington-New York area.

In an analysis story on August 24, the *Times* described it as a strategy in five parts: (1) top level briefings by the president and other officials for news executives; (2) briefings on legislative proposals for reporters around the country by administration teams; (3) special mailings to editorial writers and broadcast news directors; (4) direct appeals to the public through presidential television addresses; (5) a minimum of presidential contacts with the White House corps, with contacts almost always in formal meetings.

Several aspects of this schema need comment. It is important to notice the emphasis placed upon news executives in distinction to reporters. That means, in newspapers, editors, managing editors, and publishers; in broadcasting, news directors and station managers. This is a demonstration of the knowledgeable Herbert Klein at work. Such people are the ones primarily responsible for policy. They seldom walk into the newsroom and announce "The Line"; their attitudes come through indirect cues which are passed along through the structure. The newsman who knows that his boss sympathizes with the president, or that he was a special guest at San Clemente and rather enjoyed it, has a different attitude than one without such reminders. The only special attention for working reporters, it will be observed, is aimed at political writers outside the Washington area who would be subjected to the considerable flattery of visitation by a clutch of administration staff men talking about legislative objectives.

There were several of these elaborate briefing sessions during the summer and fall of 1970. Generally they were set up in connection with a presidential visit for some other purpose. News executives from the region were invited in for confidential talks with the president with plenty of time for questions and answers. Keeping it off the record was not difficult; there is no indication that he ever said anything genuinely newsworthy. Much of the emphasis was upon the need for media outside the Washington—New York axis to assert their independence. Broadcasters were urged to develop more independence from network news, newspapers from accepting the national agenda as presented by the *Times*.

On October 8, Nixon had such a session with editors, publishers, and broadcast executives from the northeast during a stopover in Hartford, Connecticut. On November 9, he invited nine columnists of a conservative or moderate inclination to a seventy-minute background briefing on his views of the Supreme Court and his intentions of appointing a southern conservative.

After establishing personal connections with such devices, the Nixon staff kept them warm through periodic notes—"The President asked me to tell you that he particularly liked your editorial last Sunday"—and annotated Christmas cards. This was traditional presidential behavior, of course, but at a higher level of intensity and thoroughness.

Many people never asked to a private presidential briefing got mail from his office. This writer was at that time chairman of the Journalism Department at the University of Michigan, which probably explains how his name got on a special list. One morning in the early summer of 1970 a wide-eyed secretary entered the inner office carrying with extended arms, rather like some ceremonial object, a fat parchment-like envelope with "The White House" embossed on it and an obviously hand-typed address label.

Inside were texts of two recent Nixon statements with a letter of transmittal from the director of communications. With dignified intimacy he said he realized that I knew, of course, about the attached, but that most of the reporting of them which he'd seen had been pretty sketchy, and it had occurred to him that maybe I'd like to read them in entirety. It was signed "Herb," although we had not, at that time, met. There were two or three more such packets during the following year.

One of the crueler aspects of the unremitting coverage of the United States presidency is the lack of accommodation to normal human error, to misspeaking, to an unthinking expression of irritation. Richard Nixon had several such moments. Once he pushed Ron Ziegler into the path of advancing newsmen; in a strange episode which will never be completely explained, apparently, he either slapped or stroked the cheek of a man holding a child in an airport crowd. On August 3, 1970, he committed the first such gaffe to come to public attention. The trial of Charles Manson and his "family," accused of a particularly revolting set of killings, was underway. At a meeting in Denver of law enforcement personnel, Nixon made an impromptu reference to Manson being "guilty, directly or indirectly, of eight murders without reason." Ziegler tried to undo the slip, but it was headlines within an hour or two and the tape was on the evening newscasts. Defense attorneys displayed newspapers in the courtroom in the attempt to get a mistrial declared (they failed). Attempts to explain became news in themselves. On August 6, Representative Charles Wiggins, a California Republican, declared that Nixon's comments on the Manson trial, while "wrong," had been "relatively unimportant news" and that the press had acted "irresponsibly" in reporting them.[7]

In retrospect, it seems that the congressman very possibly was correct. At no point in the popular mind, at least (which is another way of saying in the way the media handled the Manson trial) was there any other than formal possibility of Manson's innocence. Nixon, always a clumsy ad-libber, simply said what everybody else had been saying, and the media made him pay for it.

In September the congressional campaign began to heat up. Vice-President Agnew took again to the provinces with lance and thesaurus, flaying for feckless arrogance college administrators and others who had failed to keep the young and the black under control and appealing to the silent majority to arise and, through the election of Republicans, seize the power which was rightfully theirs. The president also began to warm up for a fall and winter of greater political activity; he began to speak of "thugs" and "hoodlums" on campus.

And, on September 25, Charles W. Colson wrote a memorandum to H. R. Haldeman. Colson was at that time special counsel to the president, a bland title which conveyed little of his actual role and even less of his mode of operation. A reporter once described him as the White House hatchet man. He was, at that time, a fiercely ambitious backroom fighter who took joy in smiting his enemies, whether inside or outside the administration—and his enemies included almost everybody except his immediate superiors, Haldeman and Nixon. Them he tried hard, almost obsequiously, to please.

He fed material and witnesses to a *Life* reporter writing an exposé of Senator Millard Tydings of Delaware. Court testimony during 1974 indicated it was Colson who ordered the forgery of State Department cables to implicate John Kennedy in the assassination of Ngo Dinh Diem. He was generally considered the originator and guardian of the White House "enemies" list. He hired E. Howard Hunt, later to be convicted as a conspirator in the Watergate break-in, as a White House consultant. In 1972 he said he would walk over his own grandmother if it would help reelect Richard Nixon.

In his book *The Politics of Lying,* David Wise sees Colson, rather than Ziegler, as the primary force in squeezing Herbert Klein out of power. He describes Colson as the real director of public relations and a central figure of the "Image" committee, a group officially known as the Plans Committee, which met weekly during the early years of the administration. It was Colson who arranged for construction workers to present Nixon with a hard hat, who organized a group of Vietnam veterans to counteract the antiwar movement among them; he even took on the job of leading cheers for Phase II, a set of economic controls directed against high prices and inflation.

On the personal level, Colson could be biting about the

people with whom he worked. When a junior member of the administration once made a comment to him about Clay T. Whitehead, director of the Office of Telecommunications Policy, he snapped back "why do you pay any attention to him? He doesn't know a damn thing and he speaks for nobody."

All told, Colson (perhaps one should say the old Colson; in 1974 he underwent a religious conversion) was an unlovely man. This was very evident in the memorandum of September 25, 1970, in which he reported his visits with the heads of the networks. There was an oddly embarrassing combination of obsequiousness and arrogance; it had the tone of an eager underling not only trying to please his chief—Haldeman—but to establish that the two of them share a unique and intimate superiority. It made clear at least one approach to what the administration saw as the continuing problem of the networks.

Basically, Colson's (and apparently the administration's) tactic at the time was to discourage any favors for the opposition. Agnew had attacked "instant analysis," contending strongly that the president should have the right to make his arguments without immediate rebuttal. Now, with Colson's visit to the top executives of the networks, the White House was moving to suppress any kind of activity which was identifiable as presentation of an opposition case (one remembers Patrick Buchanan's single-mindedness on the subject). CBS had provided the flash point.

Some time earlier that network had announced that it would provide a series of prime-time opportunities for the voice of the "loyal opposition." This was one more facet of the unending confusion surrounding the good-hearted but vague Fairness Doctrine of the Federal Communications Commission. To maintain their licenses, broadcast stations must be "fair" in their treatment of controversial subjects, but they have no further guidelines. As owners of highly profitable television stations in the biggest markets, the networks always have been jittery about the possible impact of fairness complaints, and 1970 was a bad year. In August, Senator William Fulbright, chairman of the Senate Foreign Relations Committee, introduced legislation which would give Congress, on demand, access to national television, a legal right paralleling the unlimited access given the president as a courtesy by the networks. At the same time the FCC had under advisement rulings on cases brought by a meat cutter's union and the Democratic National Committee; the union had wanted to buy radio commercials to encourage support of a boycott, and the Democratic committee to buy fund-raising television commercials, and both had been refused on the grounds that the material was too controversial.

The networks, of course, opposed both the Fulbright legislation and any change in the FCC rules which left most decisions about access to the broadcaster. It was an unpleasant position, and they felt surrounded by enemies with no friends on the horizon. It was within this context that "Chuck" Colson went to New York to lean on them.

> The harder I pressed them, the more accommodating, cordial, and almost apologetic they became,

Colson said in his memo to Haldeman.

> They were startled by how thoroughly we were doing our homework—both from the standpoint of knowledge of the law, as I discussed it, but more importantly, from the way in which we have so thoroughly monitored their coverage and our analysis of it . . . .
> There was unanimous agreement that the President's right of access to TV should in no way be restrained. . . . All agree that no one has a right of "reply" and that fairness doesn't mean answering the president but rather is "issue oriented." This was the most important understanding we came to.
> CBS does not defend the O'Brien appearance. Paley wanted to make it very clear that it would not happen again and that they would not permit partisan attacks on the President.

The reference to O'Brien is to Lawrence O'Brien, chairman of the Democratic National Committee, who had served as the party's spokesman in the first of the rebuttal sessions for which

CBS had provided time. Democrats had been almost as unhappy with O'Brien's low-key, rather wooden performance as Republicans with the extension of the privilege.

Colson went on to set out differences among the three networks about the best ways in which to provide an outlet to the opposition which, by inference, would be acceptable to the administration. NBC, according to Colson, felt that some kind of device for giving Congress access occasionally would serve, "ABC will do anything we want," but CBS did not feel that access for Congress was enough. "On this critical point," Colson wrote, "which may be the most critical of all, we can split the networks in a way very much to our advantage."

It is Colson's picture of fawning and intimidated media giants that is most striking, however.

> Stanton for all his bluster is the most insecure of all. . . . (Paley is in complete control of CBS—Stanton is almost obsequious in Paley's presence) . . . .
>
> I had to break up every meeting. The networks badly want to have those kinds of discussions which they said they had had with other Administrations but never with ours. They told me anytime we had a complaint about slanted coverage for me to call them directly. Paley said he would like to come down to Washington and spend time with me anytime that I wanted. In short, they are very much afraid of us and trying hard to prove they are "good guys." . . .
>
> The only ornament on Goodman's [Julian Goodman, president of NBC] desk was the Nixon Inaugural Medal. Hagerty [James Hagerty, former Eisenhower press secretary and vice-president of ABC] said in Goldenson's [Leonard Goldenson, president of ABC] presence that ABC is "with us." This all adds up to the fact that they are damned nervous and we should continue to take a very tough line, face to face, and in other ways.

Colson concludes by proposing a careful and continuing monitoring of network news performance with Ziegler, Klein, or Colson calling to protest any detected slanting. This policy was carried out energetically in succeeding years. Colson also promised that he would pursue with ABC and NBC the matter of their issuing a policy statement on presidential rights on television which would back CBS into "an untenable position." No such statements were issued.

Colson also indicated he would discuss with Dean Burch, chairman of the FCC, the possibility of a ruling which would hold, in effect, that when the president was on television he was acting as president and was thus above the political considerations of the Fairness Doctrine. Colson assumed, however, that such a ruling would be possible only "as soon as we have a majority [on the FCC]." No such ruling was ever made. (Complete text of the memo begins on p. 274.)

It would be naive to accept at face value Colson's description of the behavior of the network executives to whom he talked. Those who are in a position to provide contrary information are not likely to do so; any humiliation they may have felt, or affected, in the presence of the Nixon emissary must have been trivial compared with what they felt when the memorandum became public during the Watergate hearings in the fall of 1973. In any case, the revelation of Colson's own personality and character which it provides is more graphic than anything he said about anybody else. Considering the role he played for more than three years in shaping the American people's perception of their president, it is a disquieting revelation.

A bright young systems engineer named Clay Thomas Whitehead became director of the Office of Telecommunications Policy in the fall of 1970. He was thirty-two. He had a classic American background, but one which somehow never became much of a stereotype in our culture. Everybody knows about the small, tough band of rich sons and daughters with a social conscience who have played a large role in the management of this society; and about the *wunderkinder* from the Bay area and the Bronx and the Chicago suburbs, mathematicians and physicists and conceptualizers of the new technology; and the poor boys from the farm who fight their way into the seats of power (there are fewer of these, one suspects, than the folklore indicates). But few analysts, social or literary, have paid attention to the nonsuburban, nonrural small town youngsters who are bright and highly motivated and quickly shoot out of the pack.

Towns such as Columbus, Kansas (where Whitehead grew up), and the larger adjoining city of Parsons (where he finished high school) have good schools, thoughtful counselors, well-run small businesses, municipal libraries big enough to open windows in the mind and yet small enough for an occasional seventeen- or eighteen-year-old to have read everything they hold that is worth reading. Such places reflect the world of power, comfortably miniaturized. Yet there is a curious, endemic limit to the aspiration they usually stir. Few graduates of Parsons High School have gone to the Massachusetts Institute of Technology, or any other elite school; few even think about it.

Whitehead took a bachelor's degree and a master's degree in engineering at MIT, but his interests began to move toward less clinical activities. He earned a Ph.D. in management at MIT, working in the summers at the Rand Corporation, and then worked full time with that organization.

In the spring of 1968, the presidential campaign of Hubert Humphrey, oddly enough, brought Whitehead into a field he had thought about very little—politics and government. Somebody attempted to recruit him for the Humphrey staff. He refused, but the offer triggered some self-analysis and he decided, he told a *Times* interviewer, that he was a "political animal." He also decided that he was closer to Richard Nixon than Humphrey and went to work with the Nixon campaign. He worked on speeches and carried out various chores of analysis. He then stayed on after the election in the tooling-up phase of the new administration and, after the inauguration, became a member of the White House staff.

There he had the leading role—in great part at his own initiative, apparently—in the development, from the framework of an old service agency, of a new enterprise called the Office of Telecommunications Policy. Since 1961 there had been within the General Services Administration a division of Transportation and Communications Service, the latter subdivision a reorganization of the former Office of Telecommunications. In both incarnations it was a small, administrative management organization which was responsible for "planning and coordinating the development, design, establishment, and operation of the Federal civil agencies' communications programs."[8] That is, it saw to the efficient operation of the mechanics of transmission and reception in the internal communications system of the civil arm of the national government.

In September, 1970, this office was reorganized through a White House order as an agency in the Executive Office of the President and its name changed back to the earlier form—the Office of Telecommunications—with the immensely significant word *policy* added. "Tom" Whitehead was named as director at a salary of $40,000 a year and his appointment confirmed by the Senate.

There is a tendency to overestimate the neatness with which OTP articulates with other White House strategies directed against the media. Whitehead seems to be the bright, profoundly innocent technician giving unquestioning obedience to what he guesses to be the wishes of his superiors, who invented a master scheme only part of which they have revealed to him. As the grand scheme evolves, their calculations prove to be imperfect, the responses to their initiatives less predictable than anticipated, the whole enterprise not quite as useful as hoped; and the bright young man in charge is shunted aside, with only a nod of institutional gratitude, as the big men move toward other devices.

This may have been the way it happened, but the story also is that of a useful idea diverted to shortsighted political ends. As an attempt to bring pressure on the broadcasting business, it was very briefly successful; it then collapsed and, if anything, for all practical purposes ended by strengthening both the spirit—and the reputation—of the institutions it was intended to damage. It was a thrust that backlashed. The pity is the greater because it might well have been the administration's greatest contribution to a more responsible role for the media in American society.

The mandate which OTP was given at the time of its

formation was very broad. It was to do all the management chores of the former agency and, beyond, serve as "the adviser to the president of the United States on all telecommunications matters," in the words of a grumpy Senator Pastore when he opened a critical Senate committee hearing in February, 1973.[9] Specifically, it undertook to provide the information necessary for policymaking in such areas as common carrier communications (including satellites), cable television, public broadcasting, license renewal procedures, the use of the Fairness Doctrine and the problem of access, new technology, computers and communication, international systems and facilities, the United States role in international communication organizations, and, inevitably, "future plans and policies." It had substantial funding and, within a short time, a staff of sixty-seven.

To anyone with some knowledge of the regulation of broadcasting in this country, the list set out above has a curious quality of overlap about it; most of these things, other than international relations, seem to be within the province of the Federal Communications Commission as described in the Communications Act of 1934. In fact, there was a developing sense of competition between the two from the time the new agency was established. The lack of enthusiasm for OTP and Whitehead on the part of Dean Burch, chairman of the FCC, was obvious from the beginning. In addition, there is a traditional belief within the independent regulatory agencies that the executive branch constantly seeks more control of their affairs, particularly through the Office of Management and Budget. Whitehead's casual put-downs of the FCC as "flabby" worsened the atmosphere. From the FCC's point of view, the new instant empire, established under the president's protection and with close ties to him, represented at best second-guessers with license to tinker.

Yet there were good reasons for OTP's establishment. The Federal Communications Commission, particularly since the full coming of television, has had a demanding administrative load. The basic business of broadcast license renewals and transfers, along with the development of ways of regulating new broadcast forms such as cable, is all a small staff with a small budget can handle. Philosophical inquiry and basic research go by the boards, yet few social institutions have such need for continuing analysis and thinking-through.

Furthermore, the independent regulatory agency in this government is bipartisan by law (no more than four of the FCC's seven members can be of the same political party) and cannot indulge in advocacy. Although the president does appoint its members and chairmen, this does not necessarily make them the president's men. As in the case of many appointments to the judiciary, FCC members often develop a strong streak of independence. Dean Burch, although he poked into a couple of fires in search of presidential chestnuts early on, increasingly took a stance of his own.

If the president desired a platform and a spokesman as a means of exerting more direct pressure on the way broadcasting goes in this country—and Richard Nixon decided that he did—a new agency was needed. Apart from the technical administration of the government's own communication system, it was set up with no actual powers. It was advisory and a device for jawboning. It also was free of many of the restrictions of power which affect every action of the FCC; it could float trial balloons, underwrite speculative research, dig into such thorny matters as the relative efficiency of monopoly and competition in given situations without developing the tremendous pressure constantly generated by any moves of the other agency.

By the end of 1970, the new Office of Telecommunications Policy was well underway. It had let six contracts totaling over a million dollars. Five of these were concerned essentially with engineering. The sixth, a modest $86,000 arrangement with the National Academy of Sciences, was "to continue to provide guidance to the Director of Telecommunications Policy in formulating a methodology for determining the economic and social value of the electro-magnetic spectrum in such a way that these values may be incorporated into the spectrum management process."

There is a quality of ignorance in action, in Goethe's phrase, in the notion that NAS—or anybody else—could develop a "methodology" for "determining" economic and social values of any sort, but it indicated that Whitehead and his staff were thinking big and, at least, attacking noteworthy problems.

Meanwhile, the director was warming to his role as spokesman for the president in matters relating to broadcasting. He was blunt, acerbic, and sometimes flashed a stabbing wit.

Clay Whitehead was to have a curious role in the Nixon administration before it ended. The speech which brought him most to public attention was delivered in late 1972 and is discussed later in this study. Early in 1973 he was out front in laying out the administration's position on public broadcasting. After that, oddly, he seemed to fall not only from public attention but from any kind of significant role in the White House establishment. From late spring of 1973 until the end of the Nixon regime he was said to be on his way out, anxious to resign.

Then he began to appear again in major roles. In early 1974 a report concerning the development of cable television appeared, produced by a committee chaired by Whitehead; it was widely regarded as an excellent piece of work. In July the White House sent to the Congress a new proposal for the funding of public television which was to a great extent his work, both in preparation and in persuading Richard Nixon to like it.

At the time of the release of the cable television report, Les Brown of the *New York Times* wrote:

> Some observers in Washington attribute the idealistic character of the cable-TV proposals to circumstances created by Watergate. Mr. Whitehead, having seen the power of his office diminished with that of the Administration, and having seen other bright young loyalists disgraced in the Watergate hearing, has decided to leave government service.
>
> One theory is that Mr. Whitehead stayed on to see through the issuance of a statesman-like cable-TV report to counter his negative image with a positive deed.[10]

In fact, Whitehead was to stay on through the last days, almost eight months later. His final service to government was to him distasteful, but of importance.

In May of 1974, Philip Buchen, a former law partner of

Gerald Ford and staff director of a committee working on problems of privacy, decided it was unlikely that Richard Nixon would survive as president and took it upon himself to begin the planning for an orderly transition (he did not tell Ford). According to James Naughton of the *New York Times,* Buchen decided to approach Whitehead for help for two reasons. Whitehead had been a member of the team set up by Nixon in the fall of 1968 to plan the transition from Lyndon Johnson's administration, and hence had something resembling experience. He also "was one of the few Nixon aides that Mr. Buchen knew well—and thought he could trust with a large secret."[11]

Whitehead still felt loyalty to Nixon and was reluctant to face the project, but finally consented and organized a three-man team which, working out of his kitchen, prepared a checklist of things that had to be done when the moment came. Meanwhile he had delivered his resignation and was preparing—more than a year after the rumors started—finally to leave government service. He was packed for departure and a camping trip to Colorado on August 7 when the word came that there indeed would be a presidential resignation. Ford hurriedly had chosen a group of five close friends to manage details. Whitehead sat in with them. The meeting was held in his office, and he was still dressed in boots and blue jeans.

Those melancholy days were a long way ahead, however, in 1970, as the young man who had decided that he was a political animal set out to make the Office of Telecommunications Policy a force to be reckoned with.

FOUR

Year 1971

I don't give a damn how it is done, do whatever has to be done to stop these leaks and prevent further unauthorized disclosures. I don't want to be told why it can't be done.

Richard Nixon on the Pentagon Papers,
as quoted in Charles Colson's affidavit

J. David Singer, professor of political science at the University of Michigan, had invited a young researcher named Anthony Russo to come to Ann Arbor as an assistant on a project in December, 1970; but while Russo's books and papers arrived from California, Russo did not.

"I kept writing and calling," Singer said later. "And I couldn't figure what the hell was going on. His excuses were always vague and unsatisfactory. He was occupied with something else, but didn't make clear what it was. Now I know. He was spending his free time running a Xerox machine."

He was indeed, and so was a friend of his named Daniel Ellsberg. The Xerox machine was leased by a small advertising agency belonging to a friend of Russo's, Linda Sinay. Ellsberg rented the copying machine from Sinay first in the fall of 1969 and kept it busy for more than a year after that. He had a great deal to do: several copies each of some 7,000 typescript pages which made up a forty-seven volume historical analysis of the origins of United States involvement in Vietnam.

The story of the Pentagon Papers has been told in several publications,[1] and there is no need to do so again here. For our purposes, the most important parts of the story are those related to the administration's decision to make a case in the courts for censorship and the details of the case which they made.

In terms of the Nixon offensive against the media, the great significance of the Pentagon Papers case was—with apologies for the cliché—that it was the watershed. Until June of 1971, the actions of the administration in intimidating and harassing the press were ad-lib and eclectic. That generalization stands despite Magruder and Colson memos, despite Agnew speeches. The memos were the work of men who knew how their bosses felt about the media and sought to ingratiate themselves; the first Agnew speech grew largely out of a suggestion from Klein, the second out of an obvious need to even up the blame. With the beginning of the publications of the Papers, however, the administration was forced to develop a legal and philosophical stance toward the media and their role in the processes of government. Traces of the Pentagon Papers crisis repeatedly appear in the antimedia activities for the remainder of the first Nixon term.

The Nixon administration's successful invocation of prior restraint in connection with the Pentagon Papers in 1971 was the first time since the expiration of the Alien and Sedition Acts in 1803 that the government had gone to court for such a cause. Several newspapers were briefly muzzled by executive fiat during the Civil War, including *Harper's Weekly* for publishing drawings of the defense works of Washington. World War I saw many prosecutions of individuals because of their exercising, in one way or another, freedom of expression. John D. Stevens, an authority on the period, has estimated that between fifty and sixty people were sentenced to prision terms, although most were released shortly after the end of the war.

Ethnic chauvinism was never so great, perhaps, as during World War I; it was a period when, in all seriousness, sauerkraut was renamed "liberty cabbage" and the Battenbergs in the English royal house became Mountbattens and any German-language publication (of which there were many at the time) was automatically suspect. Eager state legislatures outdid themselves passing repressive laws aimed at anything German. That unhappy situation was made worse at the federal level by the passage of the Espionage Act of 1917 (amended in 1918). This vaguely worded and intellectually sprawling legislation is still with us, and was invoked by the government in the Pentagon Papers case. It provides for prosecution of statements which might cause insubordination or disloyalty in the armed forces or obstruct enlistment. Its application to the media never has been firmly established. During the hysteria of the World War I period prosecutions were carried out by state authorities under either state statutes or the Espionage Act.

Apart from these cases, the tradition of unlimited freedom in political journalism has held firm in this country, and in connection with them a qualifying explanation leaps to mind. *But that was different,* the civil libertarian finds himself thinking immediately, *that was wartime.* Richard Nixon felt that the country was at war at the time of the Pentagon Papers case, too, and the government contended that the publication of the material gravely threatened national security. There simply was much less consensus in national attitudes and the action of 1971 seems much more "political" than during the fever of 1917.

Three aspects of the Pentagon Papers case seem particularly relevant to this history: (1) the background of the decision to attempt to stop publication; (2) the nature of the government's case; and (3) the implications for the continuing viability of the First Amendment as protector of free expression.

The last of these is discussed at some length in chapter 7 as a part of the effort at an overall assessment of the effects of government's offensive against the media. The first of the three is the least significant but is perhaps the most intriguing.

One is struck first of all by the strangely delayed-action response in almost all quarters to the beginning of the *Times*'s series. On Sunday, June 13, the *New York Times* published the first installment, made up of a detailed summary narrative written by Neil Sheehan and the texts of selected documents. There was very little reaction. Despite the *Times*'s role as the agenda-setter for the news business, few other papers picked it up—even among those who had special access through subscription to the *New York Times* news service and in whose newsrooms the *Times*'s teleprinters were rolling out copy. The Associated Press and United Press International also ignored the story, for all practical purposes, for the first thirty-six hours.

The disinterest affected reporters as well as deskmen. Melvin Laird, secretary of defense, who was scheduled to appear on the "Face the Nation" television program that afternoon, spent some frantic hours trying to prepare for the onslaught of questions based upon these revelations of scheming, duplicity, and incompetence. To his relieved astonishment, he was asked no questions which indicated that the reporters who interviewed him had even heard of the Pentagon Papers. Hubert Humphrey was on ABC's "Issues and Answers." He, too, was asked nothing.

There was no response whatever from government that Sunday. John Mitchell, the attorney general, seems to have learned about it through Laird's phone call requesting advice before the television show. Mitchell counseled calm, and did nothing until the beginning of the working week the next day.

Several factors went into this great wave of apathy. The *Times*'s makeup played a role. The display on the front page was a modest four columns wide and five inches deep with a sizeable but uncatchy headline: "Vietnam Archive: Pentagon Study Traces 3 Decades of Growing U.S. Involvement." There were bylines for Sheehan, and also for Hedrick Smith over his story of the lengthy cloak-and-dagger process through which the *Times* series was developed and written. (There was nothing at all at this stage about how the Papers were acquired, however; Ellsberg was in hiding, and his identity would not be known for several days.)

Normally one does not expect much of the general news section of the Sunday *Times;* it is a wraparound, generally quite thin, for an astonishing mixed bag of feature sections, magazines, and advertising inserts. Little news is made on Saturday, other than disaster or crime stories, and the section commonly is full of rather gummy features about the altered circumstances of the caribou, or the finding of a new clutch of pottery shards in Colombia, or an update on the Kurdish rebels. The word "archives" in a headline is very much in keeping with what one expects of the first section of the Sunday *Times*. It seems likely that a great many people, including some eventually to be much affected, simply glanced at the headline, made a note to read it later, and flipped back to "Arts & Leisure" or "The Week in Review."

It was not necessary to read more than a few lines, however, to realize the major dimensions of the event. And the failure of the wire services to pick up on the story is almost inexplicable. There is a tendency in the news business to try to downgrade others' exclusives by ignoring them. The decision-making slots on the wire services are not manned by all-stars on Sundays in June; they may have decided that it was just another of those interminable *Times* Sunday pieces. The failure of other newspapers to recognize the importance of the occasion perhaps has to be explained the same way, if there is to be any explanation at all. But the publication which sees itself as the *Times*'s major competitor made no such error; with the agony of biting on an aching tooth, the national editor of the *Washington Post,* Ben Bagdikian, set his best people to work rewriting what the *Times* was carrying—with due credit.

It is not yet known when and how Richard Nixon first realized the importance of the documents. Sanford J. Unger, in *The Papers and the Papers,* reports that the president originally was against any attempt to take action to stop further publication, and that the Republican National Chairman Robert Dole, was pleased with the beginning of the series. Dole felt—quite accurately—that Democratic administrations would be shown in a bad light, while his own substantially escaped, and he contented himself with trying to establish the label "The Mc-Namara Papers." Mitchell apparently was quite unconcerned when Laird called him for guidance before going on camera on Sunday. The member of the Justice Department who had the most direct responsibility, Robert C. Mardian, chief of the Internal Security division, was in California and did not see the *Times* at all; Mitchell did not summon him back. (Mardian was indicted by a federal grand jury in March, 1974, on charges growing out of the Watergate break-in.) Mardian arrived home Sunday night but, because of the decision of other media to ignore the Papers, knew nothing of them until he picked up the *Times* in his office on Monday morning and saw the second installment. He immediately went into action, calling Mitchell and William H. Rehnquist, assistant attorney general.

The Justice Department was operating in the dark. A high department official told Unger later "there wasn't a soul at Justice who had ever heard of the Pentagon Papers, much less seen them."[2] Meanwhile the president was maintaining his calm. As late as Tuesday morning he told those attending his regular breakfast with Republican congressional leaders that he felt the revelations would damage the Democrats and were no threat to his own administration.

Why, then, was the decision suddenly made to undertake an activity so controversial and so shocking as attempting to stop the presses of the *New York Times*? Amid the considerable amount of material now available about the Pentagon Papers there is very little relating to the key White House decision. Unger makes a persuasive case for pressure from what he carefully calls "key White House advisers, especially in the office of Henry Kissinger."[3]

That seems to have been part of the explanation, at least. It is clear that Kissinger was deeply concerned—John Ehrlich-man later described him as "quite agitated"[4]—about leaks generally. He was a willing participant in the business of placing wiretaps on the phones of his closest assistants, and he had a major role in the setting up of the White House "plumbers" unit which carried out as an early assignment the burglary of the office of Daniel Ellsberg's psychiatrist.

At that point Kissinger had no knowledge of what was in the Papers. The question of what might turn up in tomorrow's installment must have been unnerving, to say the least. This was especially true because some extraordinarily sensitive negotiations were underway at the time which eventually would turn around policies fixed since the onset of the cold war. Kissinger was working for an invitation to Peking to lay the groundwork for the Nixon visit which finally came about in February, 1972. He also was negotiating in Paris for a cease-fire with representatives of North Vietnam. Both of these activities were, of course, secret (the ease with which they were concealed is a commentary both on the willingness of the media to accept cover stories and the administration's ability to shut off leaks).

On June 14, the day after the beginning of the series, J. Fred Buzhardt, special counsel to the president, submitted a memo concerning implications of the publication for national security. Buzhardt was not a member, however, of the central group which consulted with Nixon on the problem; that was made up of Haldeman, Ehrlichman, and Charles Colson, in addition to Kissinger. Colson made a particularly energetic case for vigorous action not on the grounds of national security, but in terms of taking advantage of the opportunity to discredit the kind of people which, to his thinking, Daniel Ellsberg represented, along with the press and the antiwar movement in general. Haldeman and Ehrlichman apparently shared some of the same feeling, with Ehrlichman stressing the chance to make preceding administrations look bad.[5]

It was Richard Nixon who made the final decision and instructed John Mitchell to proceed with action in the courts. At this point there is no way of knowing, obviously, the weight which he gave to these various arguments. Every president wants to be a great president, and Nixon had a far greater opportunity in international affairs than Kennedy or Johnson. It has been pointed out many times that it is easiest for conservatives to make bold moves in foreign policy (it took Charles de Gaulle to get the French out of Algeria, Dwight Eisenhower to get the United States out of Korea). The reversal of the cold war and settlement of the Vietnam war—which also was his greatest domestic political problem—clearly were of the highest priority. Publication of a spate of sensitive documents in the press might upset the prospects for both.

Such an argument is persuasive, although its real merit is

something else. The Papers did get published after an attempt at suppression, which succeeded only in focusing more attention on them and the government's inability to control the situation. Yet the détente came about, the visits to Peking and Moscow took place, and although there were frequent hitches, the opposition in Vietnam kept talking until the United States devised a face-saving way to get out of the war.

The question thus becomes: was it worth it? Was a risk which, even without the benefit of hindsight, was problematical, worth carrying into the courts an attack upon one of the fundamental freedoms upon which the American system is based? Whether or not any other administration would have done so is an idle question. This administration acted. In the early evening of Monday, June 14, the attorney general of the United States transmitted the following telegram to the *New York Times:*

> I have been advised by the Secretary of Defense that the material published in the *New York Times* on June 13, 14, 1971, captioned "Key Texts from Pentagon's Vietnam Study" contains information relating to the national defense of the United States and bears a top-secret classification. As such, publication of this information is directly prohibited by the provisions of the Espionage Law, Title 18, United States Code, Section 793. Moreover, further publication of information of this character will cause irreparable injury to the defense interests of the United States. Accordingly, I respectfully request that you publish no further information of this character and advise me that you have made arrangements for the return of these documents to the Department of Defense.

The *Times,* after a certain amount of debate which carried overtones of earlier arguments about publishing the Papers in the first place, respectfully declined and in its issue dated June 15 (published first on the evening of June 14) carried the third installment of Sheehan's series. That night the Justice Department put together a request for injunction and flew it to New

York, and the next morning at the courthouse in Foley Square the United States attorney for the Southern District of New York made his case for it before Judge Murray Gurfein.

One of the muted side issues of the Pentagon Papers case was the lack of experience of the participants—plaintiffs, defendants, lawyers for both sides, judges—in such matters. The request for an injunction against the *Times* was the first time in history that the government had gone *to court* to get a stop order on publication.

A former chairman of the FCC sometimes amuses his acquaintances by telling the story of two phone calls in a single morning shortly before the FCC was to argue in federal district court for support of one of its rulings. Early in the morning the former chairman received a phone call from an FCC lawyer who was going to plead the case asking guidance on the kind of argument he should use. A few hours later he received a phone call from the judge who was going to hear it asking guidance in a possible ruling.

Judge Murray Gurfein, who presided over that first session on the Pentagon Papers, not only had no legal precedents to guide him, he was brand new in the job. It was literally his first day on the bench.

Both sides made simple arguments. The chief reason for the simplicity was that nobody involved had much knowledge of the material about which they were arguing. All that the two government attorneys, Whitney North Seymour, Jr., and his assistant Michael Hess, knew about the Pentagon Papers was what they had read in the *New York Times*. Alexander Bickel, a Yale law professor, had been hired by the *Times* in the middle of the night not many hours earlier when the *Times*'s regular law firm refused to handle the case. Bickel had had the advantage of some high-pressure briefing, but he could not have done much reading on his own.

Furthermore, the government asked for the injunction under the general color of a piece of legislation which had defied definitive interpretation for more than fifty years, the

Espionage Act. The extent of the government's familiarity with this weapon they took down from the wall was demonstrated in their citation of the wrong section the first time around.

The arguments thus were uncomplicated. Hess contended that publication of the Papers was inflicting "serious injuries" on the foreign relations of the United States to the benefit of other, unspecified nations, and that suspension for a few days until a full hearing could be held would hardly hurt the *Times*. He also asked that the newspaper be required to return its copies to the Department of Defense. Bickel replied that the Espionage Act was never intended to be used against newspapers, and that this was simply a case of prior restraint. He refused Gurfein's suggestion that the *Times* voluntarily stop publication until the case could be heard.

Gurfein ruled quickly. He made it clear that he was not ruling on the merits of the case, but ordered the *Times* to stop publication of the Papers because it might suffer only temporary harm at best while the interests of the United States might suffer, through continued publication, "irreparable harm." He refused, however, to order the *Times* to return its copy of the Papers; in his argument, Bickel had pointed out that the source might be determined through fingerprints. A full hearing was set for June 18, three days later.

Much happened in those three days. The *Times* management decided to obey Gurfein's order and ran no more material from the Papers, an action which disturbed Daniel Ellsberg profoundly. Ellsberg had leaked the Papers because of his conviction that the act would immediately and dramatically affect the course of the Vietnam enterprise; he had felt, according to some observers, disappointed because of the relatively modest play the *Times* gave the story in breaking it. Now he was dismayed.

"When the *Times* obeyed the restraining order," Ellsberg told Unger, "I could foresee that the thing would be stopped for weeks while it went to the Supreme Court. That would lose the momentum of it, and the Supreme Court might rule against it, in which case it would be totally blocked."[6] He therefore started seeking other outlets, offering copies to the three television networks. NBC and ABC turned them down immediately; CBS agonized for a time and said no, primarily because the House was getting ready to vote on a Commerce committee's recommendation that CBS be cited for contempt in a different matter.

So Ellsberg made a copy available to the *Washington Post.* He attached some conditions (although Ellsberg and the *Post* later disagreed about what they were), and the transaction had some overtones of nineteenth-century melodrama which involved secret flights by Ben Bagdikian, national affairs editor of the *Post,* and kitchen conferences in the Georgetown home of Benjamin Bradlee, the newspaper's editor. The *Post,* in a curious kind of way, perhaps owes much to Judge Gurfein. Without his restraining order, and the *Times*'s willingness to obey it, the *Post*—and, eventually, the *Boston Globe* and the *St. Louis Post-Dispatch* and a string of other papers—might have been forever on the periphery of one of the biggest stories of the decade, rewriting in chagrin from the pages of the *Times* one of the ultimate exclusives.

It is perhaps impossible to convey to those who do not know members of the staffs of the two papers the consummate satisfaction with which the *Post* set about preparing its own account, from materials supplied directly to it, of sections of the Pentagon Papers which the *Times* had not touched. It is a truism of the news business—and especially of its critics—that there is no competition in the newspaper industry any more; that the great papers have agreed among themselves upon sphere of exploitation, rather like the powers at the Congress of Vienna, and that all of them put out an essentially similar homogenized product.

The generalization is, for the most part, probably true. There is, however, no competition more intense and unremitting than that which does exist in the news business: *Time* and *Newsweek* for more than forty years now; the news departments of NBC and CBS; the *Detroit Free Press* and the *Detroit News;* and above all, the *Washington Post* and the *New York Times* since the close of World War II. In most business competition, the making of more money and a certain amour propre are the consequential motives involved. But the news medium which outdoes another in terms of truth, completeness, revelation—this is an exercise in superior virtue, a triumph which benefits the whole society as well as establishing superiority in intellectual competition.

In this particular contest the *Post* has been the lean and hungry one, and the competitive drive among its staff members to beat the old lady of West 43rd Street is stronger than anything reciprocated by *Times* editors. The *Times* was the country's quality paper before the *Post* even became serious, and for many years thereafter its superior resources in staff, money, authority, and tradition kept it well ahead. Relative financial positions became a good deal closer during the latter part of the 1960s as the *Post* consistently made money while the *Times* had lean years; the *Times* began cutting back on some of its spectacular practices, such as the publication of full texts of important documents. The *Post,* meanwhile, was perpetually goaded by the realization that it was the supplementary newspaper for the powerful elite which worked in its own city. It steadily improved, and the status which it acquired during the Nixon years, amplified by that administration's attacks upon it and capped by the tough-minded, persistent brilliance of its Watergate exposé, has made the game much more even indeed. It was an enthusiastic newsroom crew that went to work on the haystack of xeroxed sheets the evening of June 17.

Whatever may have been the primary impetus for the government's moving against the *Times,* it received new and powerful incentives to pursue the matter as the *Post* got ready to publish. On that same day, June 17, the FBI passed along a tip from a paid informer—a double agent—that the Soviet embassy had received a set of the Papers. It turned out not to be true, although in any case there was little for the Soviets to learn from them.

Perhaps Nixon and Henry Kissinger did not know that yet (although it seems almost unbelievable that adequate analysis had not been made by staff members four days after the break), or perhaps the simple fact that it could happen was enough, but White House activity became intense. Nixon told Charles Colson, according to an affidavit filed by Colson three years later,

> I don't want excuses. I want results. I want it done, whatever the cost.
> ... I don't give a damn how it is done, do whatever has to be done to stop these leaks and prevent further unauthorized disclosures. I don't want to be told it can't be done.[7]

Along with the creation of the so-called plumbers unit, a campaign to identify Ellsberg as part of an espionage conspiracy was begun and, according to some sources, the CIA illegally brought into domestic intelligence operations.

Meanwhile the attempts to stop publication continued. The most expeditious way for the government to move against the *Post* would have been simply to ask Judge Gurfein, in New York, to extend the injunction already issued against the *Times* to cover the Washington paper. There was no jurisdictional problem, since the corporation of which the *Post* was a part owned *Newsweek* and therefore had major offices in both cities. Unger, the best historian of the Pentagon Papers controversy, was a *Post* reporter whose beat was the Justice Department, and he stated that apparently that course of action was never even considered.

Instead, the *Post* received through a telephone call from William Rehnquist, assistant attorney general for the Office of Legal Counsel (sometimes referred to by the explanatory title "the president's lawyer's lawyer"), precisely the same formal request that Mitchell had telegraphed the *Times*—to discontinue publication and return the documents. Benjamin Bradlee of the *Post* declined. He also declined to suspend publication until the *Times*'s case was decided, and Rehnquist instructed the *Post*'s attorneys to meet with Justice Department lawyers later that afternoon at the United States District Court for the District of Columbia.

The government's case, as presented by Joseph M. Hannon

of the United States attorney's office, was substantially the same as that made by Seymour in New York three days before. It raised the possibility of threats to the security of the United States and benefits to unspecified foreign powers. It also asserted that the *Post* would suffer no injury if it suspended the series for a few days until a full hearing could be held. The same point had been made in the first New York hearing, and it was the basis of Gurfein's restraining order.

Roger Clark, the *Post*'s lawyer, took a somewhat more fundamentalist line than had Alexander Bickel for the *Times*. Although he was one of the *Post*'s regular lawyers, he had had little more time for preparation for argument than Bickel at the *Times*'s first hearing. He had argued forcefully against the *Post*'s using the Papers at all, but after Katharine Graham's decision to proceed had assumed without question the leadership of the defense.

His argument was uncompromising First Amendment gospel, but he also assured the court that the newspaper's staff had carefully gone over the material to be published and were satisfied that nothing in it represented a danger to national security. Finally, he pointed out that several copies, or portions of them, obviously already were in circulation, and that silencing the *Post* would protect nothing.

Judge Gerhard Gesell, who had once been a student correspondent for the *New York Times* and at one point a lawyer for the *Post*, first requested that the *Post* voluntarily stop publication until a full hearing could be arranged. On behalf of the newspaper Clark refused. Gesell then proceeded quickly to a decision. Interestingly, he accepted one premise of the government's argument—that damage might be done to the national security—and thus rejected both the *Post*'s assurances of disinfection and the contention that the material was in circulation in any case. He did, however, accept and affirm in ringing language the importance of the First Amendment sanction against prior restraint and cited *Near* v. *Minnesota,* the classic 1931 case in which the United States Supreme Court provided the benchmark explication of the concept of no censorship.

He thus took, in effect, the position precisely opposite from one taken later, in the fall of 1973, by the Burger court.

Gesell held that the First Amendment overrode any other consideration, at least in this case, and that he therefore could not enjoin publication. Within eighteen months, a federal court held (and the Supreme Court refused to review) that an enjoined publication must observe court-ordered restraint *even if it is clearly unconstitutional* until it can obtain a reversal on appeal. That reversal constituted major damage to freedom of expression, and, as is argued elsewhere in this book, may well be the most devastating accomplishment of government's offensive against the media during the Nixon years.

Gesell's finding for the *Post* did not stand for long. One of the striking aspects of the whole legal process connected with the Pentagon Papers is the speed with which matters moved, a clear reflection of the importance and urgency of the central issue which all parties recognized. The government immediately appealed, and by 9:45 that same evening a three-judge panel had been assembled to hear more argument. In the small hours of the morning they decided, two-to-one, to reverse Gesell and enjoin further publication of Papers material until the following Monday, June 21, when a full-scale hearing would be held.

The decision came after bitter wrangling, and the dissenting judge, J. Skelly Wright, was eloquent in defeat. He spoke of a "sad day for America" and said that the administration "has enlisted the judiciary in the suppression of our most precious freedom. As if the long and sordid war in Southeast Asia had not already done enough harm to our people, it now is used to cut out the heart of our free institutions and system of government."

At the end of the first stage, the *Post* thus stood exactly where the *Times* had three days earlier; the only difference was that it had won an inconsequential victory in the first round. Gesell had denied the government, Gurfein acceded. Prior restraint, however temporary and technically expeditious, was a reality in what had been the freest journalism in the world.

The *Times* and the government went at it full-scale on June 18, the same day the *Post* was arguing its case in the preliminary hearing. Both the *Times* and United States Attorney Seymour's staff had enjoyed the relatively luxurious span of forty-eight hours for collecting evidence and thinking matters through. The government changed the thrust of its argument, moving away from the vagaries of the Espionage Act. One professor of communications law summarized the new argument this way:

> Instead of using the statutory authority as a basis for the injunction, government attorneys argued that the President had "inherent power" under his constitutional mandate to conduct foreign affairs to take the necessary steps to protect the national security. This included the right to classify documents. Freedom of the press was not an impediment to this power, according to U. S. Attorney Whitney North Seymour Jr., who argued: "National defense documents, properly classified by the Executive, are an exception to absolute freedom of the press, and should be protected by the courts against unauthorized disclosure." Acceptance of this argument, of course, would mean that the government could stop the publication of any document—merely by stamping it classified—without proving danger to the nation.[8]

The significance of this theme was set out by William McComber, a deputy undersecretary of state, who testified that "a historic and present absolute essential to the conduct of diplomacy is the capacity for governments to be able to deal in confidence with each other and to have confidence that when they are dealing in confidence, that confidence will not be violated."

Since the Papers were historical in nature and concerned largely with details of policy discussions, it obviously was necessary for argument building to push the concept of legitimate classification beyond that of figures and drawings and weapons descriptions. Much of the overall tone of the series of government presentations might be summed up as "the Executive should have the right to conduct the affairs of his office with whatever degree of privacy he wants to establish."

It was a daring notion—the Nixon administration in its

relations with the media always was ready to think the previously unthought of, even the previously unthinkable—but not a very wise one. The *Times* countered with fifteen affidavits which laid out some of the ways in which government officials had selectively leaked classified material to the *Times* in the past to achieve their own ends. One of the strongest was by Max Frankel, chief of the Washington bureau. It appeared, slightly adapted, in the *Times*. The total weight of careful documentation in the affidavits made it devastatingly clear that the government itself had traditionally used the classification process cynically.

Despite this kind of ammunition, Alexander Bickel, the *Times*'s lawyer, took a compromising line. He agreed with the United States attorney that under certain conditions the courts might indeed legitimately exercise prior restraint—but asserted that this was no such case. It was a disturbing concession, and one is tempted to think at that point a completely unnecessary one. Oddly, by the time of the final pleading before the Supreme Court, Bickel finally moved to a strong First Amendment case, and the court, while finding for the newspapers, played back the same argument he had used in the second session before Gurfein. It made an apparent victory hollow.

At this earlier point, however, the *Times* won a clear victory. While accepting the idea that there were imaginable circumstances justifying prior restraint, Gurfein almost contemptuously made it clear that this, in his opinion, was not one of them. He also indicated his belief that the Espionage Act was not meant to apply to newspapers in any event. The *Times* began to prepare for resumption of publication, but Gurfein's decision gave the government time for an emergency appeal to the three-man appellate court. After some hurried consultation, that hearing was set for the following Monday, June 21.

Thus part of the content of both the *Times* and the *Washington Post* was suppressed by the authorities at the end of the first week. At no time in the previous history of the republic had it been true, even in wartime, that two major newspapers (in most judgments, the country's best) showed the hand of the censor at the same time.

There was little tendency in the newspapers' offices to mourn about it, however, because the big story had become not the Pentagon Papers as such, but the struggle between the media and the government over the right to print. On Monday, June 21, the three-man New York appeals court decided that the *Times* case was sufficiently important that it should be heard by the full bench. Getting eight judges together required postponement for another day, until the twenty-second. Meanwhile in Washington the *Post* was making an energetic case before Gesell for vacating the temporary injunction.

Those proceedings were considerably more interesting than the *Times*'s pleading at the same stage three days earlier. Gesell granted the government's request for what developed into several hours of secret hearings. The government again pleaded the threat to United States security in the publication of classified documents. Gesell asked the government to give examples. The *Post* had prepared an impressive rebuttal technique; as Unger says,

> . . . each time the government cited a touchy item in the Papers, *Post* Pentagon correspondent George Wilson and other reporters in the courtroom passed on to Glendon [the *Post*'s lawyer] the exact book-and-page reference to where that material had already been available to the public.[9]

The *Post* also argued, as had the *Times*, that government officials had for years leaked classified material for their own purposes and introduced affidavits from staff members including Ben Bradlee, the newspaper's editor, and its foreign affairs specialist Chalmers Roberts. The government produced witnesses from both the State Department and the military who testified to presumptive damaging effects of the publication.

As he had the first time, Judge Gesell found for the *Post* and in his oral opinion said, along with sharp chastisement of the Justice Department, "the First Amendment remains supreme."

Once again, the government appealed immediately, and a

hearing before the full nine-man bench was set for the next afternoon, June 22.

By the twenty-second, the actions against both the *Times* and the *Post* were largely symbolic (and therefore their prosecution more meaningful), since bits and pieces from the documents had appeared all over the country in what had finally become an aroused press. The *Boston Globe* started publishing from their own set on the twenty-second. Customers of the news services operated by both the *Times* and the *Post* had received material from the respective papers through that channel. Within a short time the spread was nationwide and irresistible; eleven Knight newspapers, the *Chicago Sun-Times,* the *St. Louis Post-Dispatch,* the *Christian Science Monitor,* and the wire services all were at it to some extent. The response, or lack of it, by federal attorneys in some of those cities was revealing, as we shall see. For the sake of coherence, however, it is more convenient to follow the *Times* and the *Post* through the final appellate hearings to the point where the United States Supreme Court put the two cases together for the last round of arguments.

There were close parallels between the *Times* case in New York and the *Post* in Washington by the time of the third set of arguments. Both began the same day. Both were conducted before all the judges of the circuit court—a full nine in Washington, eight in New York, where there was a vacancy. Each court was very much aware of the other's simultaneous activity, of course; not only did the presiding judges confer by telephone, but law clerks maintained frequent communication. And each knew, of course, that whatever decision they might make automatically would be appealed to the United States Supreme Court.

In New York, United States Attorney Seymour challenged, without using the precise language, the concept of the supremacy of the First Amendment over other considerations. He spoke of "stolen documents" and threats to the national security. He cited a reference in *Near* v. *Minnesota* in which Chief

Justice Hughes, in listing some hypothetical considerations under which prior restraint might be justified, spoke of the sailing times of troopships in wartime. Seymour contended that this was intended as an example of national defense considerations and that from it could be projected a wide range of other cases (such, of course, as the one at hand).

Seymour also made a direct attack upon the presence of journalists at the Gurfein hearings, indicating that their whispers and facial expressions constituted a form of pressure upon that judge. He also submitted a group of items from the Papers which he asserted were especially sensitive and affidavits from additional persons in the defense establishment.

There was at the time a considerable amount of criticism of Alexander Bickel and the case he presented in response. Don Pember speaks of the understandable desire of the defense lawyers in both cases to win a verdict under tremendous pressure of time, not to refine constitutional law.[10] Unger is critical not only of Bickel's willingness—almost eagerness—to concede hypothetical cases justifying prior restraint, but also of his courtroom manner:

> The argument before the appellate court went very badly for the *New York Times;* Seymour was agile, eloquent, and for the most part successful in his interchanges with the eight judges, while Bickel fumbled and was continually harassed by Chief Judge Henry J. Friendly.[11]

Bickel's formal case consisted of an examination of the history of the Espionage Act demonstrating that the intent of the Congress did not include restraint of newspaper publication. It also attacked the government's request for the return of the *Times*'s copy of the Papers on the grounds that it violated the attorney general's own guidelines on subpoenas directed to newsmen.*

---

*This statement, issued February 5, 1970, was one of the few actions by the Nixon administration which were clearly projournalist. Its thrust was that subpoenas should be issued only in situations where the issues involved were critical and immediate. Whatever effect it might have had was wiped out in a few months by the Supreme Court's decision in the Caldwell case, about which more will be said later in this study.

The arguments were couched in the general framework of the First Amendment, although Bickel had already given away in earlier hearings any defense of the absolutist position. The amici curiae briefs filed in support of the *Times* were a good deal more in the absolutist vein, contending that no court had jurisdiction over actions so clearly proscribed by the First Amendment.

Seymour in his oral argument again hit hard the issues of national security and stolen property. There also was an interesting reflection of the fact that the government's attorney apparently shared the suspicions, if not the developing paranoia, of the administration toward the press when he resurrected the complaint about pressures from the presence of journalists at the hearing and their unruly manners; he asserted he had been hissed when he came into the room.

More significantly, following the lead of questions from friendly judges, he set out the steps he felt the *Times* should have taken before publication of the Papers. The permission of the Defense Department to publish first should have been requested; that denied, the paper might have published editorials demanding the Papers' declassification. Alternatively, the *Times* could have filed a suit under the Freedom of Information Act to obtain their release. He blandly summed up those recommendations:

> If newspapers would follow these procedures and use whatever arguments and noise and editorializing they can muster to expedite the process, I have no doubt that even in this case much of this history, which all of us will concede is fascinating, could be published, and at the same time it could be sanitized so that the dangerous portions which really imperil military operations and diplomatic relations could be excised.[12]

A patronizing dislike for the media runs through that statement; so does a frightening view of the role of journalism in an open society.

The *Times* lost in the New York hearing, whether through Bickel's ineptness, Seymour's skill, the personalities of the eight judges, or the merits of the argument we shall never know. The actual decision, by a five to three vote, was to remand the case to Gurfein, requesting him to examine certain material identified by the government as especially sensitive. It was not a reversal, nor was the injunction upheld; the *Times* was free to publish material from the Papers which was not included in that resubmitted for examination.

There is no record of what Gurfein thought of that order, but it seems possible that he might have considered resigning the bench upon receiving word that the whole business was in his lap once more. Fortunately, the Supreme Court made it unnecessary.

Meanwhile, in Washington, the *Post* had a clean win. This, despite the appearance of Erwin Griswold, solicitor general of the United States, to argue the government's case. Attorney General Mitchell, indicating the rising White House concern, instructed Griswold to handle it on a few hours' notice.

The *Post*'s brief, like the *Times*'s, admitted that an immediate grave threat to the security of the country might be grounds for prior restraint, but that this was no such case. It defended the earlier Gesell decision as appropriate. To the argument that publication might damage delicate diplomatic relationships, an argument which ran repeatedly through all the hearings, it replied that just because other, more repressive regimes might not understand, there was no reason for abandoning a fundamental part of the American system.

The government's brief was signed by Robert Mardian, assistant attorney general for internal security. It invoked national security and asserted that the government could not be required to justify the "secret" classification and dismissed Gesell's earlier decision as indicating that he did not understand the authority of the president in dealing with foreign relations.

Griswold continued the emphasis upon the presidency in his oral argument, contending that its integrity would be threatened by undermining presidential authority through disclosure of such information. He set against the First Amendment the "equally fundamental right of the government to function." And, like Seymour in New York, he had a suggested procedure for handling the thing properly. He proposed a forty-five-day wait for declassification review, at the end of which cleared material would be available to the *Post* for publication. The *Post*'s lawyers refused. The next day, June 23, the *Post* won by a seven to two vote, including support from some conservative judges about whose judgment the paper's lawyers originally had been apprehensive.

In both cases the loser mounted immediate appeals. The *Times* appealed to the United States Supreme Court. At first Solicitor General Griswold, the loser in Washington, asked on appeal for a ruling parallel to the New York decision, which had released some material but sent presumably critical documents back to the court of first hearing for further examination. The same bank of judges heard this appeal on June 24 and disallowed it by the same vote of seven to two. At that point Griswold, as solicitor general, put the two cases together and appealed them to the United States Supreme Court as "constitutional issues of great magnitude."

Throughout the Pentagon Papers affair, the speed with which the courts acted reflected not only the universally shared perception that the issue was critically important but also, in retrospect, Holmes's observation that "great cases make bad law." Like the lower courts, the Supreme Court of the United States not only moved with great speed but at the cost of some inconvenience, a quality seldom associated with its privately regulated, glacially majestic pace. Griswold appealed the night of June 24. The court was scheduled for its last meeting of the regular term the next day, and Justice William O. Douglas already was on his way to Goose Prairie. Five justices voted that Friday morning to hold a special session the next day, June 26, to hear oral arguments. Four justices—Marshall, Black, Brennan, and Douglas, who voted by telephone—voted to refuse the case altogether and immediately release the *Post* and the *Times* from any restraint. The majority, however, voted to continue restraint on the material specified as especially sensitive by the government until a final decision.

No new arguments or perceptions appeared in the presentations the next day.[13] Griswold again argued the case for the government (somewhat better prepared by this time, one assumes), Glendon for the *Post,* Bickel for the *Times.* For those who hoped for a definitive clash on philosophical principles, the record makes melancholy reading.

For the government, Griswold moved a step further away from the argument about the sanctity of the classification system, making a kind of pro forma mention, but concentrating most of his attention upon the asserted threat to national security, secret diplomatic negotiations, and the end of the Vietnam war. He also touched again upon the matter of the Papers as stolen property. The *Post* answered the latter argument by contending that the source of the Papers was irrelevant to the central issue—the protection afforded by the First Amendment, or lack of it—and Griswold eventually conceded the point. This left the consequential argument that of threats to national security and the conduct of foreign relations.

There was no searching examination of the clash between those considerations and the freedom of the press, however. Both the *Times*'s and the *Post*'s attorneys had long since given up any attempt to argue a special primacy for freedom of expression. Bickel and Glendon did argue that First Amendment considerations were important in the case, but in effect primarily because the government's national security case was so weak. In an exchange with Stewart who, according to Unger, was seen by the newspapers' lawyers as a key justice who might go either way, Bickel spelled out just how qualified was his commitment to free expression. Stewart had posed both to Griswold and to Bickel a hypothetical question: supposing that in the material labeled supersensitive by the government there was information which could mean the death of a hundred American soldiers, what should be done? Griswold gave the predictable answer, and Bickel's first response was the reassurance that no such material would be found in the Papers. Stewart persisted: was Bickel saying that, if it were true, the Constitution requires that there be no restraint, even if the soldiers were required to die?

"No," Bickel said, "I'm afraid my inclinations to humanity

overcome the somewhat more abstract devotion to the First Amendment in a case of that sort." He also made clear at another point that the kinds of considerations which might justify prior restraint were not necessarily "of a cosmic nature."

It is not known how the journalists in the room felt about this amiable show of moderation, but there were present two outspoken believers in the primacy of the First Amendment, and one of them spoke up bitterly:

> Justice William O. Douglas later cut in to express his dismay that Bickel was apparently reading the First Amendment to "mean that Congress could make some laws abridging freedom of the press. . . .That is a very strange argument for the *Times* to be making."[14]

If not strange, it was at least bland and temporizing, and the argument was reduced to what Nelson and Teeter call a "squabble over whether or not the publication of the Papers was a sufficient threat to national security to allow the imposition of prior restraint."[15]

On June 30, the Court announced that, in effect, it found the government's proofs unconvincing. The vote was six to three. Of the six, only two opinions, those of Black and Douglas, asserted that any curb on free expression was in violation of the Constitution. The prevailing view was essentially that which had been set out by Alexander Bickel from the beginning, and the brief opinion indicated that in the opinion of the majority the Congress has the power to pass laws regulating such matters as the Pentagon Papers case, but has not yet chosen to do so.

It has been pointed out several times that, had the trial come along a few months later, with Black and Harlan gone and Blackmun and Rehnquist on the Court, the vote might have been the other way, denying even the hollow victory of June 30.

Because it was their case which went to the Supreme Court, the names of the *Washington Post* and the *New York Times* are those primarily associated with the Pentagon Papers case. Two

other newspapers, however, were brought into court, and it is
worth a look back to see how those cases differed.

The *Boston Globe* started publishing stories based on the
Papers on June 22. At 5:00 A.M. the next morning Assistant
Attorney General Robert Mardian called to inquire if there
would be further stories; he was told there would be. A few
hours later Attorney General John Mitchell called Thomas Winship, editor of the *Globe,* and asked that the paper voluntarily
suspend the series. Winship refused; Mitchell said it would not
be fair to the *Times* and the *Post* to permit the *Globe* to go
unchallenged, and that Winship would hear next from the
United States attorney.

The *Globe* fared worse than the earlier publishers at the
first hearing. Unger seems to ascribe this largely to inadequate
performance on the part of the *Globe*'s attorneys. Whatever the
explanation, Judge Julian ruled for restraint on the grounds that
"immediate and irreparable injury" might be done to national
security. More alarmingly, he approved the government's request for impoundment of the *Globe*'s copies of the documents.
The *Globe* refused to turn them over, and the order was later
modified to specify that the copy would be locked in a bank
vault with access limited to an assistant to the editor and the
Globe's lawyer. Neither Gurfein in New York nor Gesell in
Washington had acceded to requests concerning physical possession of the Papers. Furthermore, Julian's order not only
restrained the *Globe* from running stories which it originated
but also, briefly, any from the wire services. The *Post* and *Times*
had never been under any such restrictions, and when the paper
announced its intention to appeal, Julian withdraw that part of
the ruling. The Supreme Court's decision to review cut short
any further developments in the Boston case, unfortunately; it
would have been instructive to know what the circuit court
might have done with Julian's strictures on appeal.

The last paper to find itself in the courts before the
Supreme Court decision made all such matters moot was the *St.
Louis Post-Dispatch,* which acquired some parts of the Papers
and published a first installment on Friday, June 25 (the *Post-
Dispatch* is an afternoon paper). That evening the United States

district attorney in St. Louis called the managing editor and asked if there would be more. David Lipman assured him that there would, but not the next day, because the Saturday edition of the *Post-Dispatch* has a small circulation. At this point there was a curious development which suggested that the Justice Department was beginning to look for a way out. According to Unger, the department in Washington let out the word that the St. Louis paper was holding up until the Supreme Court decision was in. The *Post-Dispatch*'s editors wrathfully changed plans and put the next installment in the Saturday paper as a matter of principle. At that point the United States attorney went to the district court and obtained an order restraining publication for nine days. Long before they expired, of course, the matter had been settled in Washington.

Almost as interesting as the court rituals of the four papers which were enjoined was the response of various parts of the government to publication by newspapers which were never brought into court. When the *Chicago Sun-Times* started a series of articles based upon the Papers secondhand (its editors never were able to get a set of their own) and some related memoranda, the United States attorney's office made prompt contact and asked about future plans. They were told, in effect, to wait and see, and the series continued. There were phone calls after that, but none which the *Sun-Times* editors regarded as attempts at harassment or intimidation.

On June 24 the *Los Angeles Times* and eleven Knight newspapers published stories based upon material from the Papers. Both were one-shots, although both made clear they reserved the right to publish more when they found it appropriate. The *Los Angeles Times* received a phone call from the United States attorney who apparently was satisfied upon learning no further stories were scheduled. The Knight newspapers, scattered over the Eastern third of the country and including the major cities of Detroit, Philadelphia, and Miami, heard nothing at all from the Justice Department in any locale. The *Christian Science Monitor* started a three-part series on June 29, after the Supreme Court had heard arguments but before they issued a decision. The United States attorney in Boston asked

Erwin Canham, the *Monitor*'s editor, to suspend the series. He refused, but did outline, over the telephone, in answer to a request, the contents of the upcoming installments. The Justice Department then issued a press release explaining that the *Monitor* was cooperating and that there would be no court action.

Several explanations have been advanced, or are reasonably self-generating, for this inconsistency in the way the matter was pursued in various cities. The most obvious is a kind of pragmatism; even with the *Post*'s publication, an irreversible spread was underway, and by the time the *Globe* became involved there was no sensible prospect of stopping it. Obviously the various offices of the United States attorneys had considerable autonomy, or at least the very late action against the *St. Louis Post-Dispatch* would indicate that. Some of them may have had no stomach for the business in the first place, or, left to mind reading in the absence of imperatives from Washington, decided to wait, with the case headed from the beginning to the Supreme Court, until that body ruled.

Another obvious possibility grows out of the fact that when the case broke only a few people in Washington and a small cadre on the *Times* knew what was in the Papers. Fears of what they might contain must have been genuine, particularly in the case of some of the military and, of course, Kissinger and Secretary of State William Rogers. Within a day or two much of that deficiency was remedied, and it was apparent that little of the content was even slightly dangerous.

It has been suggested that there was an element of revenge in the choice of papers which were prosecuted. Unger points out that all were opponents of the war and generally hostile to Richard Nixon. Certainly the *Post* was an old enemy, and the *Times* had been out of fashion with presidents of the United States for a good many years. The *Post-Dispatch* was the first major daily to carry exposés of the developing disaster in Vietnam (Richard Dudman was filing devastatingly accurate reports several months before David Halberstam began his for the *Times*) and has been, of course, a classic liberal Democratic organ. The *Globe* also was early in sharp reporting from Vietnam; it opposed Nixon in 1968, and was growing in national stature under Winship.

The idea that the Nixon forces were smiting the enemy is of limited persuasiveness, however. The Knight newspapers were by that time energetically antiwar, under the ringing leadership of John S. Knight himself, and despite their 1968 endorsement of Richard Nixon, had in their Washington bureau some talented and articulate writers who made it clear they disliked the man. The *Los Angeles Times* may have escaped because of their longtime sponsorship of the political career of Richard Nixon, and perhaps the Justice Department stayed off the *Christian Science Monitor* because of the church—but how does one explain the complete escape of the *Chicago Sun-Times,* which on a point-by-point basis was as antithetical to the administration as the *Washington Post?*

This writer, at least, finds a simpler (and much less stimulating) explanation the most likely. It is based upon the unique status of the *New York Times* and a single action of that paper: its decision not to resist the first restraining order.

The scenario, to use a word popular with the Nixon administration, may well have gone like this: at the time of the first story in the *Times* it was assumed by all parties involved— including Daniel Ellsberg—that the material will appear only in the *Times.* Most of the Republican leadership, including the president himself, were not much exercised; the decision to move to the courts came only after pressure from Henry Kissinger, who was motivated by what must have been a fear of what the documents might contain as well as the belief that the Soviets had received a set. A pleading based upon the Espionage Act was cobbled together and the restraining order obtained. The *Times* obeyed it.

At this point, an angry Daniel Ellsberg went to work to get a copy into the hands of the editors of what he saw as the second most influential newspaper, the *Washington Post.* The Justice Department was trapped in its own precedent; it could hardly contend that such stuff is dangerous when published in one major newspaper but not when published in another. They moved against the *Post,* and the Ellsberg forces started moving a set into the hands of the *Boston Globe*. John Mitchell, who already was weary of the issue, explained to the *Globe*'s editors that it wouldn't be fair to the *Times* and the *Post* to let the *Globe* go unchallenged.

At this point there was no longer any real expectation that the content of the Papers could be suppressed, and it now was clear that the Papers would not give away anything important. The CIA had determined that the Soviets did not have a copy. The one thing that was important was the principle involved in national security versus the First Amendment, and the solicitor general put the two major cases together to permit that argument to come before the highest court.

That being the case, it must be pointed out that he, and through him the administration, won. Indeed, the government had the basic argument won as soon as the newspapers' lawyers presented their arguments in the courts of first jurisdiction, indicating that they agreed that there were times when prior restraint might be properly exercised, but that they were going to prove that this wasn't one of them. By the time the argument was reduced to a few hours before the Supreme Court, the only participants in the room who represented the opposition in the matter of principle, who were undeviatingly, philosophically committed to freedom of expression, were two old men named Black and Douglas.

Thus in the most significant sense the Supreme Court simply certified the victory which the government had won without contest in the beginning. It seems likely that Solicitor General Griswold, a putative loser, realized that, as did Attorney General John Mitchell, and so, indeed, did President Richard Nixon. After a time the media began to realize it, too.

During the springtime of 1971 John Ehrlichman suggested to Richard Salant that Dan Rather might have outlived his usefulness on the White House beat and should be reassigned. Rather was at that time simply a solid CBS on-the-air reporter, not yet the celebrity of a sort he eventually became through his increasingly visible distrust of the president. A kind of apogee in his later career was reached during a press conference in Houston on March 19, 1974, in a mutually waspish exchange. When Rather rose to ask President Nixon a question at a special press conference session of the National Association of Broadcasters meeting, there was a noisy round of applause seasoned with a few boos. Nixon asked: "Are you running for something?"

"No sir, Mr. President," Rather snapped back. "Are you?"

Bad manners, some people felt, but feature stories about Rather appeared in several magazines and newspapers during the next few weeks. Most of them included a reference to the fact that John Ehrlichman had requested Salant, president of CBS News, to transfer Rather from the White House.

That story was not precisely inaccurate, but perhaps it is worth straightening out here.

CBS News appears frequently in this study. Although in the first months of the Nixon administration the news department of NBC was regarded as the deepest villain (David Brinkley and his innuendos, in particular, produced recurrent fury), CBS had clearly taken over that status by the second year of the Nixon first term and maintained it to the end. It probably is only coincidence, however, that CBS also is regarded by most professionals in the news business as the best of the network news departments.

The avuncular competence of Walter Cronkite has contributed something to that, but there also is a historical inheritance. Two of the most estimable figures in United States broadcasting, Edward R. Murrow and Fred W. Friendly, served as chief executives of CBS News. They were partners, of course, in a remarkable series of documentaries and special features which established not only their reputations but a new journalistic form. Both were outspoken men of strong convictions. Murrow served as vice-president and director of public affairs. Some of his difficulties are set out elsewhere in this book. He submitted his somewhat embittered resignation to become John F. Kennedy's director of the United States Information Agency in 1961.

Fred Friendly had been Murrow's producer and close friend. He was named president of CBS News in 1964. Friendly served only two years, but he was a magnificent goad and agent provocateur whose essence was perhaps best captured by a colleague's weary "Friendly, you'll never have a nervous breakdown, but you sure are a carrier." Friendly was vivid, intense, and highly principled. He resigned in fury in 1966 when his network carried reruns of "I Love Lucy" rather than live coverage of special hearings of the Senate Foreign Relations Committee on the Vietnam war.

Richard Salant then became acting president of CBS News. He was as inconspicuous as Murrow and Friendly were famous, but he shared much of their tough-mindedness. His reaction to the suggestion that Rather be moved off the White House beat is illustrative.

CBS News had been after John Ehrlichman, then one of the two men closest to the president of the United States, for an interview for several weeks in the spring of 1971. He finally agreed, arriving in New York the evening of April 28 with his wife; they went to the theatre, and the next morning he participated in the interview. Salant arrived at his office to find a note taped to his door by the producer suggesting that Salant join him, Ehrlichman, and John Hart, who was the anchorman for the morning news, at breakfast. Salant went along and ate a second breakfast. In the middle of the small talk Ehrlichman abruptly changed the subject to Rather.

Rather, he said smilingly, was a hatchet man, and Salant might want to assign him back to Texas, where he'd come from. As a thousand photographs have demonstrated, there was something curiously off-putting about the strained broad Ehrlichman smile, and Salant simply felt uncomfortable and said nothing. As he thought about it afterward, however, he decided that Ehrlichman was serious.

He responded as strongly as he knew how. He leaked the story to newsmen, thus making it plain that Ehrlichman, in Salant's own words, "had just managed to give Dan Rather security in his White House assignment as long as Dan wanted to keep it."[16]

It was a minor skirmish which locked both sides further into mutual hostility. John Ehrlichman perhaps forgot it after a while, but Rather didn't. Nor did CBS, which left Rather in his White House assignment until Richard Nixon resigned.

The day after the Supreme Court delivered the Pyrrhic victory of its Pentagon Papers decision to the cause of freedom of the press, a subcommittee of the House of Representatives delivered another attack. By a vote of five to zero, the Special Investigations Subcommittee of the House Interstate and Foreign Commerce Committee, headed by Harley O. Staggers, Democrat of West Virginia, recommended to the full committee (of which Staggers also was chairman) that it request of the House a contempt citation of Frank Stanton, president of the Columbia Broadcasting System, for his refusal to turn over outtakes—film and video tape exposed but not used—from a CBS News documentary called "The Selling of the Pentagon." The network also was cited. Two days later the commerce committee voted twenty-five to thirteen to press the citation and take it to the full House of Representatives.

Once again, a politician had been willing to think the unthinkable, organize his forces, and bring to the decision point a question which five years before would have never crossed the mind of even the most impassioned hater of the networks. Furthermore, at the moment of the full committee's vote it looked as if he had won. Never in modern history had the House failed to sustain the vote of one of its committees to cite for contempt. Titillating as the thought of Frank Stanton in jail might have been to some in the communications business, the whole industry rose with a roar of outrage. Of all the crises for freedom of expression during the early Nixon years, this was the only one which provoked a widespread fighting response while there was still time for it to matter.

The politician centrally involved was not a member of the administration but of Congress, a previously little-known representative from the second district of West Virginia. The administration had no part in the initiative, except for its larger and continuing role in creating an atmosphere of "get the networks." That was precisely what Harley Staggers set out to do.

On February 23, 1971, CBS first broadcast the documentary entitled "The Selling of the Pentagon." It was a tightly-put-together, stinging analysis of Department of Defense expenditures for public relations, with demonstrations of the product. The associate producer of the program was Peter Davis, a young man who earlier had acquired unpopularity in some Washington circles with another documentary, "Hunger in America." The narrator in the Pentagon film was Roger Mudd, a man with a particular talent for conveying sophisticated irony. That was the dominant tone of the program; it seems to have been more infuriating to those who disliked it than a frontal assault.

There was, for example, some dwelling on JCOC (Joint Civilian Orientation Conference), a scheme through which prominent citizens (including, in that particular group, a bishop of the Methodist church) were hauled around the country and shown the armed forces from inside. Most segments concerning JCOC in the production made it look both expensive and fatuous, with a kind of high point in the babbling excitement of one of the prominent citizens over being permitted to fire military weapons, including recoilless rifles and tank cannon. There was a sequence showing children playing with military equipment in a shopping center while noncoms looked on benignly, a sequence demonstrating hand-to-hand combat before bleachers filled with applauding South Carolinians. There were interviews with press spokesmen for defense, clips from old indoctrination films produced by the department, a part of an interview of a returned POW by a fawning F. Edward Hébert, chairman of the House Armed Services Committee. There was a sequence showing a colonel discussing our foreign policy objectives in a public meeting in Peoria, Illinois, and there were, throughout, lots of dollar figures, all very large.[17]

Protests began even before the first broadcast was over, and by the next day the furor was prodigious. Vice-President Agnew attacked it bitterly (before he saw it); so, of course, did Melvin Laird, secretary of defense. Congressman Robert Dole, national chairman of the Republican party, spoke up against it. Both Herbert Klein, director of communications, and President

Nixon were described at a briefing as critical of the production. Neither Klein nor Nixon, however, spoke directly to the matter at that point, and both later were to oppose the contempt citation.

The protests touched on several issues in the broadcast. Hébert, who led the pack in terms of sheer fulmination, felt that the introduction to the film clip from his interview had been misleading. The Department of Defense (DOD) pointed out that there were not 30,000 offices in the Pentagon, as the narration indicated, and that the $12,000,000 annual budget for DOD-made films went largely for training films, and that the eminent civilians in JCOC had paid their own personal expenses. The range of criticisms was set out in three documents: an article by Claude Witze in the April, 1971, issue of *Air Force Magazine;* the answers, in memorandum form, by Daniel Z. Henkin, assistant secretary of defense for public affairs, to an extensive series of questions from Hébert, inserted in the *Congressional Record;* and a pamphlet rebutting the broadcast, prepared by the Department of Defense.

Meanwhile, CBS rebroadcast "The Selling of the Pentagon" a month later, on March 23 (to a much larger audience), with an additional twenty-minute tailpiece given over to the more eminent critics: Hébert, Agnew, and Laird, with a final defense by Richard Salant, president of CBS News.

Two sequences in the production became central. One was an interview with Daniel Henkin, who was in charge of public relations for DOD, by Roger Mudd. Here CBS edited a discussion which had taken something more than forty minutes into a two-minutes-plus segment, pasting fragments together to make a single answer of what originally had been responses to a series of questions and sometimes changing their order. Henkin was mild in his own reaction, indicating that he felt CBS had botched the editing job, but this kind of thing was to be expected and he bore no grudges. (The good public relations man, like the wise politician, wants no permanent enmity with the media; they're going to be there, and be useful, long after a given crisis has passed.)

The other critical issue involved the speech by a Colonel

MacNeill of the Army to a group made up of reservists and the general public in Peoria, Illinois. The Army, according to Mudd's narration, had a regulation which stated "Personnel should not speak on the foreign policy implications of U.S. involvement in Vietnam." The documentary then shows Colonel MacNeill talking about Chinese intentions in Southeast Asia and the future prospects of Laos and Cambodia. Again, this single passage represented a series of elisions of a long discourse, and the heart of the argument had an academic quality; the colonel had said (but CBS did not show him saying) that he was quoting Souvanna Phouma, and the question was where the Cambodian leader left off and the colonel started speaking for himself (the colonel never said).

The substantive matters quickly became unimportant, however, as the controversy developed. It centered instead on the process of editing, a process which is an essential part of the handling of news in any medium, because adequate journalism requires the gathering of far more raw material than can be used. The paper and pencil journalist makes his synthesis by setting out what amount to summary generalizations. In the case of the colonel's speech, for example, a good newspaper reporter using traditional methods would have decided which were the colonel's most important points, stated them in summary form, and seasoned the account with what he saw as particularly demonstrative quotations. A voice-over narrator on television does the same thing. Even with this procedure there is room for a great deal of dissatisfaction. Anybody who has had a speech reported in the press has found some of the quotes curiously chosen—"why the hell did he pick that? Did I really say that?"

It is far more difficult to provide a balanced and accurate summary simply by stringing together a few of the speaker's own words, which is what CBS was trying to do in these two cases. And it was not done with particular skill; the cutting of the Henkin interview was especially inept.

Critics of the program contended, of course, that the editing had been designed to mislead. The question of what things had been left out thus became paramount, and it was at this point that the Special Investigations Subcommittee and Chairman Staggers began to play a major role. On April 7, 1971, they subpoenaed from CBS "all film, workprints, outtakes, soundtape recordings, written scripts and/or transcripts utilized in whole or in part by CBS in connection with its documentary, 'The Selling of the Pentagon,' broadcast on February 23, 1971."

The subpoena did exempt "materials relating to segments not shown therein" and "official United States Government film that was utilized in the broadcast."

CBS refused to respond to the subpoena as such, saying that it raised ". . . an unprecedented issue in the history of the relationship between the Federal government and the press . . . the sole purpose of this subpoena, so far as we can ascertain, is to obtain materials which will aid the Committee in subjecting to legislative surveillance the news judgments of CBS. . . ."

As a courtesy, however, the network stated that it was providing film copies and written transcripts of the material actually broadcast in the documentary. On April 30 it also submitted an opinion prepared by its law firm. By this time the CBS position had been backed by almost every organization concerned with media affairs or civil rights, including a strong statement by the American Society of Newspaper Editors and a flood of newspaper editorials, many of which began by saying that normally they couldn't care less about what happened in television news, but in this case. . . .The *Washington Post* huffed that they considered that particular program shabby journalism, but that the Staggers' position was outrageous.

On April 22 Herbert Klein made clear his opposition to the subpoena in an interview with a Los Angeles radio station:

> I would be opposed to the action of the Staggers com-
> mittee. I believe that in going beyond what was broadcast
> and asking to get in effect notes of the program, that they
> infringe on the ability of broadcasters or print media to
> develop a story. Therefore I look upon it as highly restric-
> tive and dangerous to a free press.[18]

Klein generally supported the administration's views on the networks, of course. He was reported to have encouraged CBS affiliates to depend less on network news; he had spoken critically of "The Selling of the Pentagon," and in the interview just quoted slipped in a suggestion that the media were almost asking for punishment and that Congress might be all too willing to provide it in the form of legislation. But his central point went to the matter of principle involved, and it was a position he restated several times during the controversy.

About ten days later Richard Nixon spoke up in response to a question during his San Clemente news conference of May 1, 1971. His opposition to the subpoena also was clear:

> I do not believe that . . . network commentators or newspaper reporters—as distinguished from editorial writers who, of course, have a right to every bias and should express such bias—are above criticism. . . .When you go, however, to the question of subpoenaing the notes of reporters, when you go to the question of Government action which requires the revealing of sources, then I take a very jaundiced view of that kind of action.

He then qualified that statement by indicating that he might consider an exception a case in which a major crime had been committed and there was important evidence available only in a reporter's notes. He concluded his discussion of the subject with a characteristic, bitter personal reference:

> But as far as the subpoenaing of notes are concerned, a reporter's, as far as bringing any pressure on the networks as the Government is concerned, I do not support that. I believe, however, that each of us as a public figure has a right to indicate when we think the news coverage has been fair or unfair.
>
> Generally speaking, I also feel that I do not have to say much about that because of regardless of what I say you're going to say anything you want about me. And it usually may not be very good.[19]

Meanwhile the Special Investigations Subcommittee mulled the matter, and on May 26 wrote to Frank Stanton withdrawing the original subpoena. They ignored the fact of CBS's formal rejection of the original subpoena and accepted the material submitted by the network as satisfying four of the five items in the original request. They insisted, however, upon having the outtakes, and had decided that Stanton should come along personally and bring them with him on June 9. Staggers made his essential attitude clear:

> As I indicated in my statement of April 20, it is not this Subcommittee's desire or function to judge viewpoint or to curtail or influence in any way documentaries dealing with controversial issues or personalities. It is this Subcommittee's responsibility, however, to insure that the rights of the American people are preserved. In an area of such critical importance, the public has a right to know "whether what it is seeing on the television screen is real or simulated, edited or unedited, sequentially accurate or editorially rearranged, spontaneous or contrived," when, in the absence of appropriate disclosure, deception could result. It is my sincere desire that upon further reflection you will accede to the Subcommittee's request so that together, in a spirit of full cooperation, we can proceed directly to a solution mutually beneficial to all of the people.

Certainly by this time the content of a documentary called "The Selling of the Pentagon" was at best, a side issue. The complete text of the Henkin interview and of Colonel Mac-Neill's speech (along with a good deal of other material) had been put in the *Congressional Record* by Congressman Hébert. It thus was possible to make a completely accurate study of the ravishment of the original by CBS's editors, a point made repeatedly by the network and by Stanton. Staggers, in effect, simply waved that argument aside. The subcommittee's case reduced to the fact that broadcasting was a licensed medium, and that a small body representative of a larger one (the commerce committee), which was in turn representative of the full Congress, which represented the people (who were the licensors), had the right in their name to judge the quality of a newscaster's work. As Staggers said, with breathtaking simplification, "We can determine if what was aired was fair and accurate."[20]

The fact that broadcasting is a licensed medium made meaningless, in the subcommittee's eyes, the argument that a broadcast journalist's outtakes are comparable to a reporter's notes. They nailed it down as they saw it in a press release issued the same day as the letter to Stanton:

> . . . it appears that questionable and deceptive practices were employed in presenting to the public what purported to be a factual news documentary. The Subcommittee's inquiry has proceeded on the basis that the public has a legitimate interest in such matters, and, further, that this interest is paramount to any contention on the part of a broadcaster that these are questions better left to his sole discretion.
>
> The information requested by the Subcommittee is relevant to an evaluation of the adequacy of the present laws governing broadcasting, and in considering proposed new legislation on the subject of news programming which has been referred to the Commerce Committee.

The words "chilling effect," first used by Stanton, were to become a catch phrase in the torrent of talk about the CBS case, but nowhere were they so well justified as in reference to the last paragraph of the subcommittee's press release. Chairman Staggers kept well in mind the official commitment of congressional committees to the development of legislation, and he clearly saw the drafting of such legislation as within the competence of his particular group.

For a variety of reasons Stanton's appearance before the subcommittee was postponed until June 24. Meanwhile, on June 22, Dean Burch, chairman of the Federal Communications

Commission, notified the subcommittee by letter that, in response to their query, CBS had met the requirements of the Fairness Doctrine.

As pointed out earlier, fairness is one of a great many issues about which broadcasters have become increasingly spooky in a time of growing challenges to their licenses; the standard elaborate solicitation of replies following even the most innocuous broadcast editorials is a reflection of this. In the case of "The Selling of the Pentagon," CBS provided twenty minutes of rebuttal time following the rebroadcast on March 23, and a one-hour special panel discussion on April 18 called "Perspective: The Selling of the Pentagon" with government and military spokesman participating. On July 11, after the FCC had made its finding concerning the provisions of the Fairness Doctrine but before the final vote in the House, CBS broadcast a final discussion in a special one-hour installment of "Face the Nation," with two members of the commerce committee as guests.

Stanton's appearance before the Special Investigations Subcommittee on June 24 followed the lines predictable from the earlier statements of the principal actors. Stanton repeatedly "respectfully declined" to produce the outtakes; Staggers and the other members of the subcommittee badgered him moderately, with Staggers announcing at one point "in my opinion, you are now in contempt." The discussion ran for four hours, and sometimes grew heated. At its conclusion Chairman Staggers gave Stanton one final chance to comply with the subpoena. Stanton respectfully declined.

Staggers told a reporter after the session that the issue was "deceptions and whether they can be permitted in broadcasts. If this is permitted to happen, the era of Big Brother has arrived." He foresaw a time when the networks could ". . . control America . . . the thoughts of Americans."[21]

The next day Stanton was the *New York Times*'s "Man in the News," the subject of an admiring essay headlined "Crusading Broadcaster" with a picture captioned with a quote from an unidentified colleague: "He's a quiet renaissance man."

On June 28, CBS released to the country's newspaper and

broadcast editors copies of an internal memo headed CBS OPERATING STANDARDS: NEWS AND PUBLIC AFFAIRS. An introductory note from Stanton said: "For more than a year we have been engaged in preparing a compendium of our current operating standards . . . this memo is the result of those efforts."

Although the network had vigorously defended its editing in both the Henkin interview and the MacNeill speech, page 3 of the memo carried two particularly interesting paragraphs under the heading "Editing":

> a. If the answer to an interview question, as that answer appears in the broadcast, is in part or in whole, from the answers to other questions, the broadcast will so indicate, either in lead-in narration, bridging narration lines during the interview, or appropriate audio lines.

> b. If more than one excerpt from a speech or statement is included in a broadcast, the order of their inclusion in the broadcast will be the same as the order of their inclusion in the speech or statement, unless the broadcast specifically indicates otherwise.

In other words, although CBS had done nothing wrong, it had decided not to do it again. The timing of the release was, to say the least, felicitous. The document is thoughtful and highly detailed and there is no reason to doubt that it had indeed been in preparation for months, but it seems possible that its completion might have been a little hurried.

A summary story about the new guidelines, written by Jack Gould, appeared in the *New York Times* as an "add" to the story of the Special Investigations Subcommittee's voting on June 29, five to zero, to request the House to cite for contempt. Two days later the full commerce committee supported the request, twenty-five to thirteen.

By this time even the most lethargic toilers (and investors) in broadcasting were becoming alarmed; Congress was on the verge of assuming a role which made the already-vexatious FCC seem powerless in comparison. Harley Staggers was jubilantly confident, with history all on his side.

He was about to be, as the *New York Times* put it, "stunned and embarrassed." Carl Albert, Speaker of the House, had no intention of either letting the House investigate news broadcasting or violate its own traditions. He approached Staggers and asked him to withdraw the request for the contempt citation or to reach a private compromise. Staggers refused and insisted on a vote on July 13 (as chairman of the committe making such a request, he could set the date). Albert hurriedly made face-saving arrangements; on the day of the vote a Massachusetts Republican moved to send the matter back to the commerce committee, thus effectively killing it. The vote was 226 to 181 to recommit.

Republicans and Democrats were in about the same proportion on both sides of the issue, with conservatives in both parties voting to support (against recommittal), but there were some surprises. Both John D. Dingell and James O'Hara of Michigan, highly predictable liberals, spoke and voted against recommittal. Distrust of broadcasters, particularly the networks, makes strange bedfellows.

To Harley Staggers the most hurtful blow was the refusal of six Democratic committee chairman to support what had become a question of personal privilege. Wright Patman (Banking and Currency), Carl Perkins (Education and Labor), John Blatnik (Public Works), Melvin Price (Standards of Official Conduct), and Wilbur Mills (Ways and Means) all voted to recommit. Congressman Staggers said it was the most intense lobbying pressure he'd ever seen. He may have been right. For once the communications industries had recognized a major threat, even if it was not directly connected with profitability, and organized to help defeat it.

There were side issues running through the infighting and the dialectic of the CBS case as well. Some newsmen believed that the military had a particular interest in the outtakes because they were trying to identify those who had talked. CBS took courage from—and made capital of—what were then seen as two considerable victories for media freedom. The Supreme

Court had just held for the *Times* and the *Post* in the Pentagon
Papers case and a short time before an appellate court had ruled
that Earl Caldwell did not have to turn his notes on the Black
Panthers over to a grand jury. The Caldwell case was seen as
particularly relevant, and its parallel attribute of focusing on the
newsman's unused material probably helped form the judgment
of some in the House who voted, in effect, against the contempt
citation for Stanton.

Both of these court decisions turned out to be fleeting
triumphs at best, of course. The Supreme Court's decision in
the Pentagon Papers case became, not a stout protection against
those who wanted prior restraint, but a reminder to authority
that in the future it would have to make a stronger case. And
the same Supreme Court, when its turn came on Caldwell,
reversed the appellate finding and set it out that the reporter's
privileges in the face of a subpoena are no different from any
other citizen's. It is interesting to speculate what the vote on
the House citation might have been if that final judgment had
been available at the time.

On balance, what is to be made of the whole Staggers
affair? Perhaps the greatest lesson was for ambitious congressmen and not for the media. Harley Staggers seems, from this
distance, to have suffered the classic penalty for hubris. A single
gutsy issue has brought fame to many congressmen. The name
that leaps first to mind, of course, is Joseph McCarthy (he
found the magic of communism only after trying other issues),
but there were others; organized crime and Estes Kefauver (it
made him a vice-presidential candidate); investigation of war
production and profiteering and Senator Harry Truman; labor
rackets and John McClellan; and, of course, Representative
Richard Nixon and Communist spies. Harley Staggers perhaps
did not seize the issue of network reliability with the calculated
intent of making himself famous. It is probably more accurate
to say that he got into an issue that was too big for him and
with grim naiveté insisted on forcing it to a disastrous end, so
far as his own interests were concerned.

There were Washington rumors at the time, hinted at in
the media, that there was dissatisfaction with his chairmanship

of the commerce committee and some questions about his retaining it. It was a good time to look firm and in charge. Although there is no record of the executive session talk of the Special Subcommittee on Investigations, he certainly was strongly encouraged by at least two other members of that five-man group. J. J. Pickle of Texas was a classic southern conservative who had spoken out against many things, including broadcasting, and William Springer of Illinois was a longtime bitter critic of the networks. Staggers also was encouraged, of course, by the military and its friends in Congress. He also knew that a very popular man, the vice-president, had made vigorous attacks upon the media which had touched, with sensitive accuracy, a kind of mass distrust and attracted much favorable comment. There was little trace in any of the things Staggers said during the controversy of bitterness toward the media; indeed, he denied it. There was no doubt in his mind, however, that as a member of Congress he had the right to demand the networks' obedience and the clout to enforce it.

He was not particularly well equipped for the battle. The media were gentle in their coverage of Staggers himself, for the most part quoting him straight and making occasional references to his white hair. The *New York Times* did go so far as to describe him, with a straight face, as "a former athletic coach and sheriff of Mineral County." He obviously had only modest influence with the Democratic leadership, as the clumsy face-off with Albert indicated. And the battle was lost before he understood what it was about, from what might be called the parliamentary point of view. He was armed with powerful weapons and he insisted on using them. He succeeded only, even with the face-saving and history-serving device of recommittal, in embarrassing the leadership almost as much as himself.

From one point of view, therefore, the curious Staggers episode may have helped the cause of the independence of the media. At the same time it unquestionably added to what might be called the corporate nervousness not only of CBS but all the networks and, by extension, all broadcasters. The unique conception in this country of the position of broadcasting in the societal framework leaves the holders of broadcast licenses in a position rather like that of the husbands of women of very rich families. Access to vast riches costs almost nothing in terms of money; it's a matter of demonstrated charm, and persuasiveness, and ability to convince authority of one's high purposes. Once that first battle is won, a much more unsettling one begins; henceforth, acceptable behavior is everything. Any episode that suggests, however irrationally, questions about one's predictability is likely to be damaging and is to be avoided. The networks had a close call with Harley Staggers.

During the spring and summer of 1971, a team of investigative reporters from the Long Island daily *Newsday* were assembling information for a series of articles on the business activities of Richard Nixon's close friend Bebe Rebozo. *Newsday* is a rarity in the tabloid suburban press—a meaty, stylish paper with an excellent history of investigative reporting and a first-rate Washington bureau. It is owned by one of the larger communications combines, the Times-Mirror company, of which the *Los Angeles Times* is the best-known property.

Newsday's investigative team in the Rebozo story was headed by Robert Greene. Greene looks like an aging football lineman, and he talks and acts like a man perpetually aware of the danger of being had. He is physically and intellectually tough, both qualities important to the investigative reporter, and has to an even greater extent the ultimate requirement of such a workman, limitless perseverance. The Rebozo series, which appeared in September and October of 1971, was so thick with documented detail that it made slow reading.

Collecting the information was a difficult process made more difficult by the people from whom it had to be extracted. Greene was never sure to what extent this represented impersonal, inefficient bureaucracy and to what extent the planned building of special roadblocks.

There was, for example, the glacial slowness of agencies within the Department of the Interior. The Rebozo series centered about various land deals, some of them involving federal property. The obtaining of documents of record for inspection required weeks. Each document had to be cleared, in effect, before it was handed over; in the case of appraisals of Everglades land which the Rebozo combine had bought, that meant going through six steps. Often when a file was requested the documents were cleared not as a group, but serially, one at a time. Some procedures took as much as four and one-half weeks. This may have been only careful bureaucracy, but the administration did learn of the project in its early stages, and some of the officials through which the *Newsday* team had to work were known to be in communication with the White House.

Greene and his people also wanted to see the leases involved in the Nixon compound at Key Biscayne. The request was first refused by the Department of Defense on grounds of national security. *Newsday*'s reporters persisted with the General Services Administration and finally were referred to the president's staff. Gerald Warren, deputy press secretary, received the request and promised to call back. He not only failed to do so, but made himself unavailable when *Newsday* tried to follow up. At that point, the request was transferred to John Dean, the president's counsel. It took Dean five weeks to reply and when the leases were finally made available for inspection an anonymous trust was involved. Dean was asked for details about the trust. He replied that he could not answer because that particular correspondence had been lost.

There also was the odd business of the FBI interviews. One of Rebozo's business associates who figured in the series was George Smathers, a former United States Senator from Florida. Much of *Newsday*'s research, of course, was conducted through interviews. Shortly after members of the team started talking to people, Smathers was nominated as a member of the United States delegation to an upcoming round of disarmament talks. Not long after that a *Newsday* reporter discovered that one of his interviewees was expecting him when he arrived. The FBI had visited the official's office, mentioned the *Newsday* project, and asked questions which amounted to inquiring about what the respondent planned to tell them. To Greene this had a ring of intimidation and he began to demand explanations. Eventually he was told that the FBI was making a routine investiga-

tion of Smathers in connection with the disarmament delegation appointment; that they knew of the *Newsday* research for
the projected series; and that, as a matter of thoroughness, they
were trying to find out what *Newsday* had found out about
Smathers.

The Smathers nomination later was withdrawn without
explantion. There is no evidence that it was ever seriously
considered. By any standards of background or specialized
competence, Smathers was an improbable nominee, and so far
as thoroughness of the investigation was concerned, he was
hardly unknown. Not only had he been a senator, he also had
been the personal friend of three United States presidents,
including Richard Nixon.

Bebe Rebozo himself made a suggestion to the White
House staff after the series began to run which revealed a
remarkable naiveté about how newspapers—particularly rich and
honest ones—operate. Early on, the White House had decided
that Ed Guthman, national editor of the *Los Angeles Times,* the
dominant paper of the group of which *Newsday* was a part, had
been involved in the planning of the series. Rebozo suggested
that both Guthman and Robert Greene were "Kennedy loyal-
ists," in the language of a memorandum from Jack Caulfield to
John Dean,[22] and that the series might have been financed by
the Kennedy Foundation through Bill Moyers (of the Foundation) who had been publisher of *Newsday*. The matter was
investigated, but it was the opinion of Caulfield, the chief
investigator, that Rebozo's theory wouldn't wash. He did feel,
however, that something about the Guthman-Greene affiliation
with the Kennedys could be used to discredit the series:

> I would suggest, however, that consideration be given to
> an oblique Nofziger drop vis a vis the Kennedys, Newsday,
> the L. A. Times et al—a sort of alert that we are aware.

"Nofziger" was Franklyn (commonly called Lyn) Nofziger, who
at that point was a deputy assistant to the president. Operationally, he was the White House lobbyist, working closely with
Congress, and he was regarded by his colleagues as a very good
one.

His particular specialty, however, was planting material in the media, a political art form at which he was regarded as a master. This skill grew out of his background as a newsman. Like Herbert Klein, he had been a Washington bureau chief for the Copley newspapers; he then became press secretary to Ronald Reagan. He came on the White House staff in the summer of 1969. The reference in the memo to "an oblique Nofziger drop" means the covert placement of provocative gossip on a subject about which it had proved impossible to build a hard case. It also would serve as a warning to *Newsday* that the administration was prepared to give them trouble.

More ominous was the White House decision to pursue the possibility of antitrust action against the *Los Angeles Times.* Caulfield made preliminary inquiry at Dean's request and re-ported back that the *Times* was planning a new "street edition" which might stifle newspaper competition in southern California. The source of this information was Nofziger. A long memo from Donald Wilson on Dec. 1, 1971, found the prospects of a successful action dim. It reminded Dean of the kinds of sin necessary for prosecution under the Sherman and Clayton acts and pointed out the lack of supporting evidence.

No antitrust action was lodged against the *Los Angeles Times*. It is true, however, that plans of the World Publishing Company—a major book publisher also owned by the Times-Mirror corporation—to publish the Rebozo series as a book suddenly were abandoned. Some newsmen believed that the two nonevents were not unrelated.

In any event, Robert Greene was still scheduled for punishment. In early January of the following year he was informed by the New York State Internal Revenue Division that, at the request of federal authorities (a form of reciprocity common in tax investigations), his income tax return for 1970 was to be audited. Greene hired an accountant for the appointed day at a cost of $100. After a routine examination, his return was found to be in order.

The action was ordered by the White House. Other *Newsday* staff members also were audited, and so, eventually, were the books of the newspaper. Even those initiatives did not upset the *Newsday* management as much as the last gesture of punishment. Marty Schram, the paper's Washington bureau chief, was stricken from the list of correspondents accompanying Nixon to Peking. Schram had been on every major presidential trip since he began in the job. It was made clear in high-level, off-the-record conversations that the reason for this was the Rebozo series (see page 194).

"When those babies spank you," one *Newsday* staff member said later, "they want to be sure that you know you've been spanked."

It is easy to become bemused by the evidence of petulant ill-will and the search for a means of revenge in the story of the White House response to the Rebozo articles, but the most telling aspect rests in the way it demonstrates the personal seriousness with which Richard Nixon's staff, at least, took newspaper stories which touched hardly at all on the real concerns of the presidency. Nixon was not treated badly in the series, although there is, of course, an unmistakable inference of criticism. But the series was directed at the operations of a group of men who were outside government, and particularly at one man who never occupied any position, either formal or informal, in the administration or the government; who was substantially unknown to most Americans; who had no perceptible public influence, no meaningful role in the conduct of the nation's business. He was simply the president's good friend, and that was enough for the president's men.

By this time in the melancholy history of the Nixon administrations relations with the media the word "paranoia" had begun to appear, and it began to acquire some credibility.

Another newsman was feeling the pressure of authority during the late summer and fall of 1971, but, unlike Robert Greene, he never had his punishment underlined. That may have been because both he and his employer understood from the beginning the connection between his activity and the pressure. Neil Sheehan had been the leading member of the *New York Times*'s Pentagon Papers team. He apparently had a role in the acquisition of the Papers, and his byline was on the opening story of the series. He continued to write the running summary accounts.

The federal grand jury sitting in Boston began to investigate Sheehan and his wife, Susan, almost immediately. The inquiry went on for months and since, as David Wise points out in his *Politics of Lying,* some of the Supreme Court opinions in the Pentagon Papers case seemed to indicate a possible receptivity to the idea of prosecution of newsmen under the espionage statutes, it increasingly seemed possible both to Sheehan and the *Times* that he might well be indicted. Lawyers were hired to prepare a defense, and, according to some reports, the *Times* alone spent more than $25,000.

Neither Sheehan nor his wife were ever called to testify, however, and no indictments were ever handed down. Either of two possibilities, equally ugly, would seem to provide an explanation. Either it was an attempt to harass on the part of the Justice Department—as was the subpoenaing of the financial records of the Beacon Press by the same grand jury shortly after the announcement of their publication of the complete text of the Papers—or there was serious and prolonged consideration of yet another innovative attack upon the right of the journalist to exercise freely his profession.

Year 1971 ended with a minor contretemps about a major issue between the administration and its old particular enemies, the *Washington Post* and the *New York Times.* It exacerbated an already prickly relationship and the tone of the talk provides an intensity marker for, as John Dean might have said, that point in time.

On December 3, India invaded Pakistan in support of a rebellious province, Bangladesh, which sought independence as a separate nation. The succeeding war lasted two weeks. It was a time of considerable discomfort for the government of the United States. Obviously this country had to remain neutral, and it did so officially, but the president and his chief adviser in international affairs, Henry Kissinger, held strong private sympathies for Pakistan. Pakistan had been a firm ally and a partner in United States military alliances almost from the beginning of its life as a nation. India had been ostentatiously neutral during much of the worst of the cold war, to the irritation of an unbroken line of secretaries of state beginning with Dean Acheson.

And there were cold war overtones, although attenuated, in the 1971 crisis; the USSR supplied equipment to the Indians and publicly supported India and Bangladesh in their claims. Furthermore, the crisis came when Kissinger had extraordinarily delicate negotiations underway with the Chinese, the North Vietnamese, and the Russians; both a Peking and a Moscow visit already were set. Complicating matters further was the common belief within the United States leadership that public opinion in this country at least vaguely favored India. Despite that, there had been repeated gossip in the press to the effect that Nixon personally disliked the Indian leader, Indira Ghandi.

Neutrality was the only possible formal stance, but the administration tried to make its weight felt offstage. One of the ways it tried to do so, as had many administrations before it, was through manipulative use of the media. In a "deep backgrounder," Henry Kissinger hinted to a group of reporters that the president might have to cancel his Moscow trip because of Russian assistance to India. The purpose, of course, was to send a hint to Moscow without a public display of détente-dampening churlishness.

The whole matter of "backgrounders" (an awful word, admittedly, but, even so, better than one particularly favored in the offices of news magazines: "situationers") has been an item of contention in the news business for years. There obviously are messages which any administration wants to get out, to inject into national discourse, without attribution to the top leadership. When the president or secretary of state is directly quoted, he cannot—with whatever disclaimer—dissociate a tentative personal opinion from his office. There have been differences in personal style, of course, but most political leaders have, in modern times, made heavy use of the various devices of anonymity.

In addition to the obvious "on" (it can be quoted directly and attributed) and "off" (it must not be mentioned) the record, there now are generally recognized two kinds of backgrounder. The simple designation "background" means that a specific source cannot be identified, but his status and position can: "A White House spokesman" is probably the most common form. "Deep background" means that the attribution must be so vague that the source is unrecognizable. "Informed circles" or "highly placed spokesman" or, indeed, "it was learned. . ." are the most common forms in this category. (Confidential one-to-one conversations are something quite different; not only are they common in all media, they are the essential device of much political reporting.)

Editors have complained about background and off-the-record sessions for many years. This writer remembers a national affairs editor of *Time* twenty-five years ago slapping the top of his desk and fuming, "I'll be damned if I'll ever let another guy go to one of these off-the-record sessions with three hundred people in the room!"

Periodically editors swear off, or issue screeds in the trade press, or even pass resolutions. The reason for the dislike, of course, is that the newsman who goes to such a session accepts the ground rules set out by the source and is bound by them, which means almost invariably that he is being used to a purpose.

Few boycotts of backgrounders ever last long, however. Many are helpful in fuller understanding of a complex situation; they often provide a tip-off to some future happening. Rarely, but sometimes, they even provide a major story. To withdraw from them simply amounts to giving one's competitors an advantage in a highly competitive enterprise.

Kissinger always had been wise about the media and by the beginning of the second Nixon term he was the only top-level figure who had reasonable rapport with journalists. The "deep background" device, in this case, was ideal for his purpose. It also was a standard example of use for manipulation, since it amounted to a way of conveying an indirect message to a single audience. The Russians would know that it came from an authoritative source; as a matter of fact, they probably could guess its identity, but the official disguise had a symbolic meaning: "look here," it conveyed, "we're honestly upset about this, and want to make sure that you understand that we are, but we have no intention of permitting a confrontation to develop."

But Kissinger could not escape his official identity in the minds of the journalists who heard him, and if Kissinger said that there was a chance the détente was reversing, that was major news. The *New York Times* strained the "deep background" rules by referring to the source as "the White House." The *Washington Post* went flat out and identified Kissinger by name.

The *Post* invoked a technicality as a defense in this particular case, but went ahead to seize the larger issue in a declaration of policy. The technicality was that no *Post* reporter was present at the briefing; Kissinger's name was obtained from another source (a reporter who was there, obviously), which meant the ground rules did not apply. Ben Bradlee, editor of the *Post,* also announced the development of some guidelines which would "get this newspaper once and for all out of the business of distributing the party line of any official of any government without identifying that official and that government."

The guidelines when issued were not so specific or emphatic. They called for the *Post* reporter in such a situation to do everything possible to get full attribution and other information on the record but, failing that, to get attribution "specific enough so that no readers can reasonably be confused."[23]

That was read by some as meaning that the *Post* would go with "background" but not "deep background." There was some ambiguity in the understanding of the *Post*'s own staff; however, Bradlee later said that the guidelines left the matter up to the reporter as a personal judgment. At a State Department briefing on December 18, *Post* reporter and Asian specialist Stanley Karnow warned the spokesman that if he put himself on "background" that, following the new guidelines, Karnow would walk out. The briefing officer, Robert McCloskey, did put some information on background and Karnow walked out. The *Post*'s regular State Department man, Murrey Marder, remained.

"The administration has more to do and think about than the machinations of the *Washington Post*," said Ron Ziegler at the next briefing. ". . . the *Post* can proceed in any way they wish, but if all the other organizations accept the procedures, then we and the journalistic community cannot accept one organization breaking those procedures."[24]

What might be done was not made clear at the time (some meetings of correspondents' associations were scheduled, but little came of them), and it is impossible to identify among the various anti-*Post* activities of the administration during the next few months anything directly traceable to the background flap. The discussion and Bradlee's ruling, however, may have had a considerable effect upon the administration's use of backgrounders. Not much inclined to talk to the press from the beginning, they may have found in the *Post*'s attitude justification for further cutbacks; in any event, the number of backgrounders diminished almost as abruptly as the number of Richard Nixon's press conferences. By early 1974, old Washington news hands were estimating that such briefings were off 80 percent, and about the only regular sessions remaining made up a ritual known as "cocktails with Clawson," the former newsman who eventually replaced Herbert Klein as director of communications.

And so ended, in a kind of indeterminate surliness, the offensive of authority against the media for the calendar year 1971. It was a modest end for a year which had seen, in the actions sparked by publication of the Pentagon Papers, an attack upon the traditional interpretation of the First Amendment unthought of since 1803; and, in the decision of the United States Supreme Court in that case, the limning of the framework by which the forces of restraint might lose the battle but win the war.

FIVE

Year 1972

The President: . . . *the main thing is the* Post *is going to have damnable, damnable problems out of this one. They have a television station . . . and they're going to have to get it renewed.*

Haldeman: *They've got a radio station, too.*

The President: *Does that come up, too? . . . it's going to be goddam active here . . . well, the game has to be played awfully rough.*

Conversation in the White House,
September 15, 1972

Save for one dark thread, Richard Nixon may well remember 1972 as the most satisfying year of his presidency. It was the year which brought to fruition a series of brilliant initiatives in foreign affairs, of triumphant visits abroad beginning with Peking, which had been not only the Forbidden City but an unthinkable one for United States leaders for a quarter of a century. It was the year when he scored one of the most convincing reelections in the history of the office; when the civil and campus strife that had marked his first term visibly diminished; when the last United States ground combat troops left South Vietnam, and the SALT talks went increasingly well; and the Dow-Jones industrial index hit 1,000 for the first time.

137

It was also, of course, the year of an event which eventually brought him deep distress—the Watergate burglary of June 17. That problem he felt to be under control, however, and steadily waning. Year 1972 was a good year.

It did not begin that way, however, in terms of the activities of his old enemies, the media. The news business was dominated during the first weeks of January by a journalistic coup that could only be described as astonishing. If there was ever an episode recently in which the exercise of freedom to publish caused even the most doctrinaire of civil libertarians to blink, it must have been Jack Anderson's series of verbatim notes from the minutes of the Washington Special Action Group.

A columnist named Drew Pearson was for years the scourge of Washington politicos who wanted to keep secrets, particularly untidy ones. His columns, originally written with Robert S. Allen under the title "Washington Merry-Go-Round," were primarily devoted to exposés and what loosely might be called political scandal, some of it grubby and inconsequential, most of it gossipy. Although Harry Truman once publicly called him a son of a bitch, Pearson had a reputation within his profession as a good reporter. If he had a problem, it lay in taste and personal style.

Most of Pearson's actual work during his later years (he died in 1969) was carried on by Jack Anderson, who would be more accurately described as his boss's alter ego than as an assistant. Anderson acquired the Pearson column after Pearson's death and continued in the old tradition (including the development of an associate named Les Whitten who became as committed and essential as Anderson had been to Pearson; we shall hear more of Whitten later). Although personally unlike Pearson in many ways, Anderson possessed the same zeal for muckraking and for smiting those he saw as evil men. In terms of the mechanics of political affiliation, Anderson, like Pearson, was essentially nonpartisan. He was, however, strongly in favor of old-fashioned morality and exposé journalism.

The problems of a columnist who deals with exclusives are considerable. Anderson's is a daily column, but because of the mechanics of distribution to his 700 clients there is a lead time of at least three days. This means he deals largely with single confidential sources who will stay confidential.

A sizeable part of these come, in the old editorial phrase, over the transom—that is, they are volunteers, some of whom may be fired by motives not altogether noble. This makes checking for accuracy critically important. Despite a remarkably good overall record, Anderson has been had on occasion. For example, his column carried charges that Thomas Eagleton, the short-lived Democratic vice-presidential nominee in 1972, had a long record of arrests for drunken driving in Missouri. The denials were sufficiently detailed and persuasive that most of the media scolded Anderson. He continued to insist that he was correct, but lamely hinted that his source had in some unexplained way double-crossed him. A Washington press corps rumor was that the source had been the Nixon administration's "dirty tricks" team. Bernstein and Woodward, in *All the President's Men,*[1] indicate that the story originally came from the Secret Service—which presumably might have been investigating Eagleton prior to taking on the job of protecting him—and was in the hands of John Ehrlichman before it appeared in Anderson's column. "Deep Throat," one of their anonymous informants, also stated that E. Howard Hunt was involved. Other newsmen had other explanations and the actual source still has not been clearly established.

As the Nixon years wore on, Anderson became increasingly evangelical about those things he considered morally outrageous. He became particularly incensed by what he and a great many other newsmen considered repressive use of the classification system. On December 30, 1972, a series of sensational columns began with this introduction:

> Publication of the secret Pentagon Papers exposed, all too late, the miscalculations and misrepresentations that entangled the U. S. in a jungle war in faraway Vietnam.
>
> Without waiting for history to overtake the Indian-Pakistan war, therefore, we have decided to publish highlights from the series of White House papers dealing with the crisis.
>
> These papers bear a variety of stamps: "Secret Sensi-

tive," "Eyes Only," "Specat (special category) Exclusive," "Noforn," (no foreign dissemination) and other classifications even more exotic.

Yet astonishingly, the documents contain almost no information that could possibly jeopardize the national security. On the contrary, the security labels are used to hide the activities—and often the blunders—of our leaders.

We believe the public is entitled to know about these blunders. . . .[2]

The documents which Anderson was excerpting were notes from the minutes of the Washington Special Action Group, a group even more exclusive than the National Security Council, which was assembled during the India-Pakistan crisis. Several agencies were represented, and each representative prepared notes for the top administrator of his agency from the formal minutes. Anderson was fed two complete sets of notes prepared for the Department of Defense.

To refer to the substance of the leaked material as a record of dangerous policy blunders was, perhaps, somewhat overstated. Anderson's columns gave forceful, sometimes gamey, documentation of what everybody suspected—that Richard Nixon liked the Pakistanis and disliked the Indians, and that his security adviser Henry Kissinger supported him, frequently against the advice of career State Department officers. But the series made great reading, and Drew Pearson would have delighted in quotes such as this one attributed to Kissinger: "I'm getting hell every half-hour from the President that we are not being tough enough on India."

Out of the columns came the word "tilt" in connection with the United States position, which was described in the conversations as a tilt toward Pakistan. The columns also made much of Nixon's ordering a naval task force into the Bay of Bengal and secret attempts to get more weapons to Pakistan.

Anderson was correct in his assertions about the lack of national security considerations in the keyhole peeping, but the bothersome aspect to many was the fact that this was the record of confidential leadership sessions within a relatively few days after they were held. The matters discussed were still under consideration, their outcomes unresolved. The logical extension of that stance was that confidential sessions among policy makers in time of crisis were no longer defensible.

There were interesting echoes of the Pentagon Papers case involved, of course. It seems probable that in his decision to publish the material Anderson was reinforced by the hope that this, too, might become a national sensation. There was reason to believe that the Supreme Court decision had made such publications more respectable, if not safer. The government's failure to attempt any kind of action to stop the series, despite an intense White House reaction, must have reflected a kind of weary dismay in the Justice Department at the thought of going through all that again. There also was the difficult fact that Anderson's columns appeared simultaneously in papers all over the country; in the Pentagon Papers case, that the material became more widespread as the case wore on became an increasingly significant argument.

But there also were sharp differences between the two cases. The Pentagon Papers were made up of documents either written, or collected, for purposes of a historical record. There were no direct reports of conversations in them. None were less than four years old at the time of publication, and most of the principals involved were no longer in government. The secret classification of the Pentagon Papers seems, in retrospect, superfluous bureaucratic caution; the classification of minutes of a secret meeting a fortnight before seems almost automatic.

Both Nixon and Kissinger were reported to be dismayed and furiously angry as the Anderson columns began to appear, and the first reaction was an intensive campaign to close off the source of the leaks. Security forces were rallied throughout the government, and the FBI put together a special cadre; wiretapping was extended. Within a few days security was the tightest within the memory of newsmen.

None of these actions produced a culprit. Three years later testimony before the Senate Armed Services Committee indicated that a Navy yeoman, Charles E. Radford, who was assigned to the Special Action Group's staff, had "retained" in an unauthorized fashion copies of the notes on the minutes and passed them along to Admiral Thomas H. Moorer who "knowingly received" them. Radford was, in other words, functioning as a Navy spy. The Xerox machine is the natural predator of secrecy. It is as easy to make five copies as one. Press accounts of Radford's activities pointed out he was a member of the Church of Jesus Christ of Latter-day Saints and that Jack Anderson was an active and prominent member of the same sect. The general conviction in Washington was that Radford was indeed Anderson's source, although both Anderson and Radford denied it.

Meanwhile, Anderson himself escaped any direct punitive action, even though G. Gordon Liddy of the "Plumbers" was later reported to have suggested shooting him. He was presumably bugged and definitely tailed. He told lecture audiences with great glee of sending his children out to copy license plate numbers of the cars from which FBI agents kept surveillance of his house. Anderson is a forceful, belligerent man, and the Bangladesh materials put him very much in public view. He was far too visible to be harassed as was Robert Greene and, through his column, was in a position to hit back forcefully if he were. That was not true, however, of his close associate, Les Whitten, and when the opportunity came to jolt him, the FBI was to make use of it.

On February 2, 1972, Senator Sam J. Ervin of North Carolina issued a statement which concluded a prophetic episode. Ervin was in charge of a hearing which put him in a head-to-head confrontation with Richard Nixon and the White House, although there was much less public notice than there would be a few months later when the Watergate hearings began. During the 1972 encounter Nixon refused to let three White House staff members testify; he instead wrote a letter which said, in effect, "this is all you need to know."

Ervin, as chairman of the Subcommittee on Constitutional Rights, was in charge of an inquiry into the case of the Federal Bureau of Investigation's sortie into the personal life of Daniel

Schorr, of the CBS News Washington bureau. The story had its beginnings in the late summer of 1971, when the FBI began asking questions about Schorr of his bosses at CBS and of his friends and neighbors. The circumstances of the inquiry, its result, and the administration's explanation of why the investigation was undertaken suggested strongly that Schorr was being harassed.

The administration always insisted otherwise. The official explanation, several times repeated, was that Schorr was being investigated for a high-ranking job in the area of environmental affairs. The interviews began with Richard Salant, president of CBS News, and eventually included literally dozens of other journalists, Schorr's relatives, his neighbors, his relatives' neighbors, and a secretary or two. The questioning always centered on Schorr's loyalty and the kind of company he kept.[3] When Schorr first got wind of it he was concerned that CBS might get the impression he was looking for another job, which would undermine his position at the network. Once that was cleared up with his bosses, he proceeded to press for explanations. The full story first appeared in the *Washington Post* on November 11, 1971. Senator Ervin became interested at that point and began setting up hearings.

The administration never wavered from its assertion that the investigation grew out of the consideration of Schorr for a major post with the environmental protection agency, although various spokesmen, including Ron Ziegler and Frederick Malek, head of personnel in the White House, gave somewhat contradictory accounts. The leak system was first used in an attempt to explain; the White House let it be known that the job involved would be that of special assistant to Russell Train, chairman of the Council on Environmental Quality. The same source later leaked the idea that the whole business had to be sub rosa to avoid hurting the sensibilities of the unidentified person then holding the job.

In August, 1972, almost exactly a year from the time the FBI first called upon Richard Salant to ask about Daniel Schorr, Ronald Ziegler wrote to Schorr in reply to his request for an official explanation. Ziegler said that the job had been that of assistant to the chairman of the Council on Environmental Quality, directing and coordinating public affairs; that Schorr had been considered for about ten days before Malek decided that he wasn't quite right for the job; and that the preliminary FBI report, which was "entirely favorable," had been destroyed.

By this time Schorr was convinced otherwise; that it was a fishing expedition in an effort to get something on him. His colleague Dan Rather also found it improbable that the White House wanted to give Schorr a job. Both Haldeman and Ehrlichman regularly referred to the CBS newsman as "Daniel P. Schorr," although his middle initial is L, and Rather once asked what the P was supposed to stand for. "Prick," said Ehrlichman.[4]

Hostility toward Schorr was somewhat more difficult to understand than that directed toward someone openly abrasive and suspicious such as Rather. Schorr covered domestic affairs, particularly the Health, Education, and Welfare beat. He was a model of carefulness as a reporter, with a personal manner which suggested a kind of no-nonsense grandfather (Schorr, in his late fifties, was probably the oldest television reporter regularly on camera at that time). Shortly before the investigation began he had appeared on the regular CBS evening news to update a film clip in which Nixon apparently promised financial aid to parochial schools; there was nothing of the sort in the works, Schorr had said. The next day he was asked to the White House by Herbert Klein's assistant for television, Alvin Snyder, for a meeting with staff assistants who showed him a multitude of statistics, the point of which was not exactly clear. The same day the order for the FBI investigation came down.

It is difficult to believe that such a minor episode could have set off a process which clearly had the potential for embarrassing the administration which, indeed, eventually occurred. Information developed by the House Judiciary Committee in July, 1974, confirmed that a job was never contemplated. Whatever the real purpose of the procedure, it did not remove Schorr from the role of journalist and practicing skeptic. To most who knew him, he seemed more aggressive than ever after the FBI went away.

On February 7, 1972, the White House made clear the direction it intended for the Corporation for Public Broadcasting. Clay T. Whitehead, director of the Office of Telecommunications Policy, told the House Commerce Committee on that day the administration did not want to consider any permanent financing of noncommercial broadcasting. The implication was clear: the Nixon administration was proceeding energetically to alter, primarily through forced decentralization, the work of an organization which sometimes liked to consider itself the "fourth network."

Not only the corporation but Public Broadcasting Service, its most visible and controversial dependent, was involved; it was PBS which aspired to be a network. The anatomy of the CPB-PBS structure must be understood to evaluate what the administration's attitude meant. An agency called the Corporation for Public Broadcasting was established by Congress in late 1967; it is the basic mechanism through which the federal government has provided its support for noncommercial broadcasting.

Creation of the corporation was sparked to a considerable extent by the report of a committee of the eminent, financed by the Carnegie Corporation. The Carnegie report called for the creation of a well-funded agency which would for the most part supply services for publicly-owned stations, providing interconnection among them, facilitate exchanges of tapes and films, and perhaps provide an occasional network hookup for special occasions. The report recommended against the creation of a network which would provide a substantial amount of programming for its affiliates. It is important to remember this fact in assessing Nixon's action in 1972; he was proposing, in fact, to move the system back toward the original Carnegie recommendations.

The financing of public broadcasting has always been a

chancy business. Stations usually belong to universities or municipalities, particularly school systems. They stay alive through energy and imagination in soliciting funds—bucket drives, celebrity auctions (which often are their best-watched shows of the year), money from school budgets, and a variety of other expedients. In the days before the creation of CPB, the only significant national-level assistance came from the Ford Foundation, which pumped in millions over the years.

Congress voted CPB a budget of $30 million for its first year, an amount which, with continuing Ford support, made a formidable difference. The distribution of these funds was under the direction of a fifteen-man board appointed by the president with Senate confirmation. From the beginning, the lion's share of CPB funds went to two dependent organizations, National Public Radio and Public Broadcasting Service. The first of these, NPR, has had a relatively untroubled history of quiet excellence. It interconnects about a hundred radio stations, providing a range of programs including a little-heard, but extraordinarily good, evening newscast called "All Things Considered." It also provides some remarkable specials; after the release of the transcripts of the White House tapes concerning Watergate in the spring of 1974, NPR presented a reading of the complete text. It never came under pressure from the administration during the period of this study, although its tone was frequently critical, and its annual allocation from the corporation has held at around $3 million.

Public Broadcasting Service has a different structure and has had a different history. It, too, is a corporation, with individual public stations as members and a board of directors controlled by station managers. PBS is the operator of the interconnected system within public television; that is, it is public television's network, supported largely by CBP. It originates programs, frequently commissioning them from local stations, although other production centers are sometimes involved (for example, "Sesame Street" is produced by Children's Television Workshop, a separate entity supported to a modest extent by CPB, along with funding from foundations). The pattern of funding for PBS was for fiscal 1972: $12.1 million from the Corporation for Public Broadcasting, $9.2 million from the Ford Foundation, and $2.2 million from corporations which paid for special programs such as continuing purchases of material from BBC (Mobil Oil and Xerox have been particularly openhanded). The total national program for that fiscal year, then, was a little more than $23 million, about half of which came from CPB.[5]

From the Ford Foundation PBS not only received sizeable amounts of money, it also received the zesty attention of the foundation's chief television consultant, Fred W. Friendly. No one, and particularly not Fred Friendly, believed that the foundation's millions gave him the right to call the shots at PBS. At the same time, Friendly's clout in noncommercial broadcasting could not have been other than great; he would have been a major figure if Ford's contribution had been fifty dollars. Friendly had all the credentials. He was one of the first great professionals in documentary and public affairs television. He had led, for a time, the news division of CBS.

And he had renounced it, flayed commercial television for short-range vision and playing to the lowest tastes, and preached a vision of a different kind of broadcasting. This quality always has been an important element in public broadcasting in this country. The majority of its most visible and able people either could find no peace in commercial operations or refused to get into them in the first place. And much of the thrust of PBS in particular, has been at doing well things regular networks do badly or refuse to do at all. Interestingly, commercial television responds to this oblique arrogance by applauding public television, praising its works, and contributing money, equipment, and occasionally facilities. Cynics have pointed out this generosity may be rooted in the belief that if public television does a great deal of high-minded stuff, the pressure on the networks for uplift will be less.

Friendly was committed to the vision which the Carnegie report specifically rejected, that of a fourth network—or at least a fourth network in public affairs operations. In part because of his influence, PBS moved strongly in that direction. Bill Moyers, William Buckley, Sander Vanocur, and other substantial names became commentators and analysts (Vanocur's $85,000 salary became a favorite target of critics). The obvious need was to build audiences, which traditionally have been small to miniscule for public television, and one of the obvious ways was with well-known names. Most were of a political bent which would be generally perceived as liberal and antiadministration, with Buckley appearing to be the token conservative and Nixon defender.

As PBS placed growing emphasis upon public affairs and national politics, the Corporation for Public Broadcasting, its patron as dispenser of government money, increasingly developed a hands-off stance toward PBS programming. By 1971 the network was essentially on its own, and its conversations with the funding agency tended to be about dollar amounts rather than principles.

It seems a fair guess that most of the friends of public television liked the direction in which PBS had moved, liked the style and élan which it had developed. There were many critics, however, who continued to cite the Carnegie report and opposed the heavy emphasis upon funding national television programming. In fiscal 1972, CPB gave less than $5 million of its total $40 million appropriation to local stations, and most of these were small grants for special purposes.

It was with this group in mind that the Nixon administration made its first direct attack upon the way things were going at CPB-PBS. The spokesman was Clay T. Whitehead, director of the Office of Telecommunications Policy, who had been designated as the White House thinker on such matters.

On October 9, 1971, Whitehead spoke to the National Association of Educational Broadcasters. He openly and directly attacked PBS and played to the endemic poverty of individual noncommercial stations:

> Instead of aiming for "overprogramming" so local stations can select among the programs produced and presented in an atmosphere of diversity, the system chooses central control for "efficient" long-range planning and so-called "coordination" of news and public affairs—

coordinated by people with essentially similar outlooks. How different will your network news programs be from the programs that Fred Friendly and Sander Vanocur wanted to do at CBS and NBC? Even the commercial networks don't rely on one sponsor for their news and public affairs, but the Ford Foundation is able to buy over $8 million worth of this kind of programming on your stations.[6]

His testimony the following February before the House Commerce Committee made clear the direction the administration planned to turn CPB. Before the year was out, two major moves got the process of implementation underway.

Whitehead was testifying against a proposal then before the committee which would have provided $155 million for the next two years of CPB operations: $65 million was proposed for the current year, $90 million for the next. The proponents' basic arguments were that longer-term funding would give the system more protection from manipulation and more opportunity for planning for a coherent future. Whitehead made it clear that he was speaking for Nixon, but despite his warning, the House passed the legislation and, a few weeks later, so did the Senate with only minor modifications.

On June 30, 1972, the president vetoed the appropriation and requested that Congress reconsider his own proposal for a one-year funding at the level of $45 million, some $10 million more than the previous year. The veto obviously amounted to more than the withholding of funds. It said clearly that the administration was going to change the structural character of public broadcasting, and it meant the death of the idea of the government's providing what Douglass Cater called "venture capital" for major new initiatives free of the pressure of advertisers. On July 22, the Senate passed the Nixon recommendation after chopping another $5 million from it.

Money was the single most powerful lever available to the administration, of course, but another change also was required. The Corporation for Public Broadcasting, along with dispensing funds, had to take back control of policy and programming.

That change came in August with the resignation of John W. Macy, president of CPB, who had headed the organization since its creation.

Macy had been, more than anything else, concerned with effective administration. He was, in the nonpejorative sense of the word, a classic bureaucrat who wanted his agency to do well and left philosophy primarily to the professionals of PBS. He objected to the growing politicization of the arguments about public broadcasting and pressure from both the executive office and some elements in Congress.

He was replaced by Henry W. Loomis, a former deputy director of the United States Information Agency, who made it clear that he and the president held similar views of the proper functioning and dimensions of public broadcasting. Thomas Curtis, a former Republican senator from Missouri, became the new chairman of the board of directors, although he was not to stay long.

Several observations seem in order in assessing the actions of the Nixon administration toward shaping public television in this country. They begin with the fact that there was a widely accepted and essentially nonpolitical set of arguments favoring the decentralization and what might be called the localization of public broadcasting. This was the forceful conclusion of the special Carnegie report as well as the recommendation of the chairman of the Sloan Foundation, another body with a continuing concern in public television policy. Unlike actions such as the push for prior restraint in the Pentagon Papers case, there was nothing surprising in the administration's position. It had wide national support, including a good deal among those working within the field—particularly station managers.

Furthermore, it was highly consistent with Richard Nixon's frequently stated conviction that money is more effectively spent by small units close to the local scene than by vast central agencies. Revenue sharing, through which the federal government returns to the states some of the taxes it collects, was a favorite proposal of Nixon's during both the 1968 and

1972 campaigns. There was an obvious parallel with giving local stations more funding for improving service to their own communities.

The opposition's point of view was that the only chance for public television to build substantial audiences and live up to its potential as a force in society was through building network operations. This was particularly true in news and public affairs programs. It is all but impossible for a single public television operation to support an adequate local news unit ("Newsroom" on KQED, San Francisco, is a shining exception); even the most prosperous commercial outlets with good budgets produce a skimpy product. The kind of public affairs programming represented by Bill Moyer's "Journal" or William Buckley's "Firing Line" can be managed through the exchange of video tapes, but some of the monuments of public television, such as full prime time coverage of the Ervin committee's hearing on Watergate, are manageable only through a centralized, well-funded national operation.

The fear of the advocates of something like a "fourth network" is that money handed out in relatively small quantities to local stations will be dissipated with nothing but trivial impacts; it will help to improve slightly programs which will remain, even so, not very well done and little attended. As Douglass Cater said, "Turning public TV into a village handicraft industry would be prohibitively expensive—or deadeningly dull."[7]

Regardless of the merits of the arguments, this clearly is a policy matter which comes close to having philosophical rather then partisan overtones. It has been, as arguments over money go, almost high-minded.

The men of the Nixon administration chose not to let it remain that. In exchanges with reporters and in personal conversation various spokesmen made it clear that they considered the Public Broadcasting Service so aggressively antiadministration that it deserved punishment. There was a good deal of openly expressed personal rancor. This was particularly true of Patrick Buchanan, who from the beginning made clear his belief that media enemies should be punished and helpers rewarded. Herbert Klein also made explicit objections both to personalities and material on PBS in the general context of "shape up or else." Whitehead played the demagogue with management. There were personal attacks upon Friendly; wry remarks circulated about efforts to make PBS the network that CBS refused to be.

This kind of talk, along with the president's vetoes and appointments, made almost inevitable the growth of the impression that the administration was not so much trying to alter public television as kill it (see for example, a major piece in *Newsweek* for January 1, 1973, headed "The Nixon Network") or turn it into a propaganda outlet. Fuel for that fire was added when Thomas Curtis, who was appointed chairman of the CPB board in 1972, resigned angrily in 1973, charging that the White House constantly interfered in board decisions. The charges of an Orwellian intention sometimes became high-pitched. Ron Powers, a syndicated writer about broadcasting, was alarmed to this extent:

> The administration ... wants, in effect, to bug the entire nation—that is, to plug every TV set in America into the strategy, wishes and ideological purposes of the White House. ... The Nixon administration has already come a long way in achieving this federalization of a public resource.[8]

There is no question that structurally public television was much changed by the end of the Nixon presidency. Although the basic tone of its news and public affairs programs seems little different, some of its most conspicuous personalities are gone or were, at the time of this writing, going. PBS's regular network features were being scheduled through a kind of auction, in effect, in which stations which wished to carry the program paid a pro rata share of its cost; programs which failed to attract enough support from station managements went by the boards.

But the idea that the administration, whatever its intentions, was making CPB into a potent tool for government propaganda clearly proved to be false. They did not assign to the job either the kind of leadership or the sort of concentrated pressure needed for that; Loomis, after a somewhat noisy beginning, increasingly seemed to be bored by the whole business.

Clay Whitehead during the later Nixon years lost, until the very last, all his visibility and apparently most of his clout inside the administration. By 1973 he was widely described as being on his way out as soon as he could find a face-saving job in industry. Whether or not this was true, there was no question that he continued to work hard. Under his chairmanship and close supervision a special committee made up of members of the Nixon cabinet produced in January, 1974, a major study of cable television and a set of policy recommendations concerning its development. The recommendations startled those who had come to have a deep distrust for Whitehead and an even deeper one for the administration. They placed great emphasis upon minimum government involvement of any sort, proposed common carrier status for cable (a condition which makes air time available to any who want to purchase it, thus separating content from ownership), and strongly reinforced freedom of expression.

Then, almost at the end of the Nixon *Götterdammerung,* Whitehead's office produced a surprisingly generous bill for the financing of public television. In July, 1974, the president sent to Congress a bill which would provide five-year funding at a greatly increased level—from $70 million the first year, an increase over the then-current $47 million, to an eventual $115 million by the fifth. Both the five-year provision and the increased funds represented things earnestly sought by the leaders of public television for many years. Both also were central in the bill Nixon vetoed in 1972. His first inclination apparently was to kill the 1974 recommendation as well, but Whitehead and Alexander Haig were given credit in the media for bringing sufficient pressure to change the presidential mind.

Yet what seemed at first glance a total conversion to the former CPB-PBS point of view was far from that. The decentralization of control and the passage of power over national programming to the hands of local stations had been largely accomplished. Beginning with the fall season of 1974, PBS's national programming was determined by the willingness of local stations to pay for the national organization's productions. Whitehead and the Nixon administration had made public television into a different kind of institution, one which promised to demonstrate the values of local control and parochial concerns—at the probable expense of some first-rate talent and the passion to do well what commercial broadcasting cannot help doing badly.

The give-and-take struggle of central versus local control goes back to the beginnings of representative government, and is hardly unique to public broadcasting. The Nixon administration chose an attitude consistent with its attitudes on most related issues and with the classic conservative stance. Had its spokesmen said nothing more than that, the action would have been seen even by most political enemies as perhaps deplorable, but nevertheless an honest outgrowth of principle. The administration's eventual financial generosity confirmed that impression in the minds of most.

But that singular zest for bastinado, the lack of style and perceptiveness, the hubris that accompanied being in charge and making the most of it, did them in again, and Nixon took the blame for one more damaging thrust at the media.

On April 14, 1972, the Antitrust Division of the Department of Justice filed suit against the NBC, CBS, and ABC television networks, charging them with using their control of air time to monopolize prime time entertainment programming and to obtain valuable financial interests in such programs. Although there were four antitrust actions against the media during the period of this study, only this one carried a threat of major industry-wide damage. It is seen by many, and especially by network executives, as the most blatant of all the administration's efforts to intimidate broadcasters.

It seems a good idea at this point to emphasize a rather obvious point—that an action discussed here as part of government's offensive against the media and described as "harassment" or "intimidation" may, from some other points of view, seem justified, responsible, and in the best general interest of the society. Antitrust activity is perhaps the best established (it goes back almost a hundred years) and most widely accepted of all the reformist moves spawned by the excesses of business. In the long history of such legislation, there have been few cases of its misuse, although there have been many complaints against the failure to use it more. The tradition of the Antitrust Division of the Department of Justice in modern times has been to move only in cases where there is a solid case and the chances of winning are high. It has not been an irresponsible agency. And, at least at first look, there seem to have been elements of network practice in programming which looked like monopoly.

The involvement of networks in the programs they broadcast developed with television. Before that time, even in the so-called golden era of radio broadcasting, the networks had almost no role in the content of the entertainment programs they carried. They sold to advertisers empty air on an interconnected set of stations. The advertiser (or, more accurately, his advertising agency), bought the time and put in it what he wished. Other than providing news and public affairs coverage (which, by the late thirties, was generally superb; there are newsmen still who feel that the greatest era in broadcast journalism was that of the years around and during World War II), the networks were simply transmission channels and advertising agencies were the primary programmers.

The same general pattern held in the earliest days of television, but by the early 1950s the networks began moving into direct control and ownership of programs. The advertising agencies resisted, of course, and at one stage the president of CBS, Frank Stanton, suggested that the FCC might establish a fifty-fifty principle. Nothing came of it, and by the mid-sixties the networks had something close to total control.

They obtained this primarily through ownership of, or, more commonly, investment in, the production companies which provide the prime time series and daytime soap operas and game shows. Each of these gets on the air through a complex and highly competitive process which begins with making a pilot film and the preparation of scripts, story lines, and detailed production plans. This is an expensive process, with these costs alone sometimes reaching a million dollars. Investors are needed to provide start-up capital, and there were obvious advantages to the networks in that role. Typically, they invested a relatively small sum in each of several promising possibilities. In exchange the networks received a share of the ownership (frequently somewhat larger than the dollars contributed might seem to justify) and a guarantee of their right of first refusal. For the producer this also was a felicitous arrangement, even if it sometimes turned out that he had given away quite a lot for relatively little, because it meant that when the network was setting its final schedule the presence of the network's own money in his show was a powerful influence.[9]

The other major source of prime time material, of course, has been motion pictures, and the networks also began moving into ownership-sharing roles in movie companies and theater chains; in some cases they produced their own films ("a brand-new full-length feature made especially for television"). Add to this the fact that for some years the networks have invested in Broadway shows which are the basis of many successful movies, particularly musicals, and it's clear that almost every phase of program making could be a source of network profit. By the end of the decade this had reached the point where it was commonly assumed in the industry that no network would consider for its schedule any series in which it had no share of ownership.

Both the Federal Communications Commission and the Antitrust Division of the Department of Justice had watched these developments with interest for a good many years. A government memo refers to "an intermittent investigation of the program practices of NBC, CBS, and ABC by the Antitrust Division which commenced in the mid-1950s." The target was inviting, but apparently none of the attorneys general during more than a decade and a half felt that the matter was strong enough to press. Most curiously of all, in 1971 plans for a suit very much like the one to be brought in 1972 were approved by

Richard W. McLaren, then head of antitrust, and sent to Attorney General John Mitchell for approval. Mitchell signed the complaint, but never filed an action.

It was not until April of 1972, then, that proceedings actually got into a courtroom. The past history and present circumstances seemed strange even to many with no particular sympathy for the networks. The *New York Times* said in an editorial:

> If it were not for the timing of the start of a Presidential campaign, the anti-trust suit filed by the Justice Department against the three major television networks would be easy to view as a normal—even laudable—exercise of the Department's legal duty to combat monopoly practices. . . .
>
> . . . However, there are elements in the backgrounds of the present Federal action against the broadcasters which engender doubt whether its origins may not lie as much in politics as in zeal for law enforcement.
>
> One question in particular need of an answer is why the Justice Department chose to move now on long-ignored staff proposals that it challenge network financial controls over TV entertainment programs.[10]

In addition to the suspect timing, there were other elements difficult to understand if the government was serious. The Antitrust Division has had a reputation for careful preparation of cases, yet this one was based upon 1967 data which on the face of it no longer represented the facts.

The suit alleged, for example, that CBS substantially owned 73 percent of its prime time entertainment shows, NBC 68 percent of theirs, and ABC 86 percent. The networks probably would have disputed those figures even when they were new, but they were five years old. In between, in May, 1970, the FCC had issued a ruling forbidding network ownership of equity in any *new* programs, and substantial changes had taken place since then. In their first response to the 1972 action, the networks asserted that they were involved in less than 10 percent; CBS, according to Frank Stanton, was owner of only one, "Gunsmoke."

The networks also accused the Justice Department of seeking to return broadcast content to the exclusive control of advertising agencies and implied their belief that the actual purpose of the action was political harassment and intimidation in an election year.

During the next twenty months they proceeded to gather materials in preparation for their formal answer to the suit and the accompanying request for its dismissal. Each of the three organized its case somewhat differently from the others, but two arguments were central: first, that the actions were brought for an unconstitutional purpose, in that, although designated as antitrust actions, they actually were designed for political intimidation; and second, that the suits would bar the networks from creating and transmitting any of their own entertainment programs, which is a form of speech protected by the First Amendment.

During the months between the filing of the federal suit and the networks' reply, a good deal of evidence to support their first argument surfaced. Beginning in October, 1973, the office of Senator Lowell Weicker, of Connecticut, released a series of private White House memoranda which had come into the possession of Senator Ervin's committee investigating the Watergate matter. A good many of these referred to the networks and are discussed elsewhere in this study. Overall, they demonstrate an embittered concern and an itch for administering punishment. In addition to citing the references to use of antitrust as a threat in Magruder's "Shot-gun versus the Rifle" memo and Dean's "screw our enemies" memo, CBS produced sworn statements by Dan Rather and Frank Stanton.[11] Rather, CBS White House correspondent, stated that Ron Ziegler once told him that the networks were "anti-Nixon" and that "they were going to have to pay for that, sooner or later, one way or another." Then chief operating officer Stanton affirmed that he had been told by Colson after the government suit was filed that the administration would "bring you to your knees in Wall

Street and on Madison Avenue" in retaliation for CBS's failure to "play ball" with the administration.

As of early 1975, there still was no decision in the network antitrust case. In October, 1974, the networks moved for dismissal on the grounds that the government had refused to surrender certain documents vital to their defense. The court granted the dismissal, but without prejudice—meaning that the suit could be reinstated. Three weeks later the government did just that, indicating its continued belief in the strength of its original case. The networks prepared to come back with essentially the same defense. A searching decision, if and when one comes, might have some deep implications. If the court should rule, for example, that the Nixon administration did try to use the antitrust authority for political harassment, future activities of the division in the media field might have heavy going.

There were several happenings in the month of June, 1972, which are worth a quick note. A remark of John Ehrlichman's proved to be a peg, in the language of the newsroom, for some examination in the media of the decline of the press conference and the general throttling of sources of information. When a television interviewer in Los Angeles asked Ehrlichman why the president did not hold more press conferences, he replied that reporters ask "a lot of flabby and fairly dumb questions and it really doesn't elucidate very much."[12]

That apparently helped provoke Max Frankel, head of the *New York Times* Washington bureau, into an elaborate examination of what had happened to the press conference.

In all of 1971, President Nixon faced ad hoc questioning by the White House press on nine occasions, compared with an annual average of 24 to 36 by Presidents over the last 25 years. There have been two news conferences in 1972, the last one 12 weeks ago, compared with President Eisenhower's 13 and President Johnson's 15 in the years they sought re-election, 1956 and 1964. The last formally scheduled news conference, which allows the preparation of questions in advance and provides radio and television as well as press coverage, occurred on June 1, 1971 [more than a year before the date of the Frankel article].[13]

Frankel went on to make the point that presidential press conferences must be frequent to be of much use. The more infrequent, the more pointless the questions tend to become, consisting of rhetorical exercises which are either hostile zingers or—to use a metaphor the president himself used—soft lobs which can be hit out of the park. The Frankel essay concluded with a list of fourteen questions, the presidential answers to which the Washington bureau of the *Times* would like to have had but were quite certain they'd never get:

> Are you still confident of ending the war in your first term and pulling the rug out from under the Democrats on this issue? Why will the peace terms you get this year be better than those you might have obtained three years ago? What constitutional authority do you now possess for bombing North Vietnam and mining its harbors?

The final question went, "Do you really think the press is hostile for harboring such questions?"

Detailed discussion of the administration's refusal to provide access to information for reporters lies outside the boundaries laid down for this study. The concern here is with the dimensions and the anatomy of the attack, the initiatives undertaken by authority—not only the Nixon administration, but in one case by the Congress and in numerous cases by the courts—which might have had the effect of harassing or intimidating the media and thus affecting the quality of political journalism.

It is difficult to define the cutting off of sources of information as either intimidation or harassment. To go to the courts and plead for prior restraint (and win it); to harass reporters with FBI, Internal Revenue Service, or grand jury investigations; to threaten with contempt citations or antitrust actions; or to attack the morality of journalists and the credibility of the media as institutions—such things are intimidation. It is possible in such cases to point to the spirit of the law or, at least, tradition and conventional morality and pronounce them offended.

To say to a president "you should have been willing to talk to us more" is something quite different. That prerogative clearly lies with the man in the White House. There were presidents before Richard Nixon who were even less communicative than he: his idol Woodrow Wilson, Hoover in the last two years of his term, Eisenhower at various stages in his eight years. Not making discourse easy does not constitute harassment. The skillful attenuation of the flow of information to subordinates who in another administration could be expected to confidentially provide much of the substance of the daily report also is something quite different, even though its effect upon the quality of Washington reporting is pronounced.

This book does not try to grapple with that problem, but this does not mean that the problem is of minor importance. In 1973 the Professional Relations Committee of the National Press Club, in cooperation with American University, carried out a study entitled *The Press Covers Government: The Nixon Years from 1969 to Watergate.* It is based largely upon interviews with working newsmen, and the single quality it most reflects is a sense of outrage at the way the Nixon administration restricted the flow of information at all the levels which matter. Personal conversation with members of the White House press corps by 1973 invariably brought to the surface three sentiments on the part of these reporters which long before had passed from rational criticism to simple hostility. One was resentment of bad-mouthing the press by administration spokesmen, including the president. Unreasonably or not, reporters are not accustomed to being called liars or puppets who work for antisocial schemers. Another was an intense dislike of Ronald Ziegler, growing out of the conviction that he lied to them repeatedly. Third, and most apparent, was resentment of the way the clamping down of the flow of information made it infinitely more difficult to cover the administration.

The extent of the White House preoccupation with secrecy and controlled flow has been demonstrated many times, but especially in the elaborate wiretapping of staff and newsmen's telephones which finally came up for full examination in June of 1974. It's highly doubtful if this kind of paranoia served the administration well; there were, perhaps, fewer leaks and more successful cover-ups than in less careful regimes. It's an old principle of kitchen physics, however, that if the lid is kept on tightly while something's going on inside there sooner or later will be a blow—and it'll be a beauty. The continuing supply to Jack Anderson of summaries of top-level deliberations during the Bangladesh crisis and the later leaks from congressional committees and grand juries as the Watergate matter developed were demonstrations of this principle.

Not only Frankel, but other journalists and political scientists have cited the decline in number of presidential press conferences in the Nixon era. It is a good thermometer, perhaps; a symbol of administration attitudes. But the presidential press conference ceased to be a major source of information a good many years ago. Obviously the kind of continuing relationship with a president which would provide responses for those questions from the *Time*'s Washington bureau would be greatly enlightening, but the last time there was anything similar was during the tenure of Franklin Roosevelt. When Dwight Eisenhower's advisers decided he would be effective on television, the entire institution moved in the direction of show business and away from continuing insight into the thinking of the nation's leader as he wrestles with his job.

So far as the needs of good political journalism are concerned, silencing second- and third-level officials and tighter controls upon information officers were far more significant; so was the reduction of White House briefings from two to one a day. And perhaps a better indicator of the atmosphere at the beginning of Richard Nixon's second term than the frequency of his press conferences were the outraged complaints from a group of newsmen covering the visit of Leonid Brezhnev to this country in June of 1973. Press briefings were too infrequent, they protested, and scanty when they were provided by Ronald Ziegler (rather than Henry Kissinger as promised). The *Washington Post* carried a stinging little editorial about it headlined

"Summit News: An Embarrassing Story."[14] They had a point. The complainants were Soviet newsmen in Brezhnev's party, representing what is generally considered the most tightly controlled major news institution in the world.

Two other events occurred in June which were to have long-range effects on the media, in the first case, and on the administration of Richard Nixon. On June 29, the Supreme Court handed down an opinion (the Earl Caldwell case), which declared that journalists have no First Amendment right to refuse to tell grand juries the names of confidential sources. The implications of that decision are discussed beginning on page 224.

And, of course, in the small hours of June 17 a security guard in the Watergate complex where the Democratic National Headquarters was located noticed that a lock had been taped open.

He called the police.

Richard Nixon was renominated as the Republican party's candidate for president on August 22, 1972, but long before that the machinery of the campaign had been tuned and set in motion. Perhaps no reelection campaign in modern history was so elaborately prepared and mounted (there is a tendency to use the president's kind of metaphor when writing about him), none so well executed in detail. It proved to be a massive case of overkill with a fierce backlash. To raise amounts of money which were preposterously large it was necessary to go to illegal strategies and arrangements. The search for really gamey stuff to use against political enemies extended to break-ins (one commonly held theory asserted that the Watergate break-in was primarily a search to find material discrediting Senator Kennedy). Out of both these excesses came indictments, jail terms, the president's resignation, and a reputation for unconscionable shabbiness which probably will outlast all the good works of the administration.

A considerable part of the offensive against the media set out in the preceding pages was designed to keep any pro-

Democratic bias (as perceived by the administration, whose members perceived a lot of it) within limits in the media and whenever possible to suppress Democratic party viewpoints altogether. There was no nonsense among the Nixon staff about any marketplace of ideas. Such actions as the filing of antitrust suits in April also were widely seen as ways to lean on the networks, and there were small reminders during the campaign to keep the pressure on.

But the worries of the president's men were considerably diminished by the nomination of George McGovern by the Democrats in July. Muskie had been the candidate most feared by the Committee for the Re-election of the President, and they went to considerable lengths, including forgery, to help destroy his candidacy. Teddy Kennedy had also been a worry, but he never became a candidate. McGovern did not inspire such concern from the beginning, perhaps because he was not a popular media figure and hardly represented a charismatic threat. Patrick Buchanan and his monitoring staff watched the media closely as the summer wore on. They perceived the early coverage of McGovern as favorable, but were cheered by what they took to be a shift after Humphrey went on the attack during the final presidential primaries. After the exposure of the Eagleton medical record and the subsequent flap culminating in his removal as the vice-presidential candidate, they obviously were reassured.

The first clear sign came in a speech by Vice-President Spiro Agnew. On July 22 he told the National Newspaper Association, an organization primarily made up of weekly newspapers, that both government and the press

> . . . might do well to forego harangue and cliché in favor of discussion based on reason and the public interest.

He also assured the publishers that

> . . . the widely-heralded assumption that every allusion to press shortcomings represents an attempt to destroy

First Amendment freedoms, while understandable, . . . is unfounded.[15]

On August 9, Patrick Buchanan gave an interview to Robert Semple of the *New York Times* which amounted to an official unilateral cease-fire. Semple's article began:

> Washington, Aug. 9—At the express instructions of President Nixon, the White House's three years of intermittent conflict with the press has come to at least a temporary halt.
>
> "This doesn't mean that some of us have abandoned or will abandon some of our cherished assumptions about the press," Patrick J. Buchanan, a Presidential speechwriter, said today in an interview. "But it does mean that there is little disposition around here to make an issue of the media in the campaign."[16]

As in much of Buchanan's talk, there is remarkable candor in that statement. As long as we feel you're not hurting us, it says in effect, we won't make trouble, but that's just for the campaign; the offensive is not over. That was consistent with Buchanan's attitudes from the beginning of his service. It expressed a grim simplification of what he felt those in power have a right to expect from the media and leaves open-ended not only the possibility of punishment but its extent should their expectations not be met.

September came, and with it the campaign reached full cry. In the case of the president, it was carefully controlled, almost muted. Nixon made few outright political appearances on television. His favorite medium, particularly toward the end, was the radio address, and some of these dealt in more detail with a single area and at greater length than he normally would risk on television. Since radio audiences are small compared to prime television and generally half-listening, the decision seemed an odd one. Actually, it was astute. In the first place, the speeches were fully reported in the newspapers the next day; the message did get out. Second, he could not be faulted for isolating himself in smug incumbency based upon polls which showed from the beginning that he was going to be a big winner. He was campaigning and he was addressing issues of importance.

There was another factor which may have entered his managers' thinking. In both the Nixon campaign of 1960 and the Goldwater campaign of 1964, heavy Republican purchases of prime time had meant preempting the most favored evening television shows. The good burgher who removes his shoes at the end of the day and sets up camp in front of the set to watch a favorite program and sees instead somebody requesting his vote is likely to be irritated. (Nixon, on the Monday evening before the 1960 election, had committed the ultimate error; he took over the spot occupied by "I Love Lucy," which was at that point in our culture just short of being the state religion.) There was none of that in 1972. He campaigned, and he spoke with more substance than in 1968, when his advisers for tele-vision carefully tried to keep him from saying anything with meaning at all,[17] but he did it in a way which was nearly inconspicuous. It was not a campaign style which could have won for a contender, but it was perfect for an incumbent who'd had, from time to time, image problems.

During the summer his direct contact with the media increased; he held press conferences on June 20, another on June 22 (these on the heels of the Max Frankel article discussed earlier), and another on July 27. Only one was televised. His manner was conciliatory throughout, and when someone asked him about Ehrlichman's remark about "dumb and flabby ques-tions," he smilingly dissociated himself from it by saying he had not been aware of many soft pitches, which was fine, because he liked hard ones better anyhow.

There was an opportunity a few weeks later, however, to lean on the networks which seems to have been too inviting to resist. It involved the entertainment, not the news, side of television, and again went to an area in which the threshold of pain is low, the matter of profit.

The rise of television had devastated the traditional motion picture industry and, along with putting most companies out of business, had greatly reduced the number of jobs for craftsmen, technicians, and performers. Production for television kept a kind of modest establishment going. As costs mounted, the networks turned increasingly to the use of reruns. Despite the payment of residual rights, a single episode of a series which could serve both in, say, October and March, obviously was much cheaper than nothing but originals. By the beginning of the seventies, reruns were beginning early indeed. Sometimes the first of the season would appear during the "dead week," the one week of the year during which no ratings are taken, between Christmas and New Year's Day. The last of new episodes usually appeared in late January or February.

Reruns save money by putting people out of work, in the eyes of the entertainment unions and guilds, so in early September they requested the Federal Communications Commission to consider limiting reruns to thirteen weeks a year—twelve more weeks of originals, on the average, than provided by the networks at that time. The Screen Actors Guild, headed by John Gavin, led the fight, and it attracted some impressive support, including Senator Barry Goldwater, Governor Ronald Reagan (a veteran member of SAG himself), and Richard Nixon. The networks reacted with predictable dismay. A spokesman for CBS said the proposal would cost the networks an additional $150 million a year and force them to cut back on the chronic money losers, news and public affairs.

On September 14, 1971, Nixon wrote to the Guild stating in strong terms his support of its position, a letter more directed to the networks than to the union. It said that if reductions in reruns were not made voluntarily "we will explore whatever regulatory recommendations are in order." He pronounced reruns an economic threat to the American film industry and accused the broadcasters of failing to serve the public interest.

Since the FCC is an independent agency and the president has no connection with it other than nominations of its members, the "we" apparently referred to the Office of Telecommunications Policy, which frequently expressed its interest in matters which upset the networks. Clay Whitehead, OTP director, confirmed the assumption on September 15 by making a speech which referred to the "spreading blight of re-runs" and high profits at the networks.

The FCC always has been skittish in matters touching upon program content, and there have been no rulings concerning reruns. Richard Nixon demonstrated at other times his interest in television, particularly in his strong advocacy of legislation forbidding local blackouts of sporting events for which all the tickets have been sold. Obviously there might be some political advantage in echoing the mild but endemic consumer grumbling about repeats (which is not to say that his motives were political; as a fairly consistent entertainment viewer, the president presumably had attitudes of his own about such things). Considering the general attitudes of his staff toward applying pressure when they thought it might help, however, it seems reasonable that the move was designed in part as a nudging reminder to the networks of their infinite vulnerability as their reporting of the campaign came into the stretch. Whatever the thinking in the White House, the spectacle of a president—particularly this president—writing to a labor union, not only to support its demands but to censure its employers as deficient in understanding their obligations, was uncommon.

In September Richard Nixon was saying in private some hard things about a newspaper and setting his revenge afoot. In mid-May, 1974, a series of leaks from the House Judiciary Committee which was investigating impeachment of the president included the transcript of a taped Oval Office conversation which had been omitted from the transcripts submitted earlier by Nixon. The reason for the omission was that it was "unrelated to Watergate." It was, however, closely related to the *Washington Post,* where two young reporters named Bernstein and Woodward were producing almost daily stories on the bungled burglary of Democratic headquarters.

The conversation of September 15, 1972, involved the president, H. R. Haldeman, and John Dean.

> The President: . . . the main thing is the *Post* is going to have damnable, damnable problems out of this one. They have a television station . . . and they're going to have to get it renewed.
>
> Haldeman: They've got a radio station, too.
>
> The President: Does that come up, too? . . . it's going to be goddam active here . . . well, the game has to be played awfully rough. . . .

Later Nixon brought up the name of Edward Bennett Williams, a flashy and highly successful Washington lawyer who represented some of the *Post*'s interests.

> The President: I would not want to be in Edward Bennett William's position after this one . . . I think we are going to fix the son of a bitch.[18] [Ellipses from transcript.]

It never became clear what kind of "fixing" was fashioned for Williams, but within a few months came another suit intitiated by people close to the president challenging the renewal of the broadcast license of a *Post* television property, WJXT in Jacksonville. Three years earlier, renewal for WPLG-TV in Miami had been contested.

It should be noted, as a matter of accuracy, that the two challenges by Nixon associates were about three years apart, and the White House conversation quoted here obviously can be tied only to the second (media accounts at the time the tapes became available generally—and erroneously—indicated that *both* suits came later; so did Bernstein and Woodward in their *All the President's Men*). It is unknown, obviously, what conversations if any preceded the filing of the first challenge in 1969.

Although the Watergate affair is outside the scope of this study for the most part, the activities of the *Post* in publishing the running stories of Woodward and Bernstein did provide the focal point for the sharpest criticism of the media by Nixon lieutenants during the generally subdued campaign.

The Watergate story did not assume major proportions

until after the election, because only a few publications took it seriously. The *Boston Globe* made heavy use of the *Post*'s news service in its energetic pursuit of the story. *Time* magazine provided a good deal of coverage, and so did the *Los Angeles Times*. The *New York Times* became heavily committed, trying to establish their own distinct claim to a story which at that point was identified largely with their chief rival. In July they sent down from New York a special six-man team assigned only to Watergate. Even *Post* staff members such as Barry Sussman, special Watergate editor, thought the *Times* did a remarkably good job, but the story remained identified in the public mind with the *Post*. The lead in time, the superiority of sources, and the all-out vigorous competence of Katharine Graham's paper was too much to overcome.

Being out in front was not an altogether comfortable position. The elite dailies generally are seen in the news business as agenda setters, but this time most of the remainder of the country's news media either minimized the running developments or, in some cases, actually ignored the original exposés and played up the denials. Sussman tells in his *The Great Coverup* of the episode in late October, 1972, when a Woodward-Bernstein story about Haldeman's role in campaign spending contained a couple of errors. Ron Ziegler, who was attacking the *Post* regularly in briefings, issued a contemptuous denial the next morning. Such subscribers to the *Post*'s news service as the *Minneapolis Tribune,* the *Denver Post,* the *San Diego Union,* the *Chicago Tribune,* and the *Philadelphia Inquirer* did not carry the original story at all—but gave prominent display to the White House denial.[19]

Nor, despite White House assertions that the *Post* was working in concert with George McGovern, did Watergate ever become a substantial campaign issue. Some of McGovern's staff realized that there was dynamite down there someplace, but no one knew how to get it out. Some Democratic candidates attacked the break-in in a pedestrian fashion, and various eminent Republicans explained it away. The most comical explanation was that provided by Barry Goldwater, who assured some surprised newsmen at the airport in Muskegon, Michigan, on November 1 that the whole thing was a hoax:

> I think more and more that this is a plant by Democrats to pay $100,000 to four men to say they are Republicans and get caught in the Watergate. . . . I have a hunch that when the investigation is made and a trial held that the Democratic Party is going to be responsible for this.[20]

There were minor flaps during the campaign about security—newsmen traveling with both candidates felt that the Secret Service regularly made things unnecessarily difficult for them, and there had been earlier complaints that security clearances for admission to the Republican convention in Miami were political—but the general tone of discourse was calm. Then, shortly after the election, the old rhetoric of the offensive on the press came back with a roar, almost as if to echo Patrick Buchanan's warning that the administration's forbearance had been limited to the campaign.

On November 13, Charles Colson, special counsel to the president, emissary to the networks, and eventual prosecution witness to the sins of the administration, spoke to the New England Society of Newspaper Editors. He said that the *Washington Post* and CBS "employed tactics similar to those attributed to their old archenemy of the nineteen fifties [Joseph McCarthy], engaging in the identical kind of unproven innuendo they found so shocking 20 years ago."[21]

As for Ben Bradlee, editor of the *Post,* he was a "self-appointed leader of a tiny fringe of arrogant elitists" in journalism. Colson returned to a familiar theme, that Bradlee and his ilk sat around at Georgetown cocktail parties, hopelessly out of touch with the real America, eroding confidence in the honorable men who were conducting the business of government as well as "the confidence of a lot of fair-minded persons in the objective reporting of the *Washington Post.*" Colson himself was on his way out; within four months he resigned and was gone. He had hired E. Howard Hunt as a consultant to the White

House, and Hunt had been arrested at the break-in. At that point, the White House staff was collectively playing Caesar's wife.

The final major speech of 1972 on media matters by a representative of the White House was delivered by Clay T. Whitehead. Whitehead had been steadily gaining stature since the creation of his post in 1970 and frequently spoke directly for the president, as in his testimony regarding the prospects of a veto of funds for the Corporation for Public Broadcasting unless the structure of public television was changed. His public statements generally were taken to represent Nixon's thinking. In addition to public television, he had drawn particular attention when he addressed himself to the inadequacies of the FCC and condemned the Fairness Doctrine. Broadcasters have always found the Fairness Doctrine threatening and have no great enthusiasm for the FCC, so these two lines of argument had pleased them much. His speech of December 18, 1972, the major speech of his government career, became known as the "carrot and the stick" speech, because it included one more idea which the broadcasters liked very much and one which was almost terrifying to at least the more thoughtful among them.

The setting was a luncheon of the Indianapolis chapter of Sigma Delta Chi,[22] a somewhat improbable platform for a major policy speech. The organization is a national professional journalists' organization. Program planners for the group heard that Whitehead might be available, invited him, and somewhat to their surprise got a quick acceptance. They were told later that Indianapolis was chosen for the statement because it was a way of bucking the Eastern media establishment and because it was the heartland of America.

The speech was hardly addressed to the midwestern journalists who sat around the luncheon table in Indianapolis, however. It was directed at the owners and managers of television stations, and contained some sharp language about their responsibility for controlling the relationship between themselves and the networks.

. . . all that many affiliates do is flip the switch in the control room to "network," throw the "switch" in the mailroom to forward viewer complaints to the network, sit back, and enjoy the fruits of a very profitable business.

Please don't misunderstand me when I stress the need for more local responsibility. I'm not talking about locally produced programs, important though they are. I'm talking now about licensee responsibility for *all* programming, including the programs that come from the network.

And, as the speech came to a conclusion and its most famous phrase, it became clear Whitehead was talking especially about more pressure from affiliates on network news:

There is no area where management responsibility is more important than news. The station owners and managers cannot abdicate responsibility for news judgements. When a reporter or disc jockey slips in or passes over information in order to line his pocket, that's plugola, and management would take quick corrective action. But men also stress or suppress information in accordance with their beliefs. Will station licensees or network executives also take action against this intellectual plugola? [The text of the speech is in Documents of Significance, beginning with page 300.]

The implication was clear that if they did not take action, they might have a very hard time indeed at license renewal time. So much for the stick. But if they did, license renewals would be for five, not three years; the administration was introducing legislation to that effect (it went to the House on March 13, 1973). That, of course, was the carrot.

Some of the implications and possible effects of this line of argument are discussed in another section of this study. The immediate effect on the meeting in Indianapolis was remarkable. The Whitehead text had been released in Washington at 10:00 A.M. and sections of it had moved on the news wires. By the time the luncheon was over, the meeting was jammed with representatives from television stations from over a wide area. Eerily, when Whitehead finished, there was no applause, although the group almost routinely gave big name speakers an ovation. To the intense embarrassment of the officers at the head table, there was simply silence until questions were called for. Questions came in torrents.

A kind of one-line instant analysis was provided by an old journalist from out of town who said to the chapter's president as they left the hall, "This SOB wants to curtail our freedom."[23]

The last thrust of 1972 in the administration's offensive against the media was marvelously trivial in comparison to some of the things which had preceded it. More than that, it gave a touch of the comic, involuntary or otherwise, to the most humorless administration since Hoover. On December 15, 1972, Dorothy McCardle, society reporter for the *Washington Post,* was denied admission to the White House to cover a reception. She was told that a pool of reporters had been chosen to cover the event, and that she was not among them. The following evening she arrived to cover a formal dinner the Nixons were giving for cabinet officers. She was again informed that she was not included in the pool; a little investigation revealed that she was the only reporter excluded. On Sunday morning she failed to make the pool which was to cover White House church services, and word began to get around that, as a matter of fact, the *Post* was not going to get into White House social events until after January 20, 1973, inauguration day. Ben Bradlee, editor of the *Post,* and Howard Simon, managing editor, expressed shock and Ronald Ziegler denied everything.

Pool reporting is a common device in situations where too many reporters would interfere with the proceedings. If the event is highly newsworthy and the number of places limited, lots may be drawn. In the case of the White House and the presidency, however, things are looser than that. Traditionally pool assignments have been rotated among those interested, but with the Washington media always included. This convention grows out of the fact that they are the local papers and stations. In the case of newspaper society pages in particular, they are dealing with local news.

McCardle was not the first *Post* reporter to be excluded from a Nixon social event. One of her colleagues on the *Post*'s women's section (a term used here for convenience; the *Post* no longer calls it that) had produced one of the first confrontations between the White House and the paper. Some eighteen months earlier, Judith Martin, a columnist with a gracefully wicked wit, wrote a preview of an upcoming television tour of the White House conducted by Tricia Nixon. Martin described the president's daughter as "dressed like an ice cream cone" and mused that enough of that kind of thing "could even give neatness and cleanliness a bad name."[24]

"That," said Martin later, "got me barred from Tricia's vanilla wedding, a great newspaper scandal in its day, as the *Post* refused to send anyone else. (Its day, however, was a mighty short day. The following one, the *New York Times* published the Pentagon papers, and my cause got upstaged.)"[25]

Dorothy McCardle, however, had committed no such lese majesty. She was a dignified, established reporter who, as the *Post* rather delicately put it, had been covering White House society for five administrations. As a matter of fact, she was assured by the White House press office early in the series of exclusions that there was "nothing personal."

And there was not; it was simply one more way of making coverage a bit more troublesome for the *Post*. In answer to a series of questions at the regular press briefing on December 19, Ziegler said that, while he did not "hold a great deal of respect for the journalistic approach" of the *Post*, they would be treated fairly in future pools. He also made clear that he did not accept the idea that the White House was a local story for any paper, feeling instead it always should be covered in a national context, and announced that pools in the future would have a "fairer and broader" basis.

It is doubtful if Ziegler intended it, but this put some pressure on the *Post*'s chief local competition, the *Washington Star-News,* whose reporters had been admitted without question to the events from which McCardle had been barred. Three days later the *Star-News* requested in an editorial that the *Post* be readmitted; failing that, it said stoutly, "we should take our turn in the cold." Ziegler obliged, and for a week or two in early January neither Washington paper was represented. This led to the amusing business of the representative of an out-of-town paper periodically leaving a party and repairing to the press lobby, where the two most capable reporters in the country for that particular assignment wrote down what he told them. As the furor surrounding the inauguration rose and the number of society stories increased, restrictions were quietly dropped and the episode ended.

SIX

Years 1973–74

*Don't get the impression that you arouse my anger. You see,
one can only be angry with those he respects.*

Richard Nixon to the White House
press corps, October 26, 1973

The last twenty months of Richard Nixon's presidency were a
time of increasingly feverish activity for him and for his staff,
but no significant part of it was directed in any organized
fashion toward harassing the media. By the early months of
1973 the centralization of authority and responsibility in the
White House had reached the extreme. John Ehrlichman and
H. R. Haldeman had eliminated, often with no pretense at finesse,
others around the president of whom they did not approve. It was
a wide-ranging list, headed by two different attorneys
general. They gunned not only for the highly placed, however.
At one point there was an attempt to get Nixon's Filipino valet
and the valet's wife fired. Although that effort failed, not many
of the others did. The president had become almost inaccessible
to the staff, except for Ron Ziegler and the pair frequently
referred to in Washington as Hans and Fritz. Any kind of
significant activity which came out of the White House—or,
uncommonly, got into it from outside—went through them.

177

With more than 500 members, the White House staff was a large one, but responsibility and authority were more concentrated than at any time since Woodrow Wilson lay dying.

Once the hoopla of the inauguration and the relishing of the landslide were over, the attention of these increasingly embattled few was concentrated on matters far more demanding than media relations. The Watergate story was constantly more difficult to contain, and far more people than a pair of young men on the *Post* were asking tough questions. Big lies had been told and had to be shored up continually. Wavering staff members, or former ones, had to be reinforced for stonewalling.

The year began, however, with a touch Charles Colson, the old Colson, would have liked. On January 31, 1973, federal agents arrested Les Whitten, Jack Anderson's assistant and one of the primary producers of the Anderson column. The circumstances suggested harassment.

In November of 1972 a group of militant Indians occupied the Bureau of Indian Affairs for six days. When they left they took large numbers of documents with them. For a few weeks afterward, the Anderson column touched upon the material in the stolen files several times. Anderson indicated that they were, by this time, scattered in secret locations all over the country as part of a native American underground. The columns mentioned Whitten's role in developing the story, but denied his receiving the documents or encouraging the break-in.

On the thirty-first Whitten went to the apartment of Hank Adams, a Sioux who was one of the leaders of the group. According to Whitten, after the interview Adams indicated that he was heading off to return several boxes of the material to the Bureau of Indian Affairs. Whitten volunteered to help load the material into Adams's car. When they reached the sidewalk outside the apartment, federal agents materialized and arrested both of them. The charge was receiving, concealing, and retaining stolen government property valued at more than $100,000. There was no question in Whitten's mind that the agents knew who he was and were enjoying the assignment. He was put in jail for a few hours and then released.

A few days later Whitten told his story to the grand jury, and Adams backed it, saying that at no point was there a plan for Whitten to receive the papers. The grand jury refused to indict. Considering the experience of some other reporters, it's a persuasive idea that Whitten's arrest was enough in the eyes of those who arranged it. He had been spanked, and Anderson had received a demonstration that such business as the Bangladesh papers did not go unnoticed.

Most of the administration activity related to the media after Nixon's first formal recognition of the Watergate scandal was sporadic and unorchestrated. The great running story of the summer was that of the hearings conducted by Senator Sam Ervin's Senate subcommittee. Much of the more interesting comment of the papers and television newscasts was, in fact, history rather than breaking news, material which came into sight through the subcommittee's probing. Leaks and leads multiplied for both newsmen and committee staff members. A recurrent story of particular interest to the media, for example, was that of the wiretaps associated with the establishment of the unit the White House nicknamed the "plumbers." It began to come clear during the summer of 1973 just how much the administration, and particularly Henry Kissinger, had been alarmed after the appearance of the Pentagon Papers in 1971, and just how extensive the efforts had been to contain leaks. The precise number of taps and the identity of the tapped was a continuing half-speculative story. Most of the unknowing subjects were government officials, including some very close to Kissinger, but a few newsmen were included. Eventually, the consensus held that at least Marvin Kalb of CBS, William Beecher and Hedrick Smith of the *New York Times,* and Henry Brandon of the *London Times* had been monitored (the monitors apparently heard nothing of importance). Some of the taps went back to the beginning of the Nixon administration in 1969, and at least one newsman—Joseph Kraft, a syndicated columnist—apparently was a victim at that time.

Early in 1973 both the president and vice-president made

rather surprising gestures of conciliation toward the media; more surprising then than in retrospect, with the full circumstances of their situation understood. The opening of this book describes Richard Nixon's trip to the White House press quarters on April 30 of that year after his first televised speech on Watergate. Even though the event may have been more calculated than it appeared, his tension and fatigue were apparent. That might have been explained in part by the fact that he had lied, deliberately and explicitly, in regard to the extent of his knowledge of the affair, the point at which he acquired it, and what he intended to do about it.

Three days later Vice-President Agnew, in a little-reported speech to the Maryland Press Club, indicated that the administration would like to begin serious conversations with media people to reduce the "unfortunate hostility" between them and government. He feared, he said, that the flow of information had become distorted and that everybody's credibility was beginning to suffer. He even teetered on the edge of apology, saying that, while he would not take back the substance of his attacks on newspapers and broadcasters, he now regretted the kind of language he'd used. The vice-president seems to have been speaking more to his own hopes than anything else. He had been a highly effective front man during the early days of attacks on the media, but had never done more than read speeches, and by 1973 was substantially isolated from White House decision making. Before the year was over, charges of tax fraud and kickbacks drove him to resignation.

For the most part, 1973 was a year of new revelations of old scandals and of actions taken at the lower levels of government by those who had become convinced, through almost four years of freely displayed animosity toward the press at the top level, that the media were fair game. This was particularly true in the lower courts. Some details of those actions by judges of the first jurisdiction in a variety of cases are set out in the next chapter, which deals with the effects of government's offensive against the media. The police arm of the federal establishment some-times showed signs of receiving the message as well.

On February 27, 1973, a group of militant Indians seized the village of Wounded Knee at the edge of the Oglala Sioux reservation in South Dakota, took eleven hostages, and made a series of demands upon the federal government. In reply Washington sent in federal marshals, FBI agents, and Bureau of Indian Affairs police, along with two armored personnel carriers. Roadblocks were thrown up by the federal authorities to control access and a seige developed that was to last more than two months. There were sporadic exchanges of gunfire.

Wounded Knee was difficult for journalists in several ways. South Dakota is remote; some of the national media had small bureaus in Denver and Omaha, but the nearest major offices were in Chicago (at one point United Press International sent out the bureau chief from Detroit). Day in and day out the seige was a nonstory, but constant surveillance was necessary because of the situation's volatility. The citizens of the area were hostile to newsmen from outside. Accommodations were sparse and distant—the nearest motel was in Nebraska, sixty miles away—and communication difficult.

The marshals and agents of the federal government had the same handicaps and even shorter tempers. Technically, local police and the tribal council—the official governing body for reservation affairs, also a target of the militants—were in charge and federal authorities only advising, but that pretense fooled no one ("We were supposed to believe that two hundred feds running around with machine guns were advisers?" one reporter said later). The Indians inside the compound wanted maximum public notice, of course; the authorities and the tribal council wanted them to have as little as possible. Individual journalists generally were permitted in and out through roadblocks, but they were convinced that telephones were tapped.

On April 17, with the seige almost seven weeks old, three small private planes flown by volunteers dropped food and medical supplies by parachute. Aboard one of them was Thomas Oliphant, of the Washington bureau of the *Boston*

Globe, who had been invited along by the expedition's orga-
nizers. He filed three stories in as many days. On the fourth
day, a warrant for his arrest was issued by the United States
attorney's office in South Dakota. At dawn the next day the
FBI sent out two carloads of agents to arrest Oliphant. There
was an embarrassing flaw in their intelligence, however; they
descended on his one-time home in Boston, apparently innocent
of his move to Washington some time before.

Oliphant turned himself in to federal authorities in Washington. On May 7, he and the other participants in the flight
were indicted by a federal grand jury in South Dakota. The
three counts were crossing a state line with the intent of
participating in a civil disorder, interfering with a federal marshal, and conspiracy. Oliphant was cited as the money man for
the enterprise, supposedly controlling a treasury of $10,000. In
fact, in the best tradition of the news business, he had left
Washington with five dollars in cash and a credit card.

The South Dakota indictment meant that Oliphant had to
be extradited, and the *Globe* decided to fight it. Thomas Winship, the paper's editor, wanted maximum visibility for the case
to make certain that, in his words, it "remained a visible blot on
the administration."

Eventually the Justice Department had second thoughts
about the whole matter, and Elliott Richardson, then attorney
general, ordered the charges dropped. He followed that action
with a new set of guidelines for federal authorities in their
dealings with the press which included prohibition of the arrest,
or even the questioning, of reporters without the written permission of the attorney general.

That came after, however, the confrontation with the CBS
News television crew. Five-man teams with bulky film gear were
not welcome at federal road blocks, and on the evening of May
3, 1973, the CBS unit sneaked into the compound and spent
the night. When they came out the following morning they were
taken into custody by the authorities and their cameras and
films seized. They were then turned over to local authorities.

Three paper-and-pencil journalists, including Andrew Malcolm of the *New York Times,* were attentive witnesses at the roadblock while this went on. FBI agents asked for their identifications; they produced press credentials, which were confiscated. A short time later, as Malcolm recalls it, an impressively official automobile roared up and the ranking local officer of the FBI forces got out. He demanded to know the identities of the three and the explanation of their presence. The reporters replied that they were waiting for the return of the press credentials which his agents had confiscated. The FBI chief ordered them to leave forthwith. They refused to do so until their papers were returned. A rifle-toting agent finally brought the credentials back, but remained on the scene to make certain the newsmen left.

After a good deal of argument, the CBS crew was released and their gear returned. The details of the discussion never were altogether clear; as one CBS man recalled it, before returning the film the authorities insisted upon only one condition, and that a rather odd one—that the footage be made available to other networks as well.

That conflicted, at least in spirit, with the attitude of Deputy Assistant Attorney General Hellstern, who issued a statement banning CBS indefinitely from returning to the village. Access to the media, he said, interfered with negotiations. The tribal council, not surprisingly in agreement, also announced the network's banishment. Bureau of Indian Affairs police escorted the crew to their chartered jet.

The public appearance of John W. Dean III, a former presidential counsel, before the Ervin committee during June produced more evidence of the oddly sophomoric thinking of the White House staff, including an "enemies" list which eventually totaled 550. It included a number of media people, the identity of most of whom was predictable. There was a good deal of joking within the profession to the effect that those who hadn't made it had lost face. The primary tactic contemplated for use against the enemies, apparently, was the harassing tax audit—the method used on Robert Greene of *Newsday,* which Dean cited in his televised testimony.

If revelation was the main theme of the summer and fall of 1973, angry bickering was its accompaniment. There were continuing attacks upon the media for unfair presentation, and particularly for what was seen by many as the attempt to get Nixon at all cost. Washington was full of leaked documents and rumors; some kind of source could be found for almost any assertion, however wild. The Ervin committee followed standard practice in sensitive investigations, hearing witnesses in secret and then staging for the public (and, in this case, television cameras) somewhat abbreviated repetitions. Like all congressional committees under pressure, this one was leaky, and reports of what had been heard in the executive sessions circulated constantly. Many of them reached the media. As early as May, Senator William Proxmire of Wisconsin, although convinced of Nixon's guilt and far out of sympathy with him, attacked *Newsweek* for a story which said that Dean's secret testimony proved that Nixon was involved in efforts to cover up the Watergate break-in. The accusation that the president was being lynched became common. Chancellor W. Allen Wallis of the University of Rochester said "reactions by journalists and politicians to the Watergate break-in has been morally even more corrupt than Watergate activities themselves," and Patrick Buchanan asserted that the chancellor had not put it strongly enough. Nothing, he said, could keep the liberal press from sinking its teeth in the president; he found this particularly despicable because they were doing to Nixon precisely what Joseph McCarthy had done to his opponents. They had expressed horror at McCarthy, but refused to acknowledge their hypocrisy.[1] Editors received the most abusive mail some of them had ever seen, and continued to receive it until after Nixon resigned. The solid core of Nixon supporters apparently was somewhere around 25 to 30 percent of the population. They hated the media, and they were given to communication.

The unvarying response to this was that Richard Nixon

and his staff were in deep trouble because of what they, not the press, had done. There seemed little else to say.

The president's most intense personal attack on the media came during one of his rare news conferences, this one on October 26. At the time, the common assessment was that his temper simply got the better of him. He had, after all, been winging ad-lib barbs at the press for years. In this case he seemed to fall into some incidental criticism and then, carried away, lapsed into the hyperbole from which he never could seem to escape in moments of great emotion: "I have never seen," he said, "such outrageous, vicious, distorted reporting in 27 years of public life."

As the atmosphere became more steamy, Robert Pierpoint of CBS News asked Nixon why he was so angry with reporters. "Don't get the impression that you arouse my anger," the president said. "You see, one can only be angry with those he respects."

The session concluded with an exchange which some television viewers feared was about to lead to blows. Clark Mollenhoff of Cowles publications, a huge man who had been at one time on the White House staff, sought recognition in a microphone-rattling roar a half-dozen times before a contemptuous Nixon recognized him with a remark about being unable to avoid it. Mollenhoff was standing near the rostrum, and an apprehensive Ron Ziegler moved toward the neutral ground between. Mollenhoff asked an essentially rhetorical (and insulting) question, and the president turned it aside and broke off the session.

James Reston, in his *New York Times* column the next day, indicated that he figured it was a temper tantrum; so did *Newsweek* in its next issue.[2] Some two weeks later, however, the *Times* carried a story which cast doubt on that belief. Sid Feders, a television producer for CBS, had fallen into conversation with the president shortly before he entered the room—a conversation which cooled rapidly, according to Feders, when

Nixon learned he was from CBS. As the president walked away, he said: "Cronkite's not going to like this tonight, I hope."[3]

Regardless of the amount of spontaneity in the scene, there was an elaborate pattern of follow-up on the part of the administration and some continuing waves within the news business. The charge of lying and vicious reporting was picked up by the National News Council, as described elsewhere in this book. Patrick Buchanan appeared on a morning talk show, referred to the press conference scene as a "bearpit," and demanded that the networks be forced to more responsible reporting by all possible means within the law. On October 29, Gerald Warren, deputy press secretary, held a long session with reporters during which he lectured them on responsibility and argued in justification of the president's remarks. Ken Clawson, the former *Washington Post* reporter who had inherited the title of director of communications from Ron Ziegler, put other defenders on the road, including David Eisenhower.

While some television viewers may have been offended by the manners demonstrated by journalists on October 26, there is little evidence that either the original Nixon attack or the follow-ups made much difference. Only a fragment of the United States press was by that point supporting Richard Nixon. Even such dependable stalwarts as the *Chicago Tribune* and the *Detroit News* were calling for his resignation.

Five days after the press conference, the office of Senator Lowell Weicker began to make available the internal White House memos, some of which are reproduced in the Documents of Significance section of this work, which laid out the anatomy of the attacks upon media and journalists. With their publication, whatever impulse was left in the administration for pressing the offensive obviously began to wither. Actions which once might have been defensible as expressions of principle henceforth were suspect as conniving self-service; much of the credibility necessary for effective attack was gone.

Thus it is not surprising that the most effective jolt of the year against network broadcasting came not from the White House but from the Federal Communications Commission. On

December 3, that agency handed down a ruling which had overtones of Harley Staggers in it.

In September of 1972 the National Broadcasting Company had produced a documentary called "Pensions: A Broken Promise." It was one of the early exposés in a field which has continued to attract critics. The documentary concentrated on the flaws in private pension plans and, although some affirmative statements about them were included, the general tone was made clear by the title.

A complaint was brought to the FCC by a group called Accuracy in Media, a citizens' organization which had been particularly vigilant in protecting conservative causes. There were no allegations of tricky editing or misstatement; they simply contended that the program gave an unbalanced and prejudicial view of private pension plans and thus violated the requirements of the Fairness Doctrine.

The commission agreed, saying that the network gave "overwhelming weight" to the negative aspects and neglected the plans' "positive aspects." NBC was ordered to provide in some unspecified way "a reasonable opportunity for opposing viewpoints." The vote was five to zero; Commissioners Nicholas Johnson and Rex Lee abstained.

The rulings of the Federal Communications Commission, like those of all the independent regulatory agencies, can be appealed to the courts, and NBC filed such an appeal in the District of Columbia.

NBC argued that such a ruling, if it became a precedent, would do much to supress investigative reporting by broadcasters. It also made a strong case for the ruling's constituting a violation of the First Amendment, since it tried to enlarge the Fairness Doctrine as an element in news judgment. The "Pensions" decision did not enunciate a new principle, nor was it as threatening as Harley Staggers's effort to set up a congressional committee as super-editors of news programs, but it did represent another large increment in the pressure which broadcasters were beginning to say was stifling.

The least troublesome response, in many ways, to such an

order would have been simply to broadcast another program which would present the "other side" of the pensions issue. That is what CBS did with "The Selling of the Pentagon"— twice, as a matter of fact. But that was an extraordinarily sensitive issue not likely to be repeated; the NBC case was network routine.

The network's courtroom argument rested, fundamentally, on the fact that network news time is scarce and expensive. For this reason there has been an increasing effort, particularly in documentaries, to provide sufficient balance within a given program to satisfy the requirements of the fairness rule while still exercising the journalist's right to come to a conclusion and have an opinion. Not only is the network reluctant to give away time and spend money on rebuttal presentations, there is also an obvious good-sense limit on how much programming should be given over to private pension schemes or whatever other issue may stir up dissent. The effect of the decision, if allowed to stand, would be to push the networks further into the role of inoffensive neuters and encourage the takeover of the editorial function by a combination of vague rules, irritable special interest groups, and corporate timidity. NBC's decision to dig in its heels and fight helped crystallize the conflict and bring about a decision on principle. It also produced a victory. The court of appeals held in September, 1974, that documentary producers must be given wide latitude in making their own decisions about fairness.

The final thrust—it is doubtful if the White House had any role in it—came in the beginning of 1974. On January second, the Justice Department announced its intervention with the FCC to urge denial of license renewals for broadcasting stations in Des Moines, Iowa, and St. Louis, Missouri. The department contended that in both cities powerful newspaper interests—the *Post-Dispatch* in St. Louis, Cowles Communications (the *Des Moines Register*) in Des Moines—also owned the dominant broadcasting stations, and that the breakup of such combinations had long been an objective of the department. This was quite correct. Policy statements drawn up during the Johnson administration took such a stand in principle, on the grounds not only of broadening ownership but also providing a wider range of views. The FCC had indicated similar convictions occasionally, and the notion had wide support outside of the communications industries.

Nevertheless, there were reasons for suspecting punitive politics. The *Post-Dispatch* was an ancient Nixon enemy, of course. The *Des Moines Register* had been consistently Republican for decades and supported Nixon in his three presidential campaigns, but reversed their stand as the Watergate affair developed. The bitterness of the Cowles's Washington bureau chief, Mollenhoff, toward his former colleagues in the White House was clear and they reciprocated.

Otherwise, why these particular cities? The *Post-Dispatch* is one of the country's best newspapers; the *Register*, although not so visible nationally, is also first-rate by any standards. The broadcast properties they own are well-managed and independent in their operations. In both cities there is also vigorous and profitable major competition in broadcasting, and the *Post-Dispatch* has newspaper competition, although it does share an operating agreement with the *Globe-Democrat* under the Newspaper Preservation Act.

To some observers this added up to political vengeance. One of these was Nicholas Johnson, who as an FCC commissioner had worked vigorously for such breakup action but apparently could not accept this intervention at face value.

Meanwhile, there was rising talk within the broadcast business which demonstrated how difficult it is to change the nature of the American corporation through regulation. Owners of roughly comparable properties were said to be investigating the possibility of trades among themselves, with suitable adjustments. For example, a Des Moines television station might be traded for one in St. Louis, fulfilling the requirements of the regulation for both companies at the same time.

As of the summer of 1975, no ruling on the license

renewals had been made, and no new interventions with the FCC had been made by the Justice Department.

To say that the license renewal intervention was the final shot in the offensive against the media—if indeed it was—is not to say that Richard Nixon ignored them afterward. His last few months in office were marked by a fitful, sometimes almost gauche campaign to regain popular support by making news. In early December of 1973 something the White House called "Operation Candor" was set afoot with the release of details of his personal finances. It was not a good beginning; the news accounts which followed stated that Nixon's net worth had tripled while he was in office and that he had some highly dubious tax deductions. Shortly afterward, the Internal Revenue Service began reviewing the deductions.

The Nixon family flew to San Clemente for the Christmas holiday on a commercial flight, giving the press corps the slip. The president enjoyed himself greatly with the passengers and posed for their cameras. The trip got far more coverage, although poorer photographs, than would have the standard expedition on *Air Force One*. Background stories upon his return referred to his zesty determination to take personal charge of building a new image and getting the American people's minds off Watergate. The term "Operation Candor," however, was abandoned. The State of the Union Address later in the month contained some unusual devices. The president began by announcing in dramatic tones a new international meeting to attack the then-pressing oil crisis (in fact, the meeting had been publicly announced several days before) and concluded with some ad-lib remarks about the Watergate affair which assured his audience that the matter was in hand, or near it, and that "one year of Watergate is enough."

From a long period during which the regular White House press corps had found almost impossible access to anybody who knew anything, the administration moved to suprising availability with good spokesmen who seemed anxious to talk—Ken Clawson, Bryce Harlow, and especially the president's new lawyer, an attractive and persuasive man named James St. Clair.

The number of presidential press conferences increased. At one point Ziegler announced a regular schedule of every two weeks, although that frequency never developed.

The president also began traveling, particularly to locales where a friendly reception could be expected. He spoke to businessmen in Chicago, who cheered him when he told them that the Watergate stories in the papers were "all lies." He appeared at the opening of a new auditorium housing the Grand Old Opry in Nashville and performed on the piano, playing "Happy Birthday" for his wife and "God Bless America." In between, among other things, he played with a yellow yo-yo. He departed to a storm of applause and fervent vows of support from tearful banjo pickers and country fiddlers. He went to Houston, where he spoke to the National Association of Broadcasters, had a brief dustup with Dan Rather, and dropped into a restaurant in the early morning for a cup of coffee and some photographs. The waitress refused to let him pay.

In early April he went out to campaign for a Republican congressman in Michigan's "thumb" area, normally safely Republican. He avoided the city of Saginaw, but was received with roars of delight by the small-town crowds. His man lost. At the end of the month he turned over transcripts of the Oval Office tapes in a televised speech, posing with an enormous stack of handsome blue notebooks which, it developed, contained not the millions of words which their appearance suggested but the equivalent of a normal book-length manuscript.

And in June he carried out a spectacular tour of the Middle East in connection with United States initiatives toward an Arab-Israeli settlement, climaxed by a reception by literally millions of cheering citizens of Egypt. He was an old hand at international tours and parades by that time, and this was the greatest in his career.

None of this changed anything. The problem was not one of faulty communication technique—indeed, the Nixon staff, in its way, was more skillful than any which preceded it. They knew that colorful news stories about the president which produced good photos and film would get good play, regardless of the sentiments of editorial writers or individual reporters. It worked that way. There was a touch of a snicker in some treatments of the Grand Old Opry episode, but accounts of most happenings appeared substantially as the president must have wanted them. This was particularly true of the running stories of the Middle Eastern tour, which were highly favorable; the American press always has been a trifle dazzled by what is perceived as summitry.

The reason that none of it helped, of course, was that during the same period there emerged a sorry log of indictments, convictions, exposed lies, and generally shabby past behavior. The cosmetic diversions were not enough.

On the same day that Richard Nixon resigned, the Associated Press carried, coincidentally, a story by John Lengel which provided an inventory of the legacy which the Nixon administration left to the cause of independent journalism and freedom of expression. Proposals to impose restraints on the press made up part of a wide-ranging revision of the federal criminal code proposed by the White House in the fall of 1972. Specific statutes recommended to the Congress included, as Lengel summed them up:

> An Official Secrets Act [the name was borrowed from a British statute] which would make it a crime to publish any national defense information about the "military capability of the United States or an associate nation." Opponents say such legislation would enable the government to prosecute the news media for almost any story about the Defense Department published without government authorization.
>
> Revision of the Espionage Act [which, it will be remembered, proved to be a weak reed in the government's Pentagon Papers arguments] to prohibit publication of any information that might be used to prejudice interests of the United States. Existing legislation makes it a crime to publish such information only if the government can prove it was obtained with intent to harm the country.
>
> ... The Nixon administration ... said the Secrets Act

and the Espionage Act revisions were necessary to plug security leaks.

Opponents said the administration proposals would have prevented publication of stories about the Mylai massacres, C-5A cost overruns and the Pentagon Papers.[4]

In addition, the Justice Department had begun work on a proposal made earlier in the year by the president. This would narrow sharply the applicability of the Supreme Court's Sullivan decision of 1964, which held that public officials had grounds for libel actions only where malice could be proved. Had legislation of the sort suggested by Nixon been in effect earlier, such suits, or the threat of them might have at least delayed many of the Watergate disclosures. The Official Secrets Act and the revision of the Espionage Act were buried in the judiciary committee during the late spring and summer of 1974 while that body worked on impeachment. That done, the committee almost immediately had the responsibility for conducting investigations and hearings on the nomination of Nelson Rockefeller to the vice-presidency. Full consideration of the revised criminal code had to wait until the fall of 1975, at which point the media began finally to organize a counterattack.

In his last public appearance as President of the United States, Richard Nixon began with a final barb for the press. When he entered the East Room of the White House to say goodbye to the Executive Department staff, the several hundred people there rose and applauded warmly and at length. When the applause finally stopped, the president, eyes glistening, said:

> . . . I think the record should show that this is one of those spontaneous things that we always arrange whenever the President comes in to speak. And it will be so reported in the press—

He paused, fumbling.

> and we don't mind, because they've got to call it as they see it.[5]

It almost seemed a charitable observation from a man who felt that from time to time everybody had to subvert the truth to live up to his job.

It seems appropriate to conclude this brief history by noting some obvious things which are not in it, and explaining why they are not. The working Washington newsman inevitably would find, as indicated elsewhere, that it puts far too little emphasis upon the orchestrated concealment of information—the choking off of sources, the centralizing of clearance, the use of classification. This is, indeed, important to the newsman trying to do his job. It makes it harder, but it is not punitive and in no way threatens the structure of the media, their philosophical base, or their role in this society.

Similarly, there has been very little attention given here to actions which are directed at favoring one paper over another, a particular broadcaster over his competitor. The selective passing out of favors is part of an old tradition in the politics-journalism symbiosis, and the Nixon administration brought only one new thing to it. The outside observer might be tempted to find that, on balance, a good rather than a bad thing. In the past, a dismayingly large share of exclusive interviews and important leaks have gone to the *New York Times.* The practice has been self-reinforcing, to the point where the *Times,* particularly from the Eisenhower years forward, sometimes had been seen as crypto-official. (Europeans had tended to see the relationship as stronger than that, and so had some *Times* staff members.) There was nothing unique about the *Times* after two or three years of Nixon; the White House loved it no more than the *Washington Post.* Particularly in the later months of the first term and throughout the aborted second, the administration favored the *Washington Star-News,* giving it exclusive interviews and making the road generally easy.

Both the *Post* and the *Times* occasionally were omitted from an important briefing. *Newsday* and the *Boston Globe,* with excellent Washington bureaus and always represented on presidential trips, were excluded from the most newsworthy trip of the decade, the trip to Peking. *Newsday* had published the Rebozo series during the previous autumn and its bureau chief was made to understand there was some connection. Ron Ziegler's explanation to the *Globe*'s Washington bureau chief was somewhat more vague. He called Martin Nolan to his office shortly before the release of the list of approved correspondents.

"There are three criteria for this trip," Ziegler said. "Whether you made the [past] foreign trips, whether you cover us here regularly, most of the time, and whether you covered most of the President's domestic trips into the country."

Nolan protested that the *Globe* did, indeed, meet all those criteria. Ziegler studied his list again.

"Well," he said, "there must be other standards."

"What standards?"

Ziegler did not reply.

"We wish we had two more seats," he said finally. "You almost made it."[6]

There were, during the period covered by this study, many such episodes, but the tradition is an old one. Both politicians and reporters play favorites, both sometimes act spitefully. Such standard elbow-jostling has gone unnoted here, except for an occasional bit too interesting to ignore, such as the exclusion from the White House of the *Post*'s society reporters.

Another element subject to editorial judgment, and one which this writer has found most troubling, is that of finding appropriate emphasis for Richard Nixon's expressions of dislike and distaste for the media. It would have been very easy to string together various episodes out of the man's bitter off-the-cuff remarks as a kind of connective tissue for the narrative. Because he disliked reporters, he not only spoke of his lack of respect for them, but sometimes could not resist lashing them with contempt. When he announced "peace with honor" in Vietnam in a press conference he paused, smiled grimly, and said "I know how it gags some of you to write that but, yes, peace with honor." He could illuminate a ninetieth birthday gala for Alice Roosevelt Longworth with the suggestion that she wouldn't have lived so long if she'd had to read the Washington papers. An ad-lib speech intended to praise returned P.O.W.'s ended with the denouncing of newspapers which published the Pentagon Papers, by implication, as close to traitorous. According to William Safire, Nixon had a favorite metaphor to express his satisfaction when a shot against the media hit home: "that really flicks the scab off."[7]

Some of this quality is suggested in this study, but more could have been made of it. It had much to do with reinforcing newsmen's dislike of Nixon personally; it helped heat up the battle. It is difficult to demonstrate what else this attitude did, however, and as the man became less popular—and credible—his attitude may have even worked to their credit. All presidents, to repeat an observation at the beginning of this book, sooner or later come to dislike the media; all of them make bitter remarks and sometimes take petty revenge. Nixon perhaps was more preoccupied than most. (Although that's questionable. This writer knows considerably more about Nixon's press relations than about Lyndon Johnson's, but, given that imbalance, would guess that Johnson was even more preoccupied, perhaps even more paranoid.) He clearly was more willing to make his hostility public than any of his predecessors.

To make much more of that coruscating personal dislike of the media is to run the risk of viewing most of the activity set out in these pages as part of a passion for revenge, the threat of which was removed when the man who demonstrated it ceased to be president of the United States. That would make misleadingly distant the prospect of future problems for the free press in this country.

SEVEN

Effects of the Assault

The day when the network commentators and even gentlemen of the New York Times *enjoyed a form of diplomatic immunity from comment and criticism of what they said—that day is over.*

Spiro T. Agnew

Any departure from tradition as consciously thorough as that represented by the Nixon administration's offensive against the media obviously is going to have effects. Assessing them is difficult, in great part because of the shortness of perspective at this point. There are few examples of successful intimidation, of a broadcaster or editor breaking off work on a story because representatives of government frightened him through threats or actually took action which damaged him. In more cases there are parallel lines of activity which lead strongly to a deduction about some causes and effects, but no demonstrable linkage. The most interesting, and significant, potential effects cannot be assessed at this point because it still is too early, but some speculation about them at this point seems justified.

Generally, of course, the Nixon years—especially the Watergate segment—were good years for the news media. Public opinion survey data had been showing a steady decline in status for most social institutions, including the media, for many years. As the Watergate story developed, however, attitudes toward the news media began to change. An Opinion Research Corporation poll, conducted for CBS and released in November of 1973, showed that television news correspondents were seen as credible by 63 percent of a national sample compared to 38 percent who found Nixon credible. The press in general was found credible by 55 percent and "leaders in Congress" by 50 percent.

For those who found grounds for doubt in the fact that CBS commissioned that poll, there was further evidence from the Louis Harris organization the next month. Harris found that only television news and newspapers among all social institutions had risen in public esteem during the previous year. The phenomenon was temporary, and in a short time the media rejoined government, education, and the professions in the slow continuing slide in status, but it was heady stuff while it lasted. Carl Bernstein and Robert Woodward for a time were folk heroes (rich ones), and television reporters such as Dan Rather, long overshadowed by the more visible anchormen of the networks, emerged as major figures in United States journalism.

Throughout the news business there clearly was a rise in confidence, if not arrogance, and a renewed interest in investigative reporting. As research has demonstrated several times, the typical good reporter has a touch of the reformer in him or her; the activities of the Nixon years reinforced that in many professionals. Both the open challenge from government and the models of good exposé reporting helped elevate their sense of responsibility. Insulted or not, harassed or not, it was a good time to be a journalist.

Not only the people in the field but some of the institutions changed as a result of the confrontation between government and the media; some of those institutional changes were for the better. Consider the newspaper which probably gained most in prestige. Among United States newspapers we have seen the *Washington Post* as a primary target of the Nixon forces. Its responses, although never reflecting intimidation directly, sometimes seemed to indicate the possibility that accusations of unfairness had struck home. In June, 1973, a sequence from the "Doonesbury" comic strip was omitted from the paper because it referred to former Attorney General Mitchell as "guilty" (of precisely what was never made clear, but the context was that of the Watergate hearings). It was a curious judgment, considerably milder than many implicit accusations elsewhere in the *Post,* about a possible future situation.

On another occasion the paper used in its early editions an enormous blowup (four columns wide and about nine inches deep) of a United Press International photograph of John Ehrlichman taken the first day of his testimony before the Ervin committee. The picture bore an astonishing resemblance, for the middle-aged, to the standard pictures of Mussolini of the thirties—chin up, mouth turned down in hard brackets, brows contracted in arrogant anger. It was the kind of picture a photographer will almost invariably get if he takes many shots in quick succession of an animated subject, and its impact at first glance was remarkable. Sometime between editions it was decided that the photo was unfair. The Mussolini look-alike was reduced in size and put into a cluster of several small shots, the rest of which showed Ehrlichman looking a good deal more sympathetic. The change was made before the big metropolitan editions were printed, and most *Post* readers knew nothing of the matter until Robert Maynard, the paper's ombudsman, devoted one of his columns of media criticism to it, discussing the problems of fair photo selection and fair play and conveying an implicit apology.

Along with some other papers, the *Post* also made an obvious effort to beef up its conservative material when it began carrying, in early 1973, occasional editorial page contributions by George Will, Washington editor of the *National Review.* Maynard's press pieces frequently seemed to reflect some of the discussion among the paper's staff members about the balance of their coverage of the administration.

Obviously the management of the *Post* did not make such changes because they were frightened, but rather because the continuing tension and the administration's attacks provoked, if not a sense of guilt, at least the impulse to worry a bit about the traditional shibboleths of daily journalism. Few would argue with the idea that the paper was improved by these changes, particularly the continuing attention to media criticism, beginning with its own news columns.

Other papers made obvious attempts to provide more certified conservative points of view. In the most conspicuous case, the *New York Times* hired a former member of the president's staff, William Safire, as a columnist at a reported salary of $55,000 a year. To start work as a defender of the president and his staff at the height of the Watergate hearings was unlucky timing at best, and the columns seemed to have a certain muffled quality for the first few months. George Will, for the *Post*, did not work under the same constraints. He was angrily contemptuous from the beginning of the break-in and its identifiable engineers and crew.

At least one broadcaster took the various administration injunctions about individual station responsibility for news seriously enough to establish an antidote. In January, 1972, WWJ-TV in Detroit, an NBC affiliate belonging to the *Detroit News,* began carrying as part of the early evening news a two-to-three minute segment called "Newswatch." The function of this commentary, according to a press release attributed to the station's general manager, was "countering subjective reporting of national and international issues" by the networks. The commentator, Fred E. Dohrs, was chairman of the Department of Geography at Wayne State University. The format of the segment consisted of the showing of a clip from an earlier NBC news broadcast, followed by criticism and rebuttal by Dohrs. The technique can be used to discredit the larger entity by concentration upon minor flaws, and Dohrs sometimes used it.

Again, this innovation hardly represented any sense of intimidation on the part of WWJ-TV's owners. The station is tied very closely to the *Detroit News,* and the organization is articulately and proudly conservative. At the point it set up the Dohrs commentary, its support of the Nixon administration was total, and it had less to fear than any other communications company in the country. White House attitudes toward the networks obviously struck its management as the source of a good idea rather than as a threat. And, while Dohr's analyses often might be seen as demagogic, the business of reminding the viewer that he shouldn't take a news broadcast at face value can only be seen as an improvement in the media-citizen relationship.

This is also true of the sudden spread of correction departments in many large daily newspapers. The traditional refusal to set errors right except in the most flagrant cases always has created ill will toward newspapers. The *New York Times* especially had a reputation not only for refusing to correct errors, but for gratuitous arrogance in doing so. Since the people who sought correction were generally the very movers and shakers upon which the *Times*'s constituency was built, there was a kamikaze quality in the old tradition. Beginning in 1970, however, the clearly labeled, regular niche in a reasonably visible location became common in major dailies. The *Times*'s is labeled simply "correction," and generally appears near the bottom of the first page of the second section. The *Post* puts corrections, with an appropriate headline, as close as possible to the location of the original error. The *Louisville Courier Journal* heads corrections "Beg Your Pardon." Others combine it with the popular reader service columns for which "action line" seems to be emerging as the generic name.

Practically all corrections which appear are highly specific, relating to incorrect information, and thus do not speak to complaints which are related to the tone or point of view of a piece, when the offended citizen admits that the bare bone facts are correct, but insists that the totality is terribly wrong. Few papers yet undertake to wrestle with such claims through a corrections department.

The new willingness to admit error must also be regarded as a plus in the way the information processes function in this society, even though one of modest dimensions. No television broadcasters have demonstrated any interest in correcting error. The small "feedback" segments carried on local television news shows are generally, like those on CBS's "Sixty Minutes," devoted to expression of opposing opinions, not handling inaccuracy or unfairness. Like the other phenomena we've discussed here, it seems more the result of a stimulation of the collective professional conscience than any response to a perceived threat. Once a few major papers started such departments, others followed automatically. The Nixon administration undoubtedly had something to do with that, and that is to its credit.

Media responses which clearly reflect intimidation, as we said, are hard to come by. For understandable reasons, no media people have come forward to testify to doing things they didn't want to because they were afraid not to do them. There are in a few cases some strong inductive reasons, some situations where adding two and two is almost unavoidable, for assuming that intimidation happened.

Two of these involve the Columbia Broadcasting System. In the year of the heaviest Nixon offensive, CBS was to the networks what the *Washington Post* was to the newspapers: the primary target in that medium. Several CBS personalities seem to have been particularly grating on White House sensitivities. We have discussed earlier the haunting of Daniel Schorr and the president's distaste for Dan Rather was made clear in press conferences as well as in staff directives. Vice-President Agnew was talking about Marvin Kalb of CBS, although he did not identify him by name, in the bitterest line of the Des Moines speech, and Eric Sevareid was a dirty word around the White House even before the regime of Richard Nixon.

During the last week of the presidential campaign in 1972, CBS produced a special report on the Watergate burglary (which at that time had not become a major story). Timothy Ferris of *Rolling Stone* put together a couple of admitted facts and came to the conclusion that during the presentation CBS News had bowed its neck to the bully:

> Network news people tend to talk a lot about their relationship with the administration in terms of The Game. One put it this way:
>
> "Networks are big corporations and they talk to government like other big corporations. There's an unspoken

agreement about how far we can go. It's all right for us to take our shots on the regular program and let loose from time to time with a documentary. But not too often. If a network starts to put the heat on and stops playing the game, there will be trouble."

The administration felt that the rules had been violated last fall when CBS produced a special two-part report on the Watergate. It appeared as part of Walter Cronkite's show, with Cronkite narrating. The first installment, 14 minutes long, ran on a Friday, November 3. Before the Monday segment appeared, Charles Colson, Nixon's attorney and friend, called a top CBS executive—reportedly board chairman William Paley—and complained. The report was coming too close to the election, Colson said, and looked like an effort to embarrass the president.

Colson reportedly did not argue that anything in the show had been false. His case was simply that CBS was not being fair, not playing The Game.

Paley did not tell Colson that news is the network's business and hang up. Instead an order came down that the second installment of the Watergate report was to be cut in half. In a CBS screening room Monday afternoon the people who helped put together the show cut it down from 15 to a little over seven minutes. Deleted was an illustrated account of how money from the Committee to Re-elect the President allegedly was "laundered" by passing it through the hands of intermediaries before being paid to agents for spying on and attempting to sabotage the Democratic campaign.

Nobody in the editing room seemed surprised or indignant to be editing on White House orders. It was all part of The Game.[1]

Ferris did not name his sources, which apparently were inside CBS news, but was convinced they were accurate. Walter Cronkite, however, denied the story. Cronkite may not be a Fred Friendly in his defiance of network management but he is extraordinarily difficult to fault as anybody's lackey, and his anger over this issue was very real. News personnel might also have been concerned, even without the Colson warning (he unquestionably called Paley), about problems under Section 315 of the FCC's regulations which require equal time be made available to all candidates and political parties during a campaign, and this was only a week before election. There are several reasons, in short, other than intimidation which might explain CBS's actions. Many Washington journalists, however, including some CBS staff remain convinced the change was ordered from the top.

It is more difficult to find explanation or justification for a later network action. In early June, 1973, William Paley, chairman of the board of CBS, Inc., issued a statement concerning the scheduling of special programs to give opposition viewpoints an airing in "matters of major policy concerning which there is significant national disagreement." The reason for the policy, according to the statement, was that recent presidents were constantly making more use of broadcasting to bring their case to the public, and that fairness required appropriate setting for a considered response, generally no later than one week after the presidential statement. CBS News was to determine in each case the people to be involved in the rebuttal and the format of the presentation.

The real news in the statement, however, was not in the announcement of a new policy (which ABC and NBC said, in effect, they'd had all along), but in a one paragraph footnote which announced the immediate cessation of "instant analysis" following presidential speeches. The phrase came out of Vice-President Spiro Agnew's Des Moines speech. Alvin Krebs, of the *New York Times,* did some checking within the CBS organization at the time of the announcement:

> Mr. Paley was unavailable for comment regarding reports that the new policy on "instant analysis" represented, at least in part, a response to pressure from C.B.S. affiliated stations.

A spokesman for the network emphasized Paley's personal role in the decision, "in consultation with others, including top C.B.S. News executives."

Although Eric Sevareid, who might be regarded as the inventor of the form, was quoted as favoring the new policy, he also indicated that he suspected that he was in the minority at CBS news. Another newsman who asked that his name not be used expressed what seemed to be the majority view:

> I think the ban on analysis is catastrophic, and I think I speak for most C.B.S. newsmen. Analysis is one of the things we've always done better than the other networks. When the going got tough on this matter after Agnew's blast, C.B.S. didn't buckle, but now it has—on the executive level.[2]

One of the marks of the Nixon administration's attacks on the media has been a willingness to hit where it hurts or, as Ben Bagdikian said, to "go for the jugular." The jugular of networking is affiliate relations, although their importance is little recognized outside the business.

The regulations of the Federal Communications Commission are weighted heavily on the side of protecting the independence of the individual station. The network cannot require, for example, that an affiliate carry a particular program; the affiliate is free to reject it out of hand, or even edit it. To make both of these processes possible, programs which might be seen as controversial or questionable are previewed for affiliates before they are broadcast. The process of obtaining affiliate commitment to carry a program is referred to, somewhat confusingly, as obtaining "clearance." Clearances of major prime time entertainment programs is normally no problem, apart from occasional departures such as the two-part "abortion" episode on "Maude" during the 1972–73 season, but for other programs with smaller audiences it may be a tough problem indeed. One of the reasons for the relatively small audiences of the Dick Cavett late night talk show on ABC, for example, was the small number of ABC affiliates which were willing to carry it. The "nonclearers" found that old movies drew a better audience, thus making easier the selling of local spots as well as providing more slots for them. Similarly, though all three networks carried news broadcasts on Saturday and Sunday nights, many affiliates in major markets did not carry them, opting instead for a brief local newscast followed by a movie or syndicated material. More significantly, perhaps, network news departments have pressed from time to time for expansion of the early evening network news broadcasts to an hour from the present half hour. Such newscasters as David Brinkley and Walter Cronkite have been outspoken in their criticism of the enforced superficiality of the half hour format, but the networks, as of the summer of 1975, had never succeeded in getting enough clearances to make a one hour program worthwhile. Station managers make more money by putting something else in that slot.

Pressure from affiliates, then, is a very real force in network affairs, and although CBS's board chairman may not have been influenced by it, there is little question that many station owners and managers were sympathetic to the administration's position on "instant analysis." As a group, these people are set apart from their opposite numbers in the newspaper business by one important difference: regardless of how remote from the operational the newspaper tycoon may be, he always sees himself as being in the news business. The people who own and run television stations are generally much more like those who own movie houses; they see themselves as being in the entertainment business, and are, quite properly, concerned with attracting the widest possible audiences at all times to provide inducement for the advertisers who are their only source of income. And they are, whatever they do, badgered people. Their worst nightmare is the loss of the license to broadcast, the use of what always has been defined as a publicly-owned natural resource for their private gain, either through its being taken away by the FCC for malfeasance (a remote possibility at best) or awarded to somebody else when it comes up for review and renewal every three years. That possibility once was equally remote, but is much more real in these days of well-organized and skilled citizens groups who are mounting contests to renewal at an increasing rate. The station manager also must be constantly concerned with programming which may diminish the size of his audience. He is, in short, fearful of the FCC, of organized groups which will oppose his relicensing, of Catholics who are against abortion and Jews who are against mixed marriages, of prohibitionist groups that protest programs with too much drinking in them— of almost anybody, in short, who is likely to offend anybody else.

Add to this the fact that news operations add relatively little income to his gross, and you get a man who tends at best to bear up bravely when his news department makes waves. The attitude was strikingly described by Fred Friendly in his *Due To Circumstances Beyond Our Control,* although the situation is at the network rather than the individual station level. In the salad days of "See It Now," Edward R. Murrow and Friendly tackled with gusto a variety of controversial subjects. Friendly writes with affection and respect of the support which he and Murrow received from the same William Paley and Frank Stanton, president of the network, in the face of constant pressures and protests from dozens of groups, including affiliates and figures in government. Eventually, however:

> One brief burst of dialogue told it all.
>
> "Bill," Murrow pleaded at one point, "are you going to destroy all this? Don't you want an instrument like the See It Now organization, which you have poured so much into for so long, to continue?"
>
> "Yes," said Paley, "but I don't want this constant stomach ache every time you do a controversial subject."
>
> "I'm afraid that's a price you have to be willing to pay. It goes with the job."
>
> Nothing else that was said mattered. After seven years and almost two hundred broadcasts, See It Now was dead.[3]

Paley was inestimably more patient than most broadcast executives, but Friendly points out that his patience became noticeably shorter when CBS went public with stockholders to worry about. Most television station managers have stockholders to worry about, too.

They therefore were tantalized with Clay Whitehead's suggestion that license renewals might be stretched out for five years instead of three and that more affiliate pressure on network news departments would be a fine thing. There may have been no connection, but it was, in any case, a depressing moment for American journalism—and especially for those people who considered CBS news in a class by itself—when, at the conclusion of the first Nixon speech after announcement of the new instant analysis policy, an obviously uncomfortable Dan Rather announced that the network would have something to say about it on a later occasion.

Sevareid's approval of the dropping of "instant analysis" was based upon his feeling that comment which was genuinely instant—that is, in situations where no advance text is available and the commentator has to respond without hesitation and on the basis of a single hearing—is often bungled. This unquestionably is true. Spiro Agnew took delight in his Des Moines speech in pointing out the stunned inarticulateness of all the network commentators when, in the last moments of his speech of March 31, 1968, Lyndon Johnson announced that he would not run again.

That, however, is perhaps the only time an explosive of such force has been included in a presidential address; the general line of most presidential statements is highly predictable to insiders. An intelligent discussion is easier if an advance text is available, obviously, and the Nixon administration on occasion deliberately did not provide these. The fact that they might make withholding a regular practice may have entered into CBS management's decision. The practice has great disadvantages for any political leadership, however. Not only is the straightaway news coverage more likely to be more slipshod, the amount of it may be affected, and it seems unlikely that any administration with sharp sensitivities in such matters would adopt a regular policy of no advance texts. In the case of the Nixon administration, the failure to provide them in random cases may well have been part of a general strategy of catching the media up short occasionally as a means of reminding them of the joys of cooperation.

The CBS policy of no instant analysis lasted about five months. Morning-after analysis was regularly provided on the Hughes Rudd-Sally Quinn Morning News program which had, of course, only a fraction of the original presidential audience. Eric Sevareid continued his commentaries on the evening news broadcast. The network also arranged two "reply" programs during the period. On June 19, CBS television presented at the beginning of its regular "CBS Reports" program a set of three critical commentaries on President Nixon's economic message of June 13. On September 23, in early afternoon, the CBS radio network presented a reply by Carl Albert, Speaker of the House of Representatives, to the president's "supplemental" State of the Union message. The total national audience for Albert probably would have fitted comfortably into a medium-size Masonic temple, but this is not to fault CBS. Fitfully and timidly, they did provide an opportunity for response to the administration, including an earlier appearance by Lawrence O'Brien, national chairman of the Democratic party, which particularly infuriated some White House staff members and the Republican leadership in Congress. ABC and NBC provided, in one form or another, what could be classified as ventilation of opposing points of view, but without the formal identification of such programs as a platform for the opposition. CBS did occasionally provide that platform, in the face of great pressure from the White House, as we have seen.

In late October of 1973 the office of Senator Lowell Weicker released a set of confidential White House memoranda which included the Colson memo (reprinted beginning on page 274) describing network executives as groveling sycophants who would do anything to please. On November 13, two weeks after the memo appeared in the press, CBS announced that it would resume instant analysis. Paley announced it, as he had its suspension, saying that abstaining had been given a "fair trial." He pointed out that the continuing rapid flow of major stories about government "has made it clear that postponing news analysis under all circumstances may impair a journalistic service of far greater value to the public than we had realized." The same statement said that the policy of providing time to spokesmen for the opposition would continue.

Paley's office denied that the appearance of the Colson memorandum had anything to do with the decision to lift the ban. Whatever the reason, the CBS news department reverted to the old ways with a whoop of delight. Five days later the president had a question-and-answer session with the members of the Associated Press Managing Editors at their meeting in Florida. At the conclusion of that meeting, CBS cameras in Washington swung in on a cluster of ancient White House bêtes noires—Fred Graham, Daniel Schorr, and Dan Rather. Rather explained briskly that they had been compiling a list of "contradictions" in the president's remarks (pads and pencils were visible) and began by asking Schorr, "How many did you find, Dan?" "Two," Schorr said, "and one incomplete reference. . . ." A lot of hearts were lifted, as well as the ban.

Although it may not have directly affected William Paley's action, there is no question that the appearance of the Colson memo had great influence at the top in both broadcasting and government. It made network executives hypersensitive to any suggestion that they were being intimidated. Even if they chose not to make some overt gesture of defiance, they were left in a position where they were all but forced to back news departments and individual journalists who went after the administration hard. And the administration, as Les Brown pointed out in the *New York Times,* was nailed with "documentary proof of what had previously been suspected: that there was an orchestrated effort in the administration to pressure the networks into adopting a sympathetic attitude toward the White House."[4]

Brown also reported in the same article that the FCC was abandoning a proposal based upon an economic analysis which would divorce the networks from the five highly profitable VHF stations that each of them owns because pushing it would appear to be intimidation. The long-standing Justice Department antitrust action to get the networks out of program production continued, but spokesmen for the department repeatedly disavowed any political motivation, pointing out that the action had been started decades earlier. The networks in their counter-briefs took advantage of their new martyrdom to contend that any effort to get them out of production would interfere with their news and special events programming; they were being intimidated all over again.

The White House also was successful in bringing pressure on at least one program of the American Broadcasting Company, Dick Cavett's late-night talk show.

Cavett actually was not an employee of ABC. The network bought the program as a package from the producer, Daphne Productions (named for the Cavett family dog). The contract provided that the producer had complete control of program content; it also provided, however, that ABC had the right to decide if any given show was "acceptable." Since Cavett and his staff tended to be feisty sorts, this arrangement sometimes produced conflicts more noisy than those generated in the employer-employee relationship.

Cavett's producer handled routine liaison with the administration. He would call Alvin Snyder, a former CBS News employee serving as a television specialist on Herbert Klein's staff, if the Cavett program wanted some member of the administration as a guest. Snyder would call Cavett's producer when the administration wanted to push their people or points of view. According to one of Cavett's producers, Christopher Porterfield, "whenever Snyder felt that complaints or pressure tactics were called for, he didn't waste time on the producer but saved them for the ABC brass."[5] Cavett has indicated in his autobiography his conviction that this route was used at the time of a proposed appearance by Angela Davis.[6] The network insisted on conditions which, as it developed, ensured that Davis would refuse to appear, but clear evidence of White House pressure never surfaced.

It was much more visible in the spring of 1971 when the controversy about the supersonic transport (SST) came to its climax. The administration wanted very badly the bill which provided funding. Cavett and his staff were just as strenuously against it, and during the winter both proponents and oppo-

nents of the bill had appeared on the program. Two of the
opponents were seen by the White House as particularly damaging, Senator Birch Bayh of Indiana and Arthur Godfrey. As
the critical vote in the Senate approached, someone in the
White House—members of the Cavett staff assumed that it was
Snyder—called the top corporate levels of the network and
demanded what they described as equal time, citing a list of
opponents who had appeared. (The list was inaccurate.) Alfred
Schneider, an ABC corporate vice-president, called John Gilroy,
then Cavett's producer, and told him that ABC had decided to
require compliance from the show. The administration spokesman was to be William Magruder, of the Department of Transportation and in charge of SST development.

Cavett and his producer, Gilroy, accepted the idea and
decided to bring in William Proxmire, senator from Wisconsin,
to provide some give and take. When word of that plan got back
to Snyder, the White House spokesman, he reacted vigorously.
Over the weekend he called Gilroy at home and made it clear
that the administration wanted Magruder to appear alone and
without any atmosphere of debate. If Cavett insisted on having
Proxmire, he said, the White House would cancel Magruder
altogether and go back to the top level at the network to get its
equal time.

Cavett introduced the SST segment of his program for
March 22, 1971, thus:

> Senator Proxmire of Wisconsin was supposed to be here
> tonight to debate William Magruder on this subject; but
> certain powers-that-be in Washington brought it to my
> attention that, with the recent appearances of Arthur
> Godfrey and Senator Birch Bayh, who are against the SST,
> as well as my own feelings about the SST, the show had
> given more time to the opponents of the program than to
> those in favor of it. Consequently the people in Washing-
> ton rather strongly suggested that Mr. Magruder be allowed
> to appear here tonight with no opposition—except mine.[7]

The issue was hardly monumental, and it may well have
backfired for the Nixon administration. Cavett said later that he

received a substantial number of letters from people who said they'd had no particular feelings about the SST before the show, but that after some exposure to Magruder, they became its sworn enemies.

Even though the evidence of successful intimidation may grow, its accumulated weight will be slight compared to the effectiveness of the government assault upon the notion that the press has a special and precious status in this society because of its unique role in the system's functioning.

The concept—and the actuality—of free expression in the media, as has been pointed out many times, is rare. It also is a luxury of societies stabilized by affluence, which seems to push political activity into a relatively narrow centrist range. One of the things the underdeveloped colony does first upon gaining its independence is to eliminate dissent in the press, not always because the place is run by scheming tyrants, but because its leaders feel that any confused tugging and hauling about national priorities might slow development disastrously. Media which give a continual impress of consensus, even unanimity, seem to be regarded as essential by political leadership, especially when economic development is critical or, of course, in wartime.

The founders of this republic, then underdeveloped and schismatic, sensed that, too. They also took advantage of the same kind of tactics which later leaders have used elsewhere in the world. Samuel Adams and his colleagues were powerful persuaders but, just to make doubly sure that there was no interference with their message, they made calculated use of gangs of bully boys who called themselves Sons of Liberty and who burned the printshops of editors opposing the revolution. By the time of Lexington and Concord, royalist sentiments in print were rare in the colonies and the impression of a national consensus overwhelming.

And clearly much of the early talk about freedom of expression was rhetoric. There are historians and lawyers who are convinced that the uncommon negative sanction with which the First Amendment begins—"Congress shall make no law. . ."—simply was intended at the time it was drafted to keep the national government from passing restrictive laws, leaving that right to the individual states of the new nation. Regardless of what was intended, or what may have been rhetoric and sloganeering instead of a social commitment, by the time of the expiration of the shabby Alien and Sedition Acts in 1803 there was a well-established acceptance in the courts and among political leaders that freedom of expression was an essential part of the new polity. It was an idea whose time, as the cliché has it, had come.

For all its attractiveness, however, it was a frail child, born of the Enlightenment at the peak of man's confidence in the capacity of his orderly intelligence to govern his affairs. It reflected the strength and influence of men who had read Locke and Hume and built a philosophy of action upon them. Given the optimistic view of man which was the heart of rationalism, the idea of restraining free and public examination of any idea was unthinkable.

It was, and is, the most abstract and detachable of the civil rights set out in the first ten amendments. Most of the others related to very specific gut issues for the citizens of the new country. The British had stationed soldiers in their houses without their consent; they had confiscated the weapons in the homes of colonial militiamen; colonials had been subjected to unreasonable searches and seizure, seen abuses of the trial system; there was a long experience of clerics meddling in secular government. There had been, however, very little suppression of the press—the response to the Stamp Act, for example, was so strong that Parliament repealed it almost immediately—aside from that which the patriots, as they called themselves, imposed upon Tory editors.

It's probably a safe assertion that no set of legal concepts has ever taken root so firmly in any other society as the Bill of Rights in the United States. We have been preoccupied with social change, in both theory and practice; there has been much praise of the constitution's flexibility and demonstrations of the fact. But those civil rights first defined have remained essentially rock hard. Some have turned obsolete and one has been used cynically (and successfully) by the National Rifle Association, but they have been defended by the courts and by popular acceptance with remarkably consistent tenacity.

As a part of that defense, a kind of special unspoken agreement which reflects the fragility of the freedom of the press seems to have grown up. It is an idea which has no real roots in popular support, although evidence to the contrary can be turned up in public opinion polls. Everything depends upon how the question is asked. The question "are you in favor of freedom of the press?" will produce a rousingly high percentage of yeses. But if the question is asked in some such form as "should the government have the right to keep Communist propaganda out of the newspapers and off the air?" a substantial majority again says yes. This does not prove that the populace is hypocritical; it is simply another demonstration of the familiar fact that lightly-held attitudes can be easily manipulated. Dictators found it easy to take away freedom of expression not only from the presumably disciplined Germans but from the demonstrably anarchic Italians during the 1930s without popular protest. Most people, even the well-educated, simply do not have personal reasons for protecting that kind of liberty, and even less concern with the abstract right of others. This means that any government probably is freer to take repressive measures against the media than its leadership may realize.

The chief protectors of free media in this country, therefore, have been the powerful, isolated elite which is our court system. Their actions have been rooted in, along with law, a consensus on the part of those in power that the media can be railed at, condemned, boycotted, even censored in specific instances when the offended party has enough clout, but are not to be touched through overt acts on the part of authority. It has been a given of the American system. The most severe media critics in the past have come from the group which is responsible for the consensus. So they have traditionally upbraided specific papers and broadcasters for shabbiness and arrogance and even venality, but no one—from A. J. Liebling to

Daniel Patrick Moynihan—has proposed crippling them or has attacked the fundamental assumptions of the system.

The opportunity to rupture that fragile consensus always has been there. Few institutions are so inviting of critical demagoguery as the media. The Nixon men were not able to resist the challenge. The vice-president was the first to ask, in effect, who are these people of the networks and why should they have the right to criticize? The government's arguments in the Pentagon Papers case were bent toward a reading of the United States Constitution which would give the president complete unilateral authority to suppress the publication of that which in his personal judgment might affect national security.

There simply is no way of predicting the long-term effect of a wide-ranging attack upon the principle of the freest possible press. There has been no such attack in our previous history, nor in that of the United Kingdom; both the original conception and the social context of other societies differ too much from ours to be of much use. We can only note the fraility of the notion, the lack of popular support for it, and the apparent lack of concern for its preservation on the part of many in the media. But not all are unconcerned. The serious civil libertarians of the news business should be grateful to such men as Robert Boyle, who wrote an "op ed" [opposite the editorial page] article entitled "Big Time Pressures, Smalltown Press," which appeared in the *New York Times* on March 24, 1973. It sums up the remarkable contagiousness of top-level attitudes for lower-level authorities. It demonstrates the rupture of that consensus which for many years has protected the news media in this country and the loss of which may be so meaningful.

> POTTSTOWN, Pa.—The bee stings in Washington and the pain is felt in Pottstown, too. The Government clamps Les Whitten, Jack Anderson's aide, in jail for eight hours, and the clanking jail door is heard round the world. Pottstown Council holds a secret meeting, and when it's un-

covered, the news about it is confined to Pottstown. Censorship, government controls, and secrecy aren't limited to people like Anderson. The small-town newsman is also feeling the sting.

Certainly, officials in Washington aren't telling officials in Pottstown not to cooperate with the press. But when the Government hides things from the national press, and when Government officials make remarks against the press, small-town politicians feel that they, too, should follow the leader and they institute roadblocks to limit freedom.

The label a politician or an official wears doesn't matter. Pottstown is a swing community in a solid Republican county. But both Democrats and Republicans alike have started attacking the press.

Small-town police departments suddenly are setting themselves up as censors. They become "unavailable" when the press calls them. Justices of the peace are starting to determine what cases to give to the press and what cases to hold back.

One Pottstown justice of the peace tried to stop a Mercury [Boyle's paper] reporter from using a pencil and notebook at a hearing because they were "recording devices." Use of a recording device is banned in justices of the peace courts. It took a ruling from the county solicitor before the reporter could use his pencil and notebook again.

School boards have been using the "executive sessions" ploy more and more. The public and press are barred from executive sessions. Board members decide at these sessions what course of action to follow, and then simply approve the action at a regular meeting.

The simple news story, too, is getting more difficult to come by. Recently there was a small fire in the Army officer's club of Valley Forge General Hospital. Damage amounted to $750. The Mercury tried to get an item on the fire and the story would have amounted to a paragraph or two.

But the Army refused to give any information until the "news release cleared the channels."

In Pottstown, a community of 28,000 some 35 miles from Philadelphia, the council meetings always have been open and above board. But late last year, council held a secret meeting. It wasn't advertised, the press wasn't alerted, and those who attended were told to keep it secret. The action taken at the meeting affected the entire community.

The council voted in a secret to get rid of the police chief, Dick Tracy. As God is my judge, that's his name. A group from council, including the Mayor, was selected to secretly tell the chief to look elsewhere for a job. He was told it would be in his best interest to keep the decision secret.

"Keep your mouth shut and we'll make it seem as if it is your choice to leave," he was told. "Open it and it'll make it rougher for you to get another job."

He kept his mouth shut.

But one of the participants of the secret meeting discussed it at a local bar. He was overheard and the newspaper, The Mercury, was tipped. . . .

In nearby Collegeville, a community of 5,000, the newspaper there, the Independent, was creating a stir in a nine-part expose on the Pennsylvania state prison at Graterford. The Independent doesn't make much of a splash statewide but ripples from it reached the state capital at Harrisburg. The word went out that no one from the state prison was to talk to the Independent publisher, John Stewart. Because he uncovered and published some sordid facts about Graterford he was put on the "no comment" list.

If you multiply the trouble the Mercury and the Independent are having in their small areas by the number of small papers across the country then you must recognize the press is being hamstrung nationally and on all levels.

Remarks by the Vice President and the President may be targeted at papers such as the Washington Star.

But they're also hurting the smaller papers. By design or not, those officials in Washington who are anti-Anderson, anti-the Times, anti-the Post, are also anti-Mercury and the Independent. They're antipress. Antifreedom.

The most damaging changes in attitude toward the media during the period of this study were within the legal system. From their venerable role as the media's chief defender in the past, the courts of this country turned far enough to produce the most effective attackers. Many units within the judicial system clearly have felt unleashed, in effect; the attitude of the administration seemed occasionally to have been interpreted as if it were equivalent to a Supreme Court decision.

This is hardly surprising. Two major rulings of the Supreme Court during the period clearly had great implications for freedom of expression and, interestingly enough, the one which may prove in time most damaging was at first hailed as a great victory.

Jules Witcover has a vivid account of the reaction at the *Washington Post* and the *New York Times* when the Court held on Wednesday, June 30, 1971, that the government could not suppress the Pentagon Papers.[8] At the *Times,* publisher Sulzberger and editor Rosenthal threw their arms around each other with jubilant shouts; in Washington, managing editor Patterson jumped on a desk top shouting, "We win, 6 to 3!"

It was not long after the cheering died that the prescient began to suspect that there was more loss than win in the decision. (Portions of the texts in the decision are reprinted beginning on page 289.) In substance, only two of the nine justices, as we have seen earlier, opposed without qualification any kind of prior restraint. One more, Brennan, envisioned possible exceptions, but under such rigidly narrow premises as to bring him down on the side of the classic civil libertarians.

Justice Thurgood Marshall's opinion did not touch directly on the prior restraint matter, focusing instead on the idea that the Congress had denied the power of suppression to the president and that the Court therefore should have no involvement in the question. Judging by his general attitudes, however, Marshall probably could be counted on the libertarian side.

This left five whose opinions, in the judgment of Thomas

Emerson of the Yale University Law School, "seriously under-
mined the doctrine against prior restraint."[9] All, in one way or
another, accepted the premise that immediate threat against
national security would be appropriate grounds for an injunction, and thus rejected the government's case not on the
grounds of principle but on the grounds that the threat had not
been demonstrated.

As Emerson, who filed an amici curiae brief on behalf of
twenty-seven congressmen at the time of the hearing, pointed
out, such a stance immediately implies two legal problems.
First, the concept of a threat to national security is so broad
and flexible that grounds for a temporary injunction—an order
based upon a persuasive but not proved contention—will not be
difficult to find.

Second, even if the courts should eventually apply very
strict interpretations—even if they should refuse to uphold any
injunction to come before them—the act of prior restraint
already has been accomplished through the granting of the
temporary restraining order in the first place. This is what
happened in the Pentagon Papers case; the *Times* was kept from
publishing that material for two weeks, and other newspapers
for lesser periods. In some possible cases—it is difficult to
predict sensibly the directions of such things, because they have
not been part of our national experience—suppression for a few
days, or even a few hours, would be enough to serve a government's purposes.

In light of this, it is difficult to accept the premise that
freedom of the media is in any way advanced by the decision. A
chilling confirmation of that skepticism came within a few
months, when two federal courts acted in such a fashion as to
produce the situation that Emerson had anticipated—and the
United States Supreme Court, by refusing to review, let their
actions stand. It has become generally known as the Dickinson
case, from the name of the first of the reporters named in the
original order.

On November 8, 1971, two reporters—one for the *Baton
Rouge Morning Advocate* and the other for the *Baton Rouge
State Times*—were cited for contempt in the United States

District Court in New Orleans. They had printed trial testimony in defiance of a judge's order. The order in itself was surprising. The testimony involved was given in open court during a pre-trial hearing in a conspiracy case. The right to publish testimony in a public court proceeding repeatedly has been held to be constitutionally protected. The actual citation for contempt was based upon publication of the fact that publication had been forbidden.

Appeal proceedings began immediately. In August, 1972, the United States Court of Appeals for the Fifth District in its ruling precisely fulfilled the Emerson prophecy. It declared that the District judge's order was, indeed, clearly unconstitutional. It also ruled, however, that the newspapers should have obeyed it *until the appeal procedure was completed and a reversal obtained.* The court also let the contempt citations stand, not on any constitutional issue but because the reporters had, in effect, flaunted their defiance.

Appeals procedures take months, years, sometimes literally decades. The Baton Rouge case, however, moved relatively quickly, and to a dismaying end. The United States Supreme Court in October, 1973, not quite two years later, refused to review the case and let the appeals court decision stand. With Black dead, only Douglas was left to dissent.

The sum of these two cases is devastatingly clear. The news media must obey any injunction, any court order, however patently unconstitutional in its intention to suppress and censor, until they can get a reversal on appeal. In the case of most news stories, that amounts to a censorship as effective as if a federal marshal stood in the newsroom with a gun. The principle of legal prior restraint, since *Near* v. *Minnesota* (1931) not even debatable in this country, is once again debatable. As a device available to any judge, however incompetent or ill-intentioned, it is now established.

It should be noted that the Baton Rouge case also documented again the willingness of vast institutions to contribute to their own destruction. Only a few major papers carried the story of the Supreme Court's refusal to review, and, so far as this writer can determine, no broadcasters at all. One of the few papers that did give it careful attention put it, through one of those common deficiencies of the copy desk, under a casual headline. "High Court Decision Headache for Press," the *Detroit Free Press* said. It wasn't a headache. It was a stroke—the kind that induces paralysis.*

The other major decision by the Supreme Court during the period of this study is somewhat more particularistic. It is concerned, in a sense, with the dynamics of the reporter's trade rather than echoing matters of principle. Its effect can be crippling, but essentially invisible to all but the most knowing of readers and vigilant of newsmen. It centers around an operational characteristic of the news business which seems to many critics a bit grubby, if not completely cynical.

Grubby or not, the fact is that news coverage of many kinds, particularly politics, politicians, and political institutions, is highly dependent upon confidential sources. The backbone of much good statehouse and Washington reporting is the disaffected second-level bureaucrat whose motives may have more to do with affecting the operations of his department or simply

---

*Lying somewhat outside the scope of this book is another long-running case involving government invocation of censorship which began in the spring of 1972. An ex-CIA agent named Victor Marchetti tried to write and publish a book about the agency. From the beginning he was harassed and discouraged; finally he was brought into court and, after a hearing, ordered to make any material he had prepared available to the CIA for clearance. After a series of court fights not entirely concluded at the time of this writing, the book appeared, heavily censored, under the title *The CIA and the Cult of Intelligence* (Alfred A. Knopf, 1974).

Although the American Civil Liberties Union, along with the authors and the publisher, argued that the case essentially was a First Amendment matter, the government was able to make stick its assertion that it was purely a matter of a contract and that freedom of expression was not involved. Upon beginning his career in the agency, Marchetti, like all new agents, had signed a contract promising never to reveal any of its secrets without its permission. Throughout the case the government talked only of breach of contract, asking that much material be excised because it violated the agreement. The presiding judge thus found himself ruling not on security matters, but upon what amounted to a property agreement. The book contains an account of the case.

getting even with somebody than a devotion to the people's right to know.

There are genuinely complex questions within the news professions about the whole business of confidential sources, but they tend to center more on the methods and extent of their use than the desirability of using them in principle; the need is a given of the system. Obviously the reporting of embittered gossip or sensational speculation is dubious. During the periods of intensive investigation of the Watergate affair in 1972–73, it was easy to find informants who would say outrageous things as long as their anonymity was protected. The temptation to use such fodder in an escalating story is considerable, and it is encouraged by the fact that in practice it is almost impossible to libel a public figure.

Generally, conscientious newsmen try to use confidential sources primarily as leads who identify the possibility of stories which the reporter then develops for himself. As the story unfolds, the informant also can serve as a checkpoint for authenticity of both fact and perspective; he becomes something like an invisible partner on the story. This is particularly likely to happen when the informant's primary concern is something above the vendetta level—if he is attempting, for example, to influence policy and his official role is powerless. Several such people are dealt with at length in Bernstein and Woodward's *All the President's Men,* which is probably the best single account of the role of the anonymous informant in a major story, in this case the Watergate story, in the literature of journalism. There are, however, many others. Roger Hilsman describes, in his *To Move a Nation,* Lieutenant Colonel John Paul Vann as "an energetic, idealistic, dynamic officer with strong convictions about the need for a more aggressive and efficient conduct of the war and a willingness, in order to achieve it, to tread on the toes of either his Vietnamese counterparts or his own American superiors."[10] He went about it through developing close personal relationships with David Halberstam and Neil Sheehan of the *New York Times.* He became a major source for the two reporters and, in Hilsman's phrase, "served as their litmus paper to test the progress of the shooting war." He also, in so doing, became a critical, although at that time invisible, factor in the first reporting to indicate that the war was going badly.

Something like this arrangement is behind much successful investigative journalism. Just as effective police work generally is based on informers rather than dazzling leaps of deductive insight, so good investigative reporting frequently is based not so much on the quantity of digging as the help of somebody who can point out the places to dig. Such collaboration must be based, of course, upon the newsman's ability to guarantee anonymity to his informants. If he can be forced to identify them, he'll have to do without them. One of the major decisions of the Nixon court sets out clearly that the reporter can be forced to testify and name names.

In June, 1972, the Supreme Court of the United States, in the words of Norman Isaacs, "ruled that the power of a grand jury took precedence over the heretofore presumed protection of the First Amendment."[11]   Three cases of reporters refusing to reveal sources were involved: Earl Caldwell of the *New York Times* and Paul Pappas of WTEV-TV, New Bedford, Massachusetts, both of whom had been reporting on Black Panther organizations; and Paul Branzburg of the *Louisville Courier-Journal,* who had reported details of a hashish-making operation. Caldwell's case was best known, and his name usually is attached to the ruling. Each had been required to promise confidentiality to inside informants as a part of gaining access; each had been subpoenaed by a grand jury which wanted to know details of what he'd seen and heard; each refused and was cited for contempt. The defenses varied somewhat (there was no connection among the cases until the Supreme Court grouped them together for purposes of the ruling). Attorneys for Caldwell and the *Times* did not claim absolute privilege for the newsman, but contended that certain stiff conditions should be met before a subpoena could be issued, and that the case in point did not. Pappas, in effect, simply claimed absolute privilege. Branzburg claimed protection under a Kentucky statute which presumably gave protection to reporters, but which proved not to do so in the judgment of two state courts (and thus reinforced many newsmen's skepticism about so-called shield laws).

The majority, concurring, and dissenting opinions in the final decision reflected a wide range of attitudes and concepts, from the majority opinion written by Justice Byron White which, in substance, said that reporter privilege is not guaranteed by the First Amendment to Justice William O. Douglas's contention that the decision will permit state and federal authorities to "annex" the news media as "an investigative arm of government."

Within six months after the decision in the Caldwell case more than a dozen reporters had been jailed for refusing to identify confidential sources. The case which received most attention was that of William Farr, of the *Los Angeles Herald-Examiner,* who refused to reveal the source of certain documents leaked to him during the Charles Manson murder trial and spent forty-six days in jail for it. (An appeals court decision in July, 1974, finally set aside the citation under the provisions of an amended California shield law.) The Farr matter received considerable media attention, perhaps in part because of its connection with the bizarre and much-publicized trial. The others received little more than local mention, as the media let themselves be nudged, almost without protest, down the path of suppression by institutional authority. The pace has continued without flagging; within a three-month period in 1973 a *St. Petersburg Times* reporter was sentenced to five months in jail for refusing to identify the source in a grand jury leak; a Vermont television reporter was cited for contempt for refusing to name a confidential source to the defense in a criminal trial; and a *Wall Street Journal* reporter was ordered by a Massachusetts trial judge to identify a source in a libel suit. It should be pointed out that not all subpoenas directed to reporters come from prosecutors in criminal actions; they commonly come from the defense as well, and originate in civil as well as criminal cases.

There was an attempt to counter in some state legislatures. In 1973 a total of eight state shield laws were either enacted or amended, bringing to twenty-five the number now in effect, and journalists were held by state courts to be protected by them in particular cases in Minnesota, Ohio, and California. A considerable congressional interest in a national shield law continued, and most of the professional news organizations and owner-management media trade associations managed to agree on a single version to which they could give their support.

The larger issue of the desirability of shield laws is a complex one which does not need to be discussed here. The definitive analysis is available elsewhere in a study by Vincent Blasi.[12] Despite the assembling of a loose coalition to push for a single national statute, opinion about the desirability of shield laws is split sharply within journalism. Many professionals feel that regardless of how carefully laws affecting freedom of expression are drawn, some courts and prosecutors will find ways to twist them into instrumentalities of constraint. Others fear a kind of quid pro quo; if the reporter gets special protection under the law, sooner or later special responsibilities will be laid on him. The problems of definition under a shield law can be enormous: who is a reporter, anyhow? A student on a high school underground paper? A free lance who seldom sells anything but keeps trying? Would the need for a functional definition eventually require the licensing of journalists?

Edward W. Barrett, former dean of the Graduate School of Journalism at Columbia University, has pointed out that some legal scholars regard the entire controversy as unnecessary, unmanageable, and the result of the incompetence of John Mitchell in his role as attorney general.[13] It was Mitchell who authorized the pressing of the Supreme Court case against Earl Caldwell. Mitchell's legal experience was largely that of bond lawyer (interestingly enough, his particular speciality was "moral responsibility" bonds), and his action gave the highest court, in the opinion of many lawyers, no real alternative to the kind of limited ruling which it made. Most sophisticated lawyers and jurists recognize that when two constitutional principles seem to conflict it is unwise to force a confrontation. "Every intelligent man in this field," Barrett notes, "knows that common sense plus the first amendment is far preferable to any conceivable precise legislation that tries to forsee all possible contingencies."

The terrain is boggy enough that the attitude of many professionals is summed up in the sentence "I believe in the reporter's right to go to jail." Opponents of any kind of shield law have included Ben Bradlee of the *Washington Post* and John S. Knight of the Knight newspapers, each a distinguished editor of publications particularly noted for investigative reporting.

There is no significant division within the field, however, about the necessity for protection of confidential sources. Jack Nelson of the *Los Angeles Times,* who had his own troubles with the courts, pointed out that such sources were essential to ". . . some of the nation's greatest exposés, including such modern day disclosures as the Pentagon Papers, the My Lai massacre and the Watergate bugging scandal. In fact, because confidential sources usually help uncover information other people try to conceal from the public, the stories they produce generally are considered public service journalism."[14] And he quotes Seymour Hersh, whose Pulitzer-winning My Lai stories were made possible through the confidential involvement of three Army officers, a congressman, and two congressional aides, as saying:

> At that time we still had the weight of 200 years of freedom on our side. And we weren't concerned about pressure to reveal sources. Things have certainly shifted.

They have, indeed—and most of the iceberg is still submerged. Some of its possible dimensions were hinted by another case in the clamorous fall of 1973.

In late summer of that year the *Wall Street Journal* carried a story saying that the vice-president, Spiro Agnew, had been notified by the Justice Department of possible bribery charges against him. The vice-president himself actually made the news break, releasing a statement before the *Journal* appeared. There was a touch of professional sophistication about the release; airlines long ago learned that they should be the first to announce crashes. The vice-president took advantage of the *Journal* which had informed him of the nature of the story early in the day and then sought a statement from him which he never gave; instead, he scooped them.

The story received great play, of course—press club bar talk had it that several other papers had been almost ready to go on the story, too—and the vice-president received television time for a press conference to deny any wrongdoing. During the next few weeks there was an unremitting series of leaks to the media of material putatively part of the government's case.

At the end of September, the vice-president's lawyers asked for an injunction against any further proceedings by the grand jury which was then investigating the case. A central argument grew directly out of the Caldwell decision, which was cited by the vice-president's lawyers: that Agnew could not receive a fair trial because of a deliberate plan, originating presumably someplace in the Justice Department, to prejudice his case through news leaks. His attorneys therefore requested permission to subpoena reporters to find out the identity of these confidential informers. Despite energetic opposition from the Justice Department lawyers, United States District Judge Walter Hoffman granted the request. Agnew's attorney then proceeded to subpoena a total of nine reporters from both Washington newspapers, the *New York Times* and *Daily News, Time* and *Newsweek,* and CBS and NBC.

These heavyweights immediately began to gear up an appeal, but the matter was made moot when the vice-president resigned and pleaded no contest to one charge of tax evasion. In a sense, this was a loss; if the litigation had run its course, more would have been learned about the real implications of the Caldwell decision.

More obvious than the professional handicaps involved in the loss of protected sources—and more demonstrably a threat to a basic right—has been the burgeoning of restrictions upon coverage of the functioning of the court system. The Supreme Court has never ruled directly upon the issue of a judge's right to silence publication, although there are, as we have seen, disturbing innuendos in the Pentagon Papers decision and the refusal to review in the Baton Rouge case. During the period this study covers, some lower courts, however, have taken to what the media often call "gag" rulings with enthusiasm, and in some cases have gone almost past belief.

It should be made clear that this does not reflect any direct initiative on the part of the Nixon administration. It is not a matter to which any recent attorney general has addressed himself, or even federal district attorneys. It rather reflects a conflict which goes back for many decades, and which has been particularly attended to since the mid-1960s. But the general stance of government at the top toward the media, the growth of an endemic sentiment that the media are fair game, has helped weight heavily the side of the courts in an old argument.

The argument is about the inevitable trade-off between freedom of the press and the right to a fair trial. Traditionally, the media have had an unrestricted and privileged right to report from the courtroom. Unrestricted and privileged means that they can not be held liable to any legal action growing out of their accurate reports of testimony and evidence. There was an understanding, sometimes enforced by a contempt citation, that newsmen were not to turn a trial into a circus; cameras generally have been banned, and broadcasting almost never permitted. Sometimes, when highly sensitive or particularly coarse matters were involved, the court might be emptied, or testimony taken in chambers, and the media normally respected such restrictions, albeit sometimes grudgingly. For the most part, however, the right of reporters to report was not even open to question.

In late 1966, however, a special ad hoc committee of the American Bar Association released the tentative draft of some findings and recommendations which expressed great concern about the media's potential for damaging the right of fair trial. It included an implied encouragement of more use of contempt power by the courts. Release of the draft was supposed to provoke thorough public discussion of the issues and it succeeded. The American Society of Newspaper Editors replied vigorously; joint bar-press committees were proposed at several levels and in many communities; law schools and journalism departments sponsored conferences and colloquia; and researchers began experimentally studying the effects of publicity on jurors. Very little persuasion has come out of all this and the arguments still go on, but the media have increasingly been losing the battle where it matters, in the courtroom.

In most of the cases in which coverage of a judicial proceeding, or part of it, has been forbidden, the critical issue has been the selection of an unprejudiced jury and, once chosen, its protection from information and opinion from outside the courtroom. In some of these it's very easy to empathize with a judge's concern. In the Baton Rouge case where all reporting was banned, for example, the crime was a conspiracy to murder and the presumptive defendant a civil rights worker. The presiding judge indicated a feeling that if anything was published about the case in Baton Rouge, the selection of a fair-minded jury would be impossible.

One of the most deeply rooted and widely accepted principles of trial by jury in this country holds that a defendant's previous criminal record, under normal circumstances, is not admissible evidence. Newspapers and broadcasters not only publish such material, but tend to emphasize it, which makes it extraordinarily difficult to keep the information away from jurors. Freedom of expression's true believers may feel themselves in an awkward spot when faced with this kind of thing, particularly since most of them also have strong convictions about the rights of defendants and the integrity of the judicial process. The danger begins when judges start ordering restrictions and striking at random with contempt citations, and increasing numbers of judges are doing just that.

The trial of the so-called Gainesville Eight in the summer of 1973 provided some insights into the variety of restrictions which a creative jurist can develop when he puts his mind to it, ranging from the sensible to the bizarre. The case was that of seven members of an organization called Vietnam Veterans Against the War and a nonmember supporter of their cause. They were indicted on charges of conspiring to cross state lines to incite a riot during the 1972 Republican national convention in Miami. A series of trials of radicals (all of which the government lost, as they were to lose in Gainesville) had built great media interest. This appeared to be the last of the series.

Judge Winston Arnow was prepared. Three weeks before the trial began he issued the first of a series of pretrial publicity orders which eventually included: (1) limiting the press pool to twenty-five; (2) forbidding the defendants, their lawyers, prospective witnesses, and "all persons in concert with the defendants" from communicating with the press—which seemed to mean that no member of the Vietnam Veterans Against the War, even if in no way involved in the trial, could talk to the press; and (3) prohibiting any sketches or photographs of the courtroom.

It was the last provison which led to an early contempt citation for which "bizarre" is the appropriate word. The stricture against sketching in the courtroom was in itself somewhat uncommon. Although cameras are generally banned, on the grounds that their presence is disruptive, most judges have permitted sketch artists to work since their physical activity is no more noticeable than a reporter's notetaking. Viewers of television news long have been familiar with this form of "visual" of judicial proceedings.

It soon developed, however, that Judge Arnow had something more in mind than prohibiting artists from working in the courtroom. A CBS network artist named Aggie Whelan attended a preliminary hearing in the case. A few hours later she drew—*from memory*—sketches of the proceedings which CBS broadcast. The judge, asserting that the network had knowingly violated his order, held CBS, Inc., in contempt and levied a $500 fine. Some thought is required before the outrageousness of such an action sinks in. Nowhere in our legal tradition is there a precedent for the idea that spectators at an open hearing cannot communicate their impressions to other people once it's over. It constitutes an attempt at thought control, and if the action crossed the mind of earlier judges, none had dared act upon it.

Eventually most of Arnow's orders were, in one way or

another, modified or withdrawn. A broad range of prestigious media joined with the Reporters Committee for Freedom of the Press in a formal complaint. In response, the press pool was increased to fifty and it was made clear that no journalists would be held in contempt for talking to anyone covered by the original order. NBC joined CBS in appealing the sketch order and the contempt citation. The United States Court of Appeals voided Arnow's sketch order, but let the contempt citation stand. It was finally vacated in July, 1974.

The primary cause for concern about the Gainesville trial is not what the judge finally succeeded in doing, but what he was willing to try to do; not so much in his heavy hand as his apparent perception of the First Amendment as clearly subordinate to expeditious functioning of judicial procedure. Judges simply did not think that way before the late 1960s.

More judges seemed to think that way as the 1970s wore on. There is in Washington an organization called the Reporters Committee for Freedom of the Press, which was founded in 1972. Its steering committee includes a variety of eminent journalists representing a range of political attitudes from Nat Hentoff to Howard K. Smith. It publishes a newsletter summarizing recent activities which it sees as threatening to freedom of expression, a kind of box score of harassment and outrage. The cover of *Press Censorship Newsletter No. III,* November-December 1973, carried headlines for the stories inside. To read the list also conveys some sense of how variegated and pervasive the battle was at that point, and how badly it was going:

U S SUPREME COURT APPROVES FIRST FEDERAL CONTEMPT FOR TRIAL COVERAGE

U S SUPREME COURT AUTHORIZES 30-DAY JAIL SENTENCE FOR ATTICA NEWSMAN

FLORIDA SUPREME COURT UPHOLDS CRIMINAL RIGHT-OF-REPLY LAW VS. MEDIA

ALABAMA PASSES CRIMINAL ACT ON DISCLOSING NEWS REPORTER'S INCOME

FLORIDA NEWSMAN SENTENCED TO 5 MONTHS IN JAIL FOR CRIME PROBE

FEDERAL JUDGE BANS VIETNAM VET FROM TALKING TO THE PRESS

CBS NEWS INC. HELD IN CONTEMPT FOR MEMORY SKETCH OF COURTROOM

VERMONT REPORTER CONVICTED OF CONTEMPT FOR SHIELDING NEWS SOURCE

WALL ST. JOURNAL REPORTER ORDERED TO DISCLOSE CONFIDENTIAL SOURCE

KENTUCKY REPORTER CONVICTED AND FINED FOR GRAND JURY PROBE

NASHVILLE TENNESSEAN CONVICTED OF CONTEMPT FOR CRIME REPORTING

AGNEW SUBPOENAS CONFIDENTIAL NEWS LEAKS: CASE MOOTED

PRESIDENT NIXON URGES PASSAGE OF OFFICIAL SECRETS ACT

JUST. DEPT. LIMITS ARREST OF REPORTERS: BOSTON GLOBE CASE DROPPED

PHILADELPHIA POLICE FILE $80 MILLION GROUP LIBEL VS. INQUIRER

LOUISIANA SUPREME COURT BANS NEWSPAPER FROM STATE CAMPUS

DALLAS POLICE ARREST AND JAIL UPI REPORTER

NORTH CAROLINA REPORTER SUBPOENAED FOR CONFIDENTIAL SEX SOURCE

These matters hardly cover comprehensively the antimedia activities of the courts during the period designated on the *Newsletter*'s cover, however. Too late for deadline, perhaps, was the story of the Indiana judge who successfully exercised prior restraint over the ABC network at the behest of a local manufacturer of children's furniture. ABC had scheduled for November 26, 1973, a documentary entitled "Fire!" One brief sequence showed the ignition and blazing destruction of a child's crib manufactured by the Smith Manufacturing Company of Salem, Indiana. Jules Bergman, the program's reporter, informed the audience that the whole sequence had consumed ten minutes, and that "the film you are seeing is a portion of that ten-minute test." The company was given a preview of the sequence and declined to reply in the broadcast, but did "dispute," as the narrator said, "the validity of the test." More importantly, it went to court, charged libel, and requested an injunction against broadcast of the sequence. The local court granted it, and the network decided to take no chances. The documentary appeared with nearly a minute of empty screen instead of the scripted crib burning. John J. O'Connor of the *New York Times* said:

> The effect was similar to reading a newspaper with empty white spaces or a censored letter riddled with holes. Within this reviewer's memory, and that of several news professionals in the industry, it represented the first time that a TV news department was directly affected on screen by a court order.[15]

It seems probable that it will not be the last. The trend toward better coverage of consumer interests which began in the early 1970s might be slowed by such rulings, given by judges on behalf of local industry; particularly if the media, like ABC in this case, decide to take no chances in the cause of protecting their own freedom.

Obviously all the potential effects of the 1969—74 offensives of institutional authority against the media were not wiped out by the resignation of Richard Nixon and the departure of his staff. In attempting to assess possible long-range effects, it might be sensible to begin by remembering the new weapons which have come to hand.

1. The Supreme Court decision in the Pentagon Papers case, which finds acceptable prior restraint—censorship—for cause. It also, in effect, invites the Congress to pass more restrictive legislation.

2. The Supreme Court action in letting stand the decision of a federal appeals court in New Orleans which says explicitly that whenever an injunction is issued against the publication (and, presumably, broadcast) of specified material the medium must obey—even if the ruling is patently unconstitutional—until the order can be reversed on appeal. Given the perishability of news, as pointed out earlier, this amounts to equipping judges of whatever courts with the power to censor.

3. The Supreme Court decision in the Caldwell case, which sharply affects the journalist's ability to deal with sources which must remain confidential (he can only promise to go to jail rather than talk), still stands. Serious efforts to provide some kind of privilege for newsmen through legislation continue. One of the provisions of the proposed revision of the federal code is a "shield" law, and it should be noted that the Nixon administration consistently backed more protection for the journalist confronting grand juries and prosecutors. The whole matter of shield laws is complex, however.

4. The device of the antitrust action, or even the threat of it. As we have seen, from time to time there were suggestions within the White House inner circle that it be used more, but actual applications of such pressure were sparse and casually chosen. The device can be used with much more powerful effects, and the vulnerability of the communications industries to it increases every year.

Historically, the great names among media in the United States were those of families and family-held properties. Hearst, McCormick-Patterson, Ochs-Sulzberger, Knight, Curtis, Meredith, Meyer, Paley—all these enterprises became prominent as family affairs which, at certain critical moments, drew strength from a head who had the authority to tell the rest of the world to go to hell. Two other giants which were publicly held, RCA and Time Inc., were so completely dominated by David Sarnoff and Henry Luce, respectively, that their situation was effectively the same. Not only were these in effect private operations, their interests were confined substantially to the newspaper or magazine or broadcasting business. Henry Luce opposed, at one point or another, every company initiative to move outside the

magazine business, and John Knight did the same in the newspaper field. Such companies were small compared to the real
giants. In 1960, Time Inc., was in one hundred seventy-seventh
place in the ranking of United States corporations, and CBS did
not even make the first five hundred; RCA was in twenty-fourth
place, but this primarily because of its large manufacturing
activities. To that point there had never appeared in this country anything like the standard European pattern in which publications are owned and frequently subsidized as minor appen-
dages of enterprises whose attention is directed primarily to
making motor cars, or steel, or refining oil.

The first changes in single-medium pattern began with the
coming of radio. After a brief period of attempting to fight
commercial broadcasting by elaborately ignoring it, the ownerships of publishing enterprises decided to join it and bought
stations and acquired licenses on their own. Television stations
were added during the medium's growth period after World War
II; by the middle sixties, a typical small communications empire consisted of five to ten daily newspapers and a few broadcasting stations. The pressure to expand became pressure to
diversify and invest in more properties. There were two main
reasons for this. In the case of the single-product companies,
such as Time Inc., or the *New York Times,* there was genuine
concern that diversification was necessary for survival; mass
circulation consumer magazines were going into a nosedive, as
were big metropolitan dailies. The more modest enterprises,
based upon a string of relatively small dailies and broadcast
properties, thrived—for several years now, newspapers have been
among the most profitable of American businesses—and they
sought diversification and new investments in part because of
tax advantages.

A look at the anatomy of one of the giants as of 1973
shows how far this has gone. The Times Mirror Company's best
known property is a fine and prosperous newspaper, the *Los
Angeles Times*, but it also owns the *Daily Pilot* (Orange county, California), *Newsday* (Long Island), and the *Times-Herald*
(Dallas); several specialized book publishing houses and the
World Publishing Company, which produces trade books;

forests and mills which produce lumber, paper, and wood products; *Popular Science* magazine; Denoyer-Geppert, which makes maps and globes; aviation products, commercial printing establishments, a Dallas television station, and twenty-one cable TV systems. Most of the sixteen-member board of directors were primarily identified as officers of other corporations such as North American Rockwell, Northrop, and various banking and security firms.[16]

In 1973 the Columbia Broadcasting System sold the New York Yankees, but still retained ownership of such oddments as an occasional Broadway production, the Steinway piano company, a book-publishing house, records, and, of course, five enormously profitable metropolitan television stations. The National Broadcasting Company had from the beginning been part of RCA, with its heavy interests in manufacturing all kinds of broadcasting and receiving equipment, recordings, and the operation of international telecommunications systems. More recently, the conglomerate acquired a rental car company and a book-publishing firm.

Other than its forest properties, the New York Times Company has stayed within the communications business, but its holdings range from the *Times* to small dailies, magazines devoted to international golf and tennis, Quadrangle Books, a television station, and a specialty house which reprints at high prices esoteric scholarly books and source materials for historians. The Times company also has been in and out of the almanac business.

Obviously enterprises of these dimensions and wide range of holdings are far more vulnerable to various regulatory agencies than the old-line newspaper publisher wrapped in the traditional protection of the First Amendment. Antitrust action by the Justice Department can be especially effective. The complexity and dynamics of corporate organization in this country are such that almost any large business can be legitimately investigated, and the decisions about which ones to investigate inevitably have to be made on a variety of bases beyond the evidential.

Because of the First Amendment as well as a long tradition

of noli me tangere, the media always have been rather special
cases in their institutional relationships with the law and regulatory agencies. Attempts by municipalities and state governments to levy taxes on advertising, for example, always have
failed, either because a court found the law unconstitutional or
because the city council or legislature which passed it had
second thoughts after feeling the fury of the media's reaction.
Over the opposition of the Justice Department, along with that
of many editors, a few publishers, and practically all journalism
academics, Congress passed the Newspaper Preservation Act in
1970. This curious piece of legislation, known in its original
form as the "failing newspaper" act, provides that joint operating arrangements worked out according to its specifications
between competing newspapers are exempt from the provisions
of antitrust legislation.

Despite these indicators of special status, the communications industry has been reminded of the existence of the antitrust division a good many times over the years. Most of these
cases tend to be particularistic and without larger implications.
Typically, the division will suggest that a newspaper ownership
which controls two papers with no competition in the same
market area divest itself of one of them—for example, forcing
the *Los Angeles Times* to sell the *San Bernadino Sun.* Such
elbowing is particularly likely when changes in ownership and
corporate realignments are underway.

Although there have been dozens of such cases since the
1950s, it must be said that the pattern to date has hardly been
widespread. Politicians and the agencies they control are cautious about what they perceive as the power of the media,
perhaps more cautious than they need to be. The chief explanation, however, lies in the fact that the choice of those to be
prosecuted rests largely in the hands of the director of the
Antitrust Division. As we have noted earlier, the tenants of that
office have been noted for their independence. They also have
been conditioned by the division's traditional tendency to
undertake only such actions as they feel they can win. In time,
however, both of these restraints can be avoided through the
careful choice of Antitrust Division directors. And the media, it

is safe to say, will continue to undo themselves; as they grow larger, they grow more vulnerable. The pressure of stockholders to turn a profit will push them toward caution and the avoidance of controversy; so will the threat of antitrust action by a vengeful administration. Some traces of both tendencies already are visible.

Another continuing threat to the traditional role of the media in their relationship to government lies elsewhere than in statutory powers and new legislation. In the opinion of this writer, there is great danger in the increasing co-opting of the press through the success of the methods of corporate public relations. That may seem a curious conclusion in light of the fact that those who first brought such methods to the White House were so thoroughly discredited and disgraced.

But these methods are based on the premise that there is no difference between the interactions of press and government and those of corporation and customers. They primarily seek to sell images rather than enlarge the more equitable and honorable operation of a unique system of government. They make covering government easy for the journalists whose stories are favorable and difficult for those whose are not. They call for the continuing harassment of the management which employs the difficult reporter (a condition which might be given the summary title of Paley's Stomach Syndrome). These assumptions and these methods have worked too well in too many places to be summarily dismissed by other administrations just because some of the early practitioners happened to be crooks.

In fact, these methods worked to a much greater extent than generally realized during the Nixon years. This writer conducted a series of interviews in 1973 with reporters and broadcasters who regularly worked the White House. One of these was a television network news producer. It soon became apparent that his attitudes, as a producer, were highly favorable to the White House news establishment as it then operated. He said:

These people are so much better than either the Kennedy or Johnson staff that there's no comparison. With
Johnson, you'd have the set-up for a presidential speech all
ready to go and somebody would come in two minutes
before air time and say "it's too hot in here; I want that
light out, and that one." The night Johnson made the
speech saying he wouldn't run again they stopped our
trucks two different times at the White House gates and
wouldn't even let them in—and we were responsible for the
pool that night.

But these guys are pros. During the inaugural parade last
January security wanted to keep a drum and bugle corps,
for God's sake, between my cameras and the presidential
stand. I went to Mark Goode and he worked out a set-up
which gave a clear shot. No buck-passing, no waffling. And
no drum and bugle corps.

They're simply sensational, that's all.

He was almost apologetic for not sharing the endemic attitude
among newsmen toward the White House and its works.

A newspaperman, himself bitterly critical of the administration, touched the same point a few days later:

Look, one of my best friends is the White House man
for a wire service. He thinks the way I do about almost
everything, but there's one exception. He thinks Ron Ziegler is the greatest press secretary in the history of the
republic. The service is sensational. The transcripts are fast
and accurate. Working conditions are plush. They pick you
up when you're going to San Clemente and they don't lose
your bags. If your basic job is getting out the word as it
comes from the White House, there's no question these
guys are experts.

Journalists, particularly American journalists, are not very
often corrupted by what might be vulgarly described as "the
three b's of bread, booze, and broads." They are much more likely
to be corrupted by that which makes their job easier and less

tension inducing. The will to dig it all out can atrophy. At the moment, the media ride the wave of the spirit of derring-do. That inevitably will pass away, and there will be other administrations too wise to make the mistakes of the Nixon era—but also wise enough to find in it the elements of an effective technique of gentle corruption. And over time, corruption may prove to be the most serious threat of all.

Documents of Significance

This collection of texts contains two kinds of documents. Most important, probably, are those which represent views of specific members of the Nixon administration toward the media and their suggestions about possible courses of action to curb what they perceive as media excesses. These include both internal White House memos and formal speeches. Two documents provide lists of stories which Richard Nixon, as president, found offensive, and thus give some insight into his concerns.

Sections of two major decisions by the United States Supreme Court also are included. The decision in the Pentagon Papers case already has had major, and essentially deleterious, implications for freedom of expression. The decision in the Caldwell case has potentially profound implications for the way the reporter goes about his work and the role of anonymous informers.

With one exception, which is noted, the material is arranged in chronological order. Materials from the Supreme Court decisions are, in effect, excerpts. Speech texts are largely intact, having been edited primarily to remove local, topical, and otherwise irrelevant references. The White House memos are unedited and include misspellings and grammatical slips.

October 17, 1969
The Shot-gun versus the Rifle

*This perhaps is the best known of the internal White House
memoranda which were collected by the Ervin subcommittee
investigating the Watergate affair. In addition to providing insight into the thinking of White House staff, there is particular
value in the log of requests from the president himself which
demonstrates both the span and particularity of his concern
with the media even at that early stage.*

  *Jeb Magruder was, at the time the memo was written, an
aide to H. R. Haldeman and deputy director of White House
communications. He then became deputy director of the Committee for the Re-election of the President and was one of the
first to "break" in the Watergate case.*

THE WHITE HOUSE

WASHINGTON

October 17, 1969

MEMORANDUM FOR: H. R. HALDEMAN

FROM: J. S. MAGRUDER

RE: The Shot-gun versus the Rifle

Yesterday you asked me to give you a talking paper on specific problems we've had in shot-gunning the media and
anti-Administration spokesmen on unfair coverage.

I have enclosed from the log approximately 21 requests
from the President in the last 30 days requesting specific
action relating to what could be considered unfair news
coverage. This enclosure only includes actual memos sent
out by Ken Cole's office. In the short time that I have
been here, I would gather that there have been at least
double or triple this many requests made through various
other parties to accomplish the same objective.

It is my opinion this continual daily attempt to get to
the media or to anti-Administration spokesmen because of
specific things they have said is very unfruitful and
wasteful of our time. This is not to say that they have
not been unfair, without question many situations that
have been indicated are correct, but I would question the
approach we have taken. When an editor gets continual
calls from Herb Klein or Pat Buchanan on a situation that
is difficult to document as to unfairness, we are in a
very weak area. Particularly when we are talking about
interpretation of the news as against factual reporting.

The real problem that faces the Administration is to get
to this unfair coverage in such a way that we make major
impact on a basis which the networks-newspapers and Congress will react to and begin to look at things somewhat
differently. It is my opinion that we should begin concentrated efforts in a number of major areas that will
have much more impact on the media and other anti-Administration spokesmen and will do more good in the long run.
The following is my suggestion as to how we can achieve
this goal:

   1. Begin an official monitoring system through the
FCC as soon as Dean Burch is officially on board as Chairman. If the monitoring system proves our point, we have
then legimate and legal rights to go to the networks, etc.,
and make official complaints from the FCC. This will have
much more effect than a phone call from Herb Klein or Pat
Buchanan.

   2. Utilize the anti-trust division to investigate various media relating to anti-trust violations. Even the
possible threat of anti-trust action I think would be effective in changing their views in the above matter.

   3. Utilizing the Internal Revenue Service as a method
to look into the various organizations that we are most
concerned about. Just a threat of a IRS investigation will
probably turn their approach.

   4. Begin to show favorites within the media. Since
they are basically not on our side let us pick the favorable ones as Kennedy did. I'm not saying we should eliminate the open Administration, but by being open we have
not gotten anyone to back us on a consistant basis and
many of those who were favorable towards us are now giving
it to us at various times, i.e., Ned Lewis, Hugh Sidiy.

5. Utilize Republican National Committee for major
letter writing efforts of both a class nature and a quantity nature. We have set-up a situation at the National
Committee that will allow us to do this, and I think by
effective letter writing and telegrams we will accomplish
our objective rather than again just the shot-gun approach
to one specific Senator or one specific news broadcaster
because of various comments.

I would liken this to the Kennedy Administration in that
they had no qualms about using the power available to them
to achieve their objectives. On the other hand, we seem
to march on tip-toe into the political situation and are
unwilling to use the power at hand to achieve our long
term goals which is eight years of a Republican Administration. I clearly remember Kennedy sending out the FBI
men to wake-up the Steel Executives in the middle of the
night. It caused an uproar in certain cases but he achieved
his goal and the vast majority of the American public was
with him. If we convince the President that this is the
correct approach, we will find that various support groups
will be much more productive and much more cooperative;
and at the same time I think we will achieve the goals
this Administration has set out to do on a much more meaningful planned basis.

PRESIDENT'S REQUEST --

TO:	ITEM:	DATE:
P. Flanigan	President's request that you take action to counter Dan Rather's allegation that the Hershey move was decided upon because of the moratorium. (Log 1733)	October 17
J. Ehrlichman	President's request that you talk to Ted Lewis concerning the present status of disci-pline within the Administra-tion. (Log 1699)	October 15
P. Buchanan	President's request for a report on what actions were taken to complain to NBC, Time and Newsweek concerning	October 14

	a recent article coverage on the Administration. (Log 1688)	
H. Klein	President's request for let-ters to the editor of <u>News-week</u> mentioning the President's tremendous reception in Miss. and last Sat. Miami Dolphin football game. (Log 1627)	October 10
H. Klein	President's request that you take appropriate action to counter biased TV coverage of the Adm. over the summer. (Log 1644) CONFIDENTIAL	October 14
H. Klein	President's request that you ask Rogers Morton to take action to counter Howard K. Smith's remarks concerning the three House seats lost by the GOP this year. (Log 1558)	October 8
P. Buchanan	President's request that ap-propriate columnists be in-formed of the extemporaneous character of Presidential press conferences. (Log 1551)	October 10
H. Klein	President's request that you demand equal time to counter John Chancellor's commentary regarding the Haynsworth nom-ination. (Log 1559)	October 7
H. Klein	President's request for a re-port on what action is taken concerning Sen. Muski's ap-pearance on the "Merv Griffin Show."	October 8
A. Butterfield	President's request for a re-port what resulted from our PR efforts following up the Friday Press Conference. (Log 1496)	October 3

H. Klein	President's request that we have the CHICAGO TRIBUNE hit Senator Percy hard on his ties with the peace group. (Log 1495) CONFIDENTIAL	October 3
H. Klein	President's request for letters to the editor regarding Newsweek's lead article covering the President's U.N. speech. (Log 1443)	September 30
H. Klein	President's request that we counter Ralph Nader's remarks regarding Virginia Knauer accessability to the President. (Log 1404)	September 29
H. Klein Ron Ziegler	President's request that you attack Life Magazine's editorial accusing the Administration of creating a Coherence Gap. (Log 1366)	September 27
H. Klein	President's request that you contact Howard K. Smith and give him the true record on what the Administration has done. (Log 1367)	September 26
A. Butterfield	Sen. Kennedy's Boston speech alleging that the war in Vietnam remains virtually unchanged. (Log 1292)	September 23
P. Flanigan	Ralph Nader's charge that the President pays little attention to consumer affairs. (Log 1293)	September 24
Dr. Kissinger	Article by Jack Anderson which alleges that some U.S. officers in Vietnam favor Thieu's hard line over the President's moderate policy and are sabotaging the truce efforts. (Log 1281)	September 23
H. Klein	President's request that you inform Walter Trohan about	September 20

our substantive programs and
that you place the blame for
inaction on the democratic
Congress. (Log 1246)

J. Ehrlichman   President request for a re-   September 23
port on possible answers to
Evans-Novak charge of an Administration retreat on tax
reform. (Log 1224)

Dr. Kissinger   President's request for a   September 16
report on Walter Cronkite's
comment that the South Vietnamese did not observe the
truce resulting from Ho Chi
Minh's death. (Log 1154)

November 5, 1973
Untitled Document

Although this listing of White House complaints is out of chronological sequence, it is included here because it provides another sampling of the taking of umbrage in high places. The origins of the document are curious.

There has been in existence since early 1973 an organization called the National News Council, a mixed group of media professionals and eminent citizens which has as its basic objective the investigation of complaints of shabby media performance as well as media protests about problems of access, intimidation, and illegal restraint. The group is public but unofficial and financed by foundations. Its history has not been untroubled. Both its establishment and its functioning were vigorously opposed by some within the news business, particularly the New York Times. *Most of the complaints which came its way during the early months of its existence were trivial.*

During a press conference—perhaps the steamiest of his career—on October 26, 1973, Richard Nixon referred to "outrageous, vicious, distorted reporting." Both the National News Council and the Communications Institute, another founda-

tion-supported body which had an important role in the estab-
lishment of the council, requested a bill of particulars. There is
an account earlier in this book of the efforts of News Council
executives to get the White House to provide it. After a good
deal of evasive action, Ziegler finally turned them down flatly,
with reassurances that he understood the media, because he'd
bought a lot of advertising in his time.

Meanwhile, the Communications Institute did receive a
reply in which the White House declined "to submit any formal
list of complaints" but did forward a tabulation "you might
want to utilize for guidance."

The basic news stories involved are, first, the resumption
of intensive bombing of North Vietnam in late December of
1972 and, second, the running story of the Watergate scandal in
the summer and fall of 1973.

THE DECEMBER BOMBINGS

Television

WALTER CRONKITE

"Soviet News Agency Tass said hundreds of U.S. bombers
had destroyed thousands of homes, most of them in the
Hanoi-Haiphong area."

--December 20, 1972

"And Hanoi Radio said the bombings indicate President
Nixon has taken leave of his senses."

--December 21, 1972

"...in Moscow Soviet Party Boss Brezhnev called the
bombing barbaric and said the future of Russian-American
relations hangs in the balance."

--December 21, 1972

DAN RATHER

The United States has "embarked on a large-scale terror

bombing" with the operative word, "unrestricted."

> --December 20, 1972
> CBS Morning News

Mr. Rather quoted Hanoi to the effect that the strikes were "extermination raids on many populous areas."

> --December 20, 1972

ERIC SEVAREID

"In most areas of this government...the feeling is one of dismay, tinged with shame that the United States is again resorting to mass killing in an effort to end the killing."

> --December 22, 1972

MARVIN KALB

Quoted on the CBS Morning News, Kalb said that Hanoi had opened a "savage personal attack" and that leading North Vietnamese editorials accused the United States of ordering a Hitlerian Blitzkrieg against North Vietnam, calling the President "a bellicose criminal."

> --December 28, 1972

PETER KALISCHER (At the Paris Peace Talks)

"In less than an hour, the Communist side walked out to protest what North Vietnam's VEE called unspeakable crimes against the civilian population."

"The blanket bombing of Hanoi and Haiphong residential areas."

HARRY REASONER

"...Dr. Kissinger's boss has broken Dr. Kissinger's word. It's very hard to swallow...Backing off from a cease-fire is a weight and comes very close to a breaking of faith, with Hanoi maybe, with Americans more certainly."

> --December 19, 1972

OTHER REPORTS

On ABC, December 21, 1972, Jerry Gordon, of Peace Action

Coalition stated: "...the American people understand
that their government has resumed the genocidal bombing
policy, that Nixon is committed to all-out victory."

On CBS, December 22, 1972, there was noted an interfaith
group of forty-one religious leaders who called the
bombing "madness" and the Administration of "aborting
the possibility and betraying the duty of peace."

Printed Media

JAMES RESTON

"This [the bombing] is war by tantrum, and it is worse
than the Cambodian and Laotian invasions..."

--December 27, 1972

ANTHONY LEWIS

"Even with sympathy for the men who fly American planes,
and for their families, one has to recognize the greater
courage of the North Vietnamese people..."

--January 6, 1973

"...the elected leader of the greatest democracy acts
like a maddened tyrant,..."

--December 30, 1972

"To send B-52's against populous areas such as Haiphong
or Hanoi can have only one purpose: terror. It was
the response of a man so overwhelmed by his sense of
inadequacy and frustration that he had to strike out,
punish, destroy."

--December 23, 1972

WASHINGTON POST EDITORIAL

"He has conducted a bombing policy...so ruthless and so
difficult to fathom, politically as to cause millions
of Americans to cringe in shame and to wonder at their
President's very sanity."

--January 7, 1973

JOSEPH KRAFT

"...Mr. Nixon called on the bombers -- an action in my

judgment, of senseless terror which stains the good
name of America."

                                      --December 24, 1972

On CBS, December 29, 1972, Jeff Williams interviewing Senator William Saxbe -- "You were recorded recently as saying that the <u>President had taken leave of his senses.</u>
Would you explain that?"

UNFAIR NETWORK COVERAGE

1)   John Dean, the President's accuser, was on three networks; Haldeman, Ehrlichman, the President's defenders,
higher in rank, were on one network. Millions fewer Americans saw the rebuttals, than witnessed the accusations on
the networks.

2)   CBS alone among the networks chose to put Donald
Segretti on national television; all-day, for five hours,
when he had nothing new to say; everything he talked of
was known -- was this of such moment to the Republic that
it merited five hours of daytime television time. When was
the last time CBS devoted five hours to the strategic balance, to the energy crisis, to the nation's economic problems -- which Americans by huge margins consider far more
serious than Watergate.

3)   On Thursday night, following Kissinger's press conference, NBC ran all four Kissinger answers dealing with
the charge that the President fomented the Middle East
crisis for domestic political reasons. Thrust of that
report was clearly to raise in the nation the question
of whether the crisis was a phony, the alert a phony
trumped up for political reasons.

4)   On Monday night, after the Cox firing, networks ran
19 separate attacks on the President, most calling for impeachment or resignation, and two defenses. (Bork was on
three nets, but on two the report was negative in character.) This took place the very night prior to the return
of Congress.

5)   Archie Cox was given 11 minutes of network news time
in an interview with about two minutes of news. The longest such time given an interviewee on the network news in
memory; this was Cronkite's doing; and one recalls the

only other two special interviews he has conducted were
with John Dean, and Daniel Ellsberg, two others whom one
cannot characterize as Administration stalwarts.

6)   CBS had three separate reports on Rebozo's bank and
the savings and loan application, one of them running to
eight minutes. The impression left with the American
people, from the length and number of such reports, is
that influence peddling was involved on a sweeping scale.
Yet, CBS itself has found no proof of wrong-doing, as Mr.
Pierpoint has admitted and the Washington Star-News has
written, "There is no evidence of any political influence
figuring in either federal ruling, a full check of the
files made available by the comptroller's office indicates." Why then this massive coverage -- if not to con-
vict Mr. Rebozo in the public mind of something for which
he could never be convicted in a court of law.

7)   Utter failure of networks to place matters in perspective. Where questioning of White House motives occurs
regularly, such as Brokaw report saying that with Cox admission he may have leaked the ITT story, White House had
found its opening. No such skepticism, no such context on
impeachment cries by Jerome Waldie who happens to be a
California liberal Gubernatorial candidate, running behind
in the polls, who just might be making noise to elevate
himself in the primaries.

8)   Where Goldwater's criticism of the President, and
rightly so, have been given wide media coverage, networks
were not waiting outside his door to get on film his
stinging attacks on the "hounds of destruction" in the
national press. Why not? Are only attacks upon the President newsworthy?

9)   Editor of the Santa Ana Register himself says that
some stations used their story, on the President's home
purchases, without the qualifications and careful attri-
butions their paper had used.

10)   Media has responsibility not only for informing
Americans, but for correcting misinformation. According
to polls 35% of American people believe RN knew of Watergate before it occurred; yet no one has even charged the
President with this. Have the networks made any effort
whatsoever to correct this utterly false impression --
when they themselves are surely partly responsible it
exists?

DOUBLE STANDARD

1)   Compare amount of investigative talent in Watergate, with that devoted to the alleged theft of the Presidency in 1960, via vote frauds in Texas and Illinois and possibly Missouri.

2)   Watergate is the most intensively covered story in history, with Ervin Committee getting all-day coverage, followed by ten minutes a night on the networks, followed often each week by "Specials" and the dominant story in the morning news.

3)   Press indicated where its heart lay at hearings by adopting the practice (according to Collins of Newsday) of writing up questions to be asked of witnesses, passing them on to Senators, thus engaging in a kind of collaboration wholly inconsistent with their function as "neutrals" in such controversies.

November 13, 1969 (Des Moines, Iowa)
Speech by Vice-President Spiro T. Agnew

The origins and background of this speech, the best known of all administration attacks on the media, are set out in chapter 2.

TRANSCRIPT OF ADDRESS BY AGNEW
CRITICIZING TELEVISION
ON ITS COVERAGE OF THE NEWS

The *New York Times*, November 14, 1969

Tonight I want to discuss the importance of the television news medium to the American people. No nation depends more on the intelligent judgment of its citizens. No medium has a more profound influence over public opinion. Nowhere in our system are there fewer checks on vast power. So, nowhere should there be more conscientious responsibility exercised than by the news media. The question is, Are we demanding enough of our television news presentations? And are the men of this medium demanding enough of themselves?

Monday night a week ago President Nixon delivered the most important address of his Administration, one of the most important of our decade. His subject was Vietnam. His hope was to rally the American people to see the conflict through to a lasting and just peace in the Pacific. For 32 minutes he reasoned with a nation that has suffered almost a third of a million casualties in the longest war in its history.

When the President completed his address—an address, incidentally, that he spent weeks in the preparation of—his words and policies were subjected to instant analysis and querulous criticism. The audience of 70 million Americans gathered to hear the President of the United States was inherited by a small band of network commentators and self-appointed analysts, the majority of whom expressed in one way or another their hostility to what he had to say.

It was obvious that their minds were made up in advance. Those who recall the fumbling and groping that followed President Johnson's dramatic disclosure of his intention not to seek another term have seen these men in a genuine state of nonpreparedness. This was not it.

One commentator twice contradicted the President's statement about the exchange of correspondence with Ho Chi Minh. Another challenged the President's abilities as a politician. A third asserted that the President was following a Pentagon line. Others, by the expression on their faces, the tone of their questions and the sarcasm of their responses, made clear their sharp disapproval.

To guarantee in advance that the President's plea for national unity would be challenged, one network trotted out Averell Harriman for the occasion. Throughout the President's message he waited in the wings. When the President concluded, Mr. Harriman recited perfectly. He attacked the Thieu Government as unrepresentative; he criticized the President's speech for various deficiencies; he twice issued a call to the Senate Foreign Relations Committee to debate Vietnam once again; he stated his belief that the Vietcong or North Vietnamese did not really want a military takeover of South Vietnam; and he told a little anecdote about a "very, very responsible" fellow he had met in the North Vietnamese delegation.

All in all, Mr. Harriman offered a broad range of gratuitous advice challenging and contradicting the policies outlined by the President of the United States. Where the President had issued a call for unity, Mr. Harriman was encouraging the country not to listen to him. . . .

Now every American has a right to disagree with the President of the United States and to express publicly that disagreement. But the President of the United States has a right to communicate directly with the people who elected him, and the people of this country have the right to make up their own minds and form their own opinions about a Presidential address without having a President's words and thoughts characterized through the prejudices of hostile critics before they can even be digested.

When Winston Churchill rallied public opinion to stay the course against Hitler's Germany, he didn't have to contend with a gaggle of commentators raising doubts about whether he was reading public opinion right or whether Britain had the stamina to see the war through.

When President Kennedy rallied the nation in the Cuban missile crisis, his address to the people was not chewed over by a roundtable of critics who disparaged the course of action he'd asked America to follow.

The purpose of my remarks . . . is to focus your attention on this little group of men who not only enjoy a right of instant rebuttal to every Presidential address, but, more importantly, wield a free hand in selecting, presenting, and interpreting the great issues in our nation.

First, let's define that power. At least 40 million Americans every night, it's estimated, watch the network news. Seven million of them view ABC, the remainder being divided between NBC and CBS.

According to Harris polls and other studies, for millions of Americans the networks are the sole source of national and world news. In Will Rogers's observation, what you knew was what you read in the newspaper. Today for growing millions of Americans, it's what they see and hear on their television sets.

Now how is this network news determined? A small group of men, numbering *perhaps* no more than a dozen anchormen, commentators and executive producers, settle upon the 20 minutes or so of film and commentary that's to reach the public. This selection is made from the 90 to 180 minutes that may be available. Their powers of choice are broad.

They decide what 40 to 50 million Americans will learn of the day's events in the nation and in the world.

We cannot measure this power and influence by the traditional democratic standards, for these men can create national issues overnight.

They can make or break by their coverage and commentary a moratorium on the war.

They can elevate men from obscurity to national prominence within a week. They can reward some politicians with national exposure and ignore others.

For millions of Americans the network reporter who covers a continuing issue—like the ABM or civil rights—becomes, in effect, the presiding judge in a national trial by jury.

It must be recognized that the networks have made important contributions to the national knowledge—for news, documentaries and specials. They have often used their power constructively and creatively to awaken the public conscience to critical problems. The networks made hunger and black lung disease national issues overnight. The TV networks have done what no other medium could have done in terms of dramatizing the horrors of war. The networks have tackled our most difficult social problems with a directness and an immediacy that's the gift of their medium. . . .

But it was also the networks that elevated Stokely Carmichael and George Lincoln Rockwell from obscurity to national prominence.

Nor is their power confined to the substantive. A raised eyebrow, an inflection of the voice, a caustic remark dropped in the middle of a broadcast can raise doubts in a million minds about the veracity of a public official or the wisdom of a Government policy.

One Federal Communications Commissioner considers the powers of the networks equal to that of local, state and Federal Governments all combined. Certainly it represents a concentration of power over American public opinion unknown in history.

Now what do Americans know of the men who wield this power? Of the men who produce and direct the network news, the nation knows practically nothing. Of the commentators, most Americans know little other than that they reflect an urbane and assured presence seemingly well-informed on every important matter.

We do know that to a man these commentators and producers live and work in the geographical and intellectual confines of Washington, D.C., or New York City, the latter of which James Reston terms the most unrepresentative community in the entire United States.

Both communities bask in their own provincialism, their own paro-chialism.

We can deduce that these men read the same newspapers. They draw their political and social views from the same sources. Worse, they talk constantly to one another, thereby providing artificial reinforcement to their shared viewpoints.

Do they allow their biases to influence the selection and presentation of the news? David Brinkley states objectivity is impossible to normal human behavior. Rather, he says, we should strive for fairness.

Another anchorman on a network news show contends, and I quote: "You can't expunge all your private convictions just because you sit in a seat like this and a camera starts to stare at you. I think your program has to reflect what your basic feelings are. I'll plead guilty to that."

Less than a week before the 1968 election, this same commentator charged that President Nixon's campaign commitments were no more durable than campaign balloons. He claimed that, were it not for the fear of hostile reaction, Richard Nixon would be giving into, and I quote him exactly, "his natural instinct to smash the enemy with a club or go after him with a meat axe."

Had this slander been made by one political candidate about another, it would have been dismissed by most commentators as a partisan attack. But this attack emanated from the privileged sanctuary of a network studio and therefore had the apparent dignity of an objective statement.

The American people would rightly not tolerate this concentration of power in Government.

Is it not fair and relevant to question its concentration in the hands of a tiny, enclosed fraternity of privileged men elected by no one and enjoying a monopoly sanctioned and licensed by Government?

The views of the majority of this fraternity do not—and I repeat, not—represent the views of America.

That is why such a great gulf existed between how the nation received the President's address and how the networks reviewed it.

Not only did the country receive the President's address more warmly than the networks; but so also did the Congress of the United States.

Yesterday, the President was notified that 300 individual Congressmen and 50 Senators of both parties had endorsed his efforts for peace.

As with other American institutions, perhaps it is time that the networks were made more responsive to the views of the nation and more responsible to the people they serve.

Now I want to make myself perfectly clear. I'm not asking for Government censorship or any other kind of censorship. I'm asking whether a form of censorship already exists when the news that 40 million Americans receive each night is determined by a handful of men responsible only to their corporate employers and is filtered through a handful of commentators who admit to their own set of biases.

The questions I'm raising here tonight should have been raised by others long ago. They should have been raised by those Americans who have traditionally considered the preservation of freedom of speech and freedom of the press their special provinces of responsibility.

They should have been raised by those Americans who share the view of the late Justice Learned Hand that right conclusions are more likely to be gathered out of a multitude of tongues than through any kind of authoritative selection.

Advocates for the networks have claimed a First Amendment right to the same unlimited freedoms held by the great newspapers of America.

But the situations are not identical. Where the *New York Times* reaches 800,000 people, NBC reaches 20 times that number on its evening news. (The average weekday circulation of the *Times* in October was 1,012,367; the average Sunday circulation was 1,523,558.) Nor can the tremendous impact of seeing television film and hearing commentary be compared with reading the printed page.

A decade ago, before the network news acquired such dominance over public opinion, Walter Lippman spoke to the issue. He said there's an essential and radical difference between television and printing. The three or four competing television stations control virtually all that can be received over the air by ordinary television sets. But besides the mass circulation dailies, there are weeklies, monthlies, out-of-town newspapers and books. If a man doesn't like his newspaper, he can read another from out of town or wait for a weekly news magazine. It's not ideal, but it's infinitely better than the situation in television.

There if a man doesn't like what the networks are showing, all he can do is turn them off and listen to a phonograph. Networks, he stated, which are few in number have a virtual monopoly of a whole media of communications.

The newspapers of mass circulation have no monopoly on the medium of print. Now a virtual monopoly of a whole medium of communication is not something that democratic people should blindly ignore. And we are not going to cut off our television sets and listen to the phonograph just because the airways belong to the networks. They don't. They belong to the people.

As Justice Byron White wrote in his landmark opinion six months ago, it's the right of the viewers and listeners, not the right of the broadcasters, which is paramount.

Now it's argued that this power presents no danger in the hands of those who have used it responsibly. But, as to whether or not the networks have abused the power they enjoy, let us call as our first witness former Vice President Humphrey and the city of Chicago. According to Theodore White, television's intercutting of the film from the streets of Chicago with the current proceedings on the floor of the convention created the most striking and false political picture of 1968—the nomination of a man for the American Presidency by the brutality and violence of merciless police.

If we are to believe a recent report of the House of Representatives Commerce Committee, then television's presentation of the violence in the streets worked an injustice on the reputation of the Chicago police. According to the Committee findings, one network in particular presented, and I quote, "a one-sided picture which in large measure exonerates the demonstrators and protesters." Film of provocations of police that was available never saw the light of day while the film of a police response which the protesters provoked was shown to millions.

Another network showed virtually the same scene of violence from three separate angles without making clear it was the same scene. And while the full report is reticent in drawing conclusions, it is not a document to inspire confidence in the fairness of the network news.

Our knowledge of the impact of network news on the national mind is far from complete, but some early returns are available. Again, we have enough information to raise serious questions about its effect on a democratic society. Several years ago Fred Friendly, one of the pioneers of network news, wrote that its missing ingredients were conviction, controversy and a point of view. The networks have compensated with a vengeance.

And in the networks' endless pursuit of controversy, we should ask: What is the end value—to enlighten or to profit? What is the end result—to inform or to confuse? How does the ongoing exploration for more action, more excitement, more drama serve our national search for internal peace and stability?

Gresham's Law seems to be operating in the network news. Bad news drives out good news. The irrational is more controversial than the rational. Concurrence can no longer compete with dissent.

One minute of Eldridge Cleaver is worth 10 minutes of Roy Wilkins. The labor crisis settled at the negotiating table is nothing compared to the confrontation that results in a strike—or better yet, violence along the picket lines.

Normality has become the nemesis of the network news. Now the upshot of all this controversy is that a narrow and distorted picutre of America often emerges from the televised news.

A single, dramatic piece of the mosaic becomes in the minds of millions the entire picture. And the American who relies upon television for his news might conclude that the majority of American students are embittered radicals. That the majority of black Americans feel no regard for their country. That violence and lawlessness are the rule rather than the exception on the American campus.

We know that none of these conclusions is true.

Perhaps the place to start looking for a credibility gap is not in the offices of the Government in Washington but in the studios of the networks in New York. . . .

The members of Congress or the Senate who follow their principles and philosophy quietly in a spirit of compromise are unknown to many Americans, while the loudest and most extreme dissenters on every issue are known to every man in the street.

How many marches and demonstrations would we have if the marchers did not know that the ever-faithful TV cameras would be there to record their antics for the next news show?

We've heard demands that Senators and Congressmen and judges make known all their financial connections so that the public will know who and what influences their decisions and their votes. Strong arguments can be made for that view. But when a single commentator or producer, night after night, determines for millions of people how much of each side of a great issue they are going to see and hear, should he not first disclose his personal views on the issue as well?

In this search for excitement and controversy, has more than equal time gone to the minority of Americans who specialize in attacking the United States—its institutions and its citizens?

Tonight I've raised questions. I've made no attempt to suggest the answers. The answers must come from the media men. They are challenged to turn their critical powers on themselves to direct their energy, their talent and their conviction toward improving the quality and objectivity of news presentation. . . .

And the people of America are challenged, too, challenged to press for responsible news presentations. The people can let the networks know that they want their news straight and objective. The people can register their complaints on bias through mail to the networks and phone calls to local stations. This is one case where the people must defend themselves; where the citizen, not the Government, must be the reformer; where the consumer can be the most effective crusader.

By way of conclusion, let me say that every elected leader in the United States depends on these men of the media. Whether what I've said to you tonight will be heard and seen at all by the nation is not my decision, it's not your decision, it's their decision. . . .

The great networks have dominated America's airwaves for decades. The people are entitled to a full accounting of their stewardship.

November 20, 1969 (Montgomery, Alabama)
Speech by Vice-President Spiro T. Agnew

The most interesting aspect of this speech, which follows the Des Moines speech by one week, rests in the fact that it represents the first flirting of the Nixon administration with the idea of the vulnerability of certain media corporations to antitrust action. This device was actually used only once, in the filing of the action against the networks in the spring of 1972, but the idea obviously was attractive from the beginning of the Nixon years. The chief barrier seems to have been the traditional prickly independence of the Antitrust Division of the Department of Justice, and particularly the nonmanipulable character of the head of that division during much of the first term, Robert McLaren. A kind of truculent tribute to McLaren's independence was delivered by Nixon when he was trying to get him off energetic prosecution of the ITT case during the campaign of 1972; "I never liked the son-of-a-bitch," the president of the United States said.

A major section of the Montgomery speech is not included; it dealt with the vice-president's attitudes toward American young people and, although revealing of the speaker, does not seem relevant to this study. The full text of the speech is available in several places, including the New York Times *of November 21, 1969.*

One week ago tonight I flew out of Des Moines, Iowa and exercised my right to dissent.

This is a great country—in this country every man is allowed freedom of speech, even the Vice President.

There's been some criticism of what I said . . . in Des Moines. . . . One Congressman charged me with, . . . "a creeping socialistic scheme against the free enterprise broadcast industry." . . .

On Monday, largely because of that address, Mr. Humphrey charged the Nixon Administration with a "calculated attack" on the right of dissent and on the media today. Yet it's widely known that Mr. Humphrey himself believes deeply that the unfair coverage of the Democratic convention in Chicago, by the same media, contributed to his defeat in November. . . .

. . . These attacks do not address themselves to the questions I raised. In fairness, . . . the majority of the critics and commentators, did take up the main thrust of my address.

And if the debate that they have engaged in continues, our goal will surely be reached, our goal which . . . is a thorough self-examination by the networks of their own policies and perhaps prejudices. That was my objective then, and that's my objective now. . . .

I'm opposed to censorship of television, of the press in any form. I don't care whether censorship is imposed by government or whether it results from management in the choice and presentation of the news by a little fraternity having similar social and political views. . . .

But a broader spectrum of national opinion should be represented among the commentators in the network news. Men who can articulate other points of view should be brought forward and a high wall of separation should be raised between what is news and what is commentary.

And the American people should be made aware of the trend toward the monopolization of the great public information vehicles and the concentration of more and more power in fewer and fewer hands. . . .

. . . A single company, in the nation's capital, holds control of the largest newspaper in Washington, D.C., and one of the four major television stations, and an all-news radio station, and one of the three major national news magazines—all grinding out the same editorial line—and this is not a subject that you've seen debated on the editorial pages of the *Washington Post* or the *New York Times*.

For the purpose of clarity, before my thoughts are obliterated in the smoking typewriters of my friends in Washington and New York, let me emphasize that I'm not recommending the dismemberment of the Washington Post Company. I'm merely pointing out that the public should be aware that these four powerful voices hearken to the same master.

I'm raising these questions so that the American people will become aware of—and think of the implications of—the growing monopoly that involves the voices of public opinion, on which we all depend for our knowledge and for the basis of our views. . . .

. . . When the *New York Journal-American*, the *New York World-Telegram* and *Sun*, the *New York Mirror* and the *New York Herald Tribune* all collapsed within this decade, that was a great, great political tragedy for the people of New York. The *New York Times* was a better newspaper when they were all alive than it is now that they are gone.

And what has happened in the city of New York has happened in other great cities of America.

Many, many strong, independent voices have been stilled in this country in recent years. And lacking the vigor of competition, some of those who have survived have—let's face it—grown fat and irresponsible.

I offer an example: When 300 congressmen and 59 senators signed a letter endorsing the President's policy in Vietnam, it was news—and it was big news. Even the *Washington Post* and the *Baltimore Sun*—scarcely house organs for the Nixon Administration—placed it prominently in their front pages.

Yet the next morning the *New York Times*, which considers itself America's paper of record, did not carry a word. Why?*

If a theology student in Iowa should get up at a PTA luncheon in Sioux City and attack the President's Vietnam policy, my guess is that you'd probably find it reported somewhere in the next morning's issue of the *New York Times*. But when 300 congressmen endorse the President's Vietnam policy, the next morning it's apparently not considered news fit to print.

Just this Tuesday when the Pope, the spiritual leader of half a billion Roman Catholics, applauded the President's effort to end the war in Vietnam and endorsed the way he was proceeding, that news was on page 11 of the *New York Times*. The same day a report about some burglars who broke into a souvenir shop at St. Peter's and stole $9,000 worth of stamps and currency . . . made page 3. How's that for news judgment?

A few weeks ago here in the South I expressed my views about street and campus demonstrations. Here's how the *New York Times* responded:

"He (that's me) lambasted the nation's youth in sweeping and ignorant generalizations, when it's clear to all perceptive observers that American youth today is far more imbued with idealism, a sense of service and a deep humanitarianism than any generation in recent history, including particuarly Mr. Agnew's generation."

That's what the *New York Times* said. . . .

One magazine this week said that I'll go down as the "great polarizer"

---

*Although the vice-president should have the right of free speech without being heckled by footnotes, it should be noted that later editions of the *Times* did, indeed, carry the story. The Washington edition, which was the one read by Agnew and his speech writers, closed too early for the account, but readers in New York City the next morning had it in full.

in American politics. Yet, when that large group of young Americans marched up Pennsylvania Avenue and Constitution Avenue last week, they sought to polarize the American people against the President's policy in Vietnam. And that was their right. And so it is my right, and my duty, to stand up and speak out for the values in which I believe. . . .

It's not an easy thing to wake up each morning to learn that some prominent man or some prominent institution has implied that you're a bigot or a racist or a fool.

I'm not asking immunity from criticism. This is the lot of a man in politics; . . .

But my political and journalistic adversaries sometimes seem to be asking something more—that I circumscribe my rhetorical freedom while they place no restriction on theirs.

As President Kennedy observed in a far more serious situation: "This is like offering an apple for an orchard."

We do not accept those terms for continuing the national dialogue. The day when the network commentators and even the gentlemen of the *New York Times* enjoyed a form of diplomatic immunity from comment and criticism of what they said is over. Yes, gentlemen, that day is passed.

Just as a politician's words—wise and foolish—are dutifully recorded by press and television to be thrown up at him at the appropriate time, so their words should be likewise recorded and likewise recalled.

When they go beyond fair comment and criticism they will be called upon to defend their statements and their positions just as we must defend ours. And when their criticism becomes excessive or unjust, we shall invite them down from their ivory towers to enjoy the rough and tumble of public debate.

I don't seek to intimidate the press, or the networks or anyone else from speaking out. But the time for blind acceptance of their opinions is past. And the time for naive belief in their neutrality is gone.

As to the future, each of us could do worse than to take as our own the motto of William Lloyd Garrison who said, . . .

"I am in earnest. I will not equivocate. I will not excuse. I will not retreat a single inch. And I will be heard."

February 4, 1970
From H. R. Haldeman to J. S. Magruder

July 16, 1970
From L. Higby to J. S. Magruder

In addition to the implications of the first part of the Haldeman memorandum which, in effect, encourages junior White House staff members to be imaginative in developing means to combat the perceived bias of the networks, these memos lay out some of the anatomy of the process of creating a more favorable image.

L. Higby is Lawrence Higby, staff assistant to H. R. Haldeman.

THE WHITE HOUSE

WASHINGTON

<u>CONFIDENTIAL</u>

February 4, 1970

MEMORANDUM FOR: MR. MAGRUDER

HIGH PRIORITY

A couple of points that I did not want to cover in the general meeting, but that you do need to move ahead on quickly.

First, I'm sure you have studied that TV summary done by Buchanan, which is a devastating indictment of NBC, especially of David Brinkley.

Specifically, Brinkley was completely off base factually on his budget criticism, and we need to get that one straightened out.

The need, probably, is to concentrate on NBC and give some real thought as to how to handle the problem that they

have created in their almost totally negative approach to
everything the Administration does. I would like to see
a plan from you; don't worry about fancy form, just some
specific thinking on steps that can be taken to try to
change this, and I should have this by Friday. Get Klein
and Ziegler both involved in the thinking on this, and I
would suggest also Nofziger, who could be very helpful,
and perhaps get Pat Buchanan in. In fact, I definitely
think you should get Pat Buchanan in to work with you on
it; but move quickly.

Another area is the mobilization of the Silent Majority,
which we touched on briefly in the meeting today. We
just haven't really mobilized them, and we have got to
move now in every effective way we can to get them working to pound the magazines and the networks in counter-
action to the obvious shift of the establishment to an
attack on Vietnam again. Concentrate this on the few
places that count, which would be NBC, TIME, NEWSWEEK
and LIFE, the NEW YORK TIMES, and the WASHINGTON POST.
Don't waste your fire on other things.

Next point, and this is also highly urgent priority. The
State of the Union evoked a tremendous number of very
strong editorials praising the content, delivery, etc.
Now we need, very quickly, a well-edited, well-packaged,
compellingly-presented mailing piece that summarizes the
highlights of those editorials, especially the ones from
surprising sources like Reston of the TIMES, so that we
can get out to our people especially the reaction that
the country's newspapers have had to the President's
address.

This is something that should have been automatically done
immediately, and perhaps it is underway. The point here
is that delay makes any action much less effective, since
it should be an immediate response and get out while the
speech is still alive. Our main failure in this whole
area is dullness, and let's not let this effort fall into
that category. Get it done on good paper in interesting
style, rather than just a mimeographed glob of editorial
excerpts.

This is the kind of thing our Outside Group should automatically pick up for us once we get them; but until we
have them, we have to fill the gap ourselves, and it's
terribly important to move quickly on this. Perhaps the
National Committee can help you with editorial and lay-
out facilities, but hold them to very high standards and

make it come out good. Leonard over there is probably the
best guy for this kind of thing and maybe would be the one
to get working on it, but give him about a one-day deadline, so that we get it done instead of talked about.

                              s: H.
                              H. R. HALDEMAN

CONFIDENTIAL

THE WHITE HOUSE

WASHINGTON

                              July 16, 1970

SECRET

MEMORANDUM FOR: MR. MAGRUDER

FROM: L. HIGBY   s: L

As I indicated to you the other day, we need to get some
creative thinking going on an attack on Huntley for his
statements in Life. One thought that comes to mind is
getting all the people to sign a petition calling for the
immediate removal of Huntley right now.

The point behind this whole thing is that we don't care
about Huntley - he is going to leave anyway. What we
are trying to do here is to tear down the institution.
Huntley will go out in a blaze of glory and we should
attempt to pop his bubble.

Most people won't see Life Magazine and for that reason
I am asking Buchanan to draft a statement for the Vice
President to give. We should try to get this statement on

television. Obviously there are many other things that we can do, such as getting independent station owners to write NBC saying that they should remove Huntley now; having broadcasting people look into this due to the fact that this is proof of biased journalism, etc.

Let's put a full plan on this and get the thing moving. I'll contact Buchanan and forward copies of my correspondence with him to you so that you will know what the Vice President is doing.

July 17, 1970
Memorandum for Haldeman and Klein from Jeb S. Magruder

This series of proposals from Magruder begins with a reference to a remark attributed to (but apparently never made by) Chet Huntley, at that point about to retire from the NBC network. Several memos in the set released by the office of Senator Weicker deal with this remark, and they demonstrate the overreaction of the White House to what appeared in the media. The Huntley episode is discussed in detail in chapter 3, but it might be pointed out here that the remark was buried in a magazine article and, even after being picked up by the news services, received slight general attention. Network news programs, even Huntley-Brinkley in its prime, have small audiences. (If Robert Young as Marcus Welby had said the same thing, that would be quite different.)

Magruder indicates that he feels it would be impossible to discredit Huntley as an individual—and therefore suggests turning the offensive to the media as institutions. It is precisely this quality which distinguished the Nixon administration from others in its offensive against the press.

Most of the proposals which follow are more revealing in their naiveté than their perceptiveness, although Magruder's list of journalists who could be counted on as outlets for administration views is interesting. After Watergate, most of the group became anti-Nixon. Alsop died in the summer of 1974.

THE WHITE HOUSE

WASHINGTON

July 17, 1970

CONFIDENTIAL/EYES ONLY

MEMORANDUM FOR: MR. HALDEMAN
                         MR. KLEIN

FROM: JEB S. MAGRUDER   s: JM

Enclosed is a tentative plan on press objectivity. Please
indicate your comments.

Thank you.

Enclosure

☆   ☆   ☆   ☆   ☆

TENTATIVE PLAN

PRESS OBJECTIVITY

Description: In the July 17th issue of LIFE Maga-
                    zine a prominent television newscaster
                    is quoted as making some extremely
                    disparaging remarks about the Presi-
                    dent. It is understood that the news-
                    caster intends to send a letter to the
                    editor of the magazine claiming he was
                    misquoted and will also send a letter
                    of apology to the President.

Objective: To question the overall objectivity of
                    a television newscaster who has ex-
                    pressed opinionated views in an influ-
                    ential consumer publication while
                    still employed as a supposedly objec-
                    tive television newscaster and to

question the motivation for such remarks and the possible breach of professional ethics by allowing such
remarks to be published prior to re-
tirement into private life. Further,
to extend these questions to cover
the professional objectivity and ethics of the whole media and to generate a public re-examination of the
role of the media in American life.

Tactics:

Since the newscaster enjoys a very
favorable public image and will apolo-
gize for his remarks, claiming to be
misquoted, we should not attempt to
discredit him personally. Also, since
his remarks were expressed as an individual, we would have difficulty
attacking his network directly. The
focus of our effort should be to raise
the larger question of objectivity and
ethics in the media as an institution.
To do this, we will have to turn objectivity into an issue and a subject
of public debate.

Follow-up:

Release the letter of apology to the
press along with a gracious reply from
the President. -- Ziegler

Plant a column with a syndicated columnist which raises the question of
objectivity and ethics in the news
media. Kevin Phillips could be a good
choice. -- Klein

Arrange for an article on the subject
in a major consumer magazine authored
by Stewart Alsop, Buckley or Kilpatrick.
Also, request Hobe Lewis to run a major
article. -- Klein

Through an academic source, encourage
the Dean of a leading graduate school
of journalism to publicly acknowledge
that press objectivity is a serious
problem that should be discussed.
Also, attempt to arrange an in-depth
analysis in a prestigious journal like

the Columbia Journalism Review.
-- Klein/Safire

Arrange a seminar on press objectivity
with broadcast executives and working
newsmen. Attempt to have this televised as a public service. -- Klein

Make this issue a major item at the
Radio-Television News Directors Con-
vention this Fall and at the next major
NAB meeting. -- Klein

Ask the Vice President to speak out on
this issue. He could point out that
the LIFE quote has proved his point.
-- Buchanan

Have Rogers Morton go on the attack in
a news conference. He could tie-in
the quote with the free-time grants to
the Democrats. Also, revive the WETA-
Woestendiek affair. Have him charge
that the great majority of the working
press are Democrats and this colors
their presentation of the news. Have
him charge that their is a political
conspiracy in the media to attack this
Administration. -- Klein/Colson

Have Dean Burch "express concern" about
press objectivity in response to a letter from a Congressman. -- Nofziger

Through independent Hill sources, stimulate non-partisan Congressional questioning of the issue. Place such remarks in the Record. -- Nofziger

Arrange for an "expose" to be written
by an author such as Earl Mazo or
Victor Lasky. Publish in hardcover
and paperback. -- Klein

Produce a prime-time special, sponsored
by private funds, that would examine
the question of objectivity and show
how TV newsmen can structure the news
by innuendo. For instance, use film

clips to show how a raised eyebrow or
a tone of voice can convey criticism.
-- Klein/Magruder

Have outside groups petition the FCC
and issue public "statements of concern" over press objectivity. -- Colson

Generate a massive outpouring of let-
ters-to-the-editor. -- Magruder

LIFE occasionally runs an opposition
view column entitled "Guest Privilege".
Position an appropriate writer, prefer-
ably a professor of journalism, to discuss this issue in that column.
-- Klein/Safire

Form a blue-ribbon media "watchdog"
committee to report to the public on
cases of biased reporting. John
Cosgrove, a former president of the
National Press Club, could set this
up. This group could sponsor the TV
special mentioned above, conduct a
speaking campaign to service groups
and colleges, issue press releases,
etc. -- Magruder

Have a Senator or Congressman write a
public letter to the FCC suggesting
the "licensing" of individual newsmen,
i.e. the airwaves belong to the public,
therefore the public should be protected from the misuse of these airwaves by individual newsmen. -- Nofziger

Through contacts in the ASNE and NAB,
bring up the question of a "fairness
pledge" for members. -- Klein

Project Manager -- Magruder

CONFIDENTIAL/EYES ONLY

September 25, 1970
Memorandum from Charles W. Colson to H. R. Haldeman

*During the summer of 1970 Charles Colson, special counsel to
the president, visited the heads of the three commercial broadcast networks. His primary objective was to ensure what the
White House would consider "fair" coverage of the president
and the administration. Specifically, he was concerned with the
destruction of the notion, once expressed by William Paley,
chairman of the board of CBS, that the opposition deserved a
kind of institutionalized platform to reply to administration
statements and initiatives. The reference in his note of transmittal to "FCC decisions" refers to commission interpretations of
the Fairness Doctrine.*

FYI - EYES ONLY, PLEASE

                                          September 25, 1970

MEMORANDUM FOR H.R. HALDEMAN

The following is a summary of the most pertinent conclusions from my meeting with the three network chief executives.

1. The networks are terribly nervous over the uncertain
    state of the law, i.e., the recent FCC decisions and
    the pressures to grant Congress access to TV. They
    are also apprehensive about us. Although they tried
    to disguise this, it was obvious. The harder I pressed
    them (CBS and NBC) the more accommodating, cordial and
    almost apologetic they became. Stanton for all his
    bluster is the most insecure of all.

2. They were startled by how thoroughly we were doing our
    homework -- both from the standpoint of knowledge of
    the law, as I discussed it, but more importantly, from
    the way in which we have so thoroughly monitored their

coverage and our analysis of it. (Allin's analysis is attached. This was my talking paper and I gave them facts and figures.)

3. There was unamimous agreement that the President's right of access to TV should in no way be restrained. Both CBS and ABC agreed with me that on most occasions the President speaks as President and that there is no obligation for presenting a contrasting point of view under the Fairness Doctrine (This, by the way, is not the law -- the FCC has always ruled that the Fairness Doctrine always applies -- and either they don't know that or they are willing to concede us the point.) NBC on the other hand argues that the fairness test must be applied to every Presidential speech but Goodman is also quick to agree that there are probably instances in which Presidential addresses are not "controversial" under the Fairness Doctrine and, therefore, there is no duty to balance. All agree no one has a right of "reply" and that fairness doesn't mean answering the President but rather is "issue oriented." This was the most important understanding we came to. What is important is that they know how strongly we feel about this.

4. They are terribly concerned with being able to work out their own policies with respect to balanced coverage and not to have policies imposed on them by either the Commission or the Congress. ABC and CBS said that they felt we could, however, through the FCC make any policies we wanted to. (This is worrying them all.)

5. To my surprise CBS did not deny that the news had been slanted against us. Paley merely said that every Administration has felt the same way and that we have been slower in coming to them to complain than our predecessors. He, however, ordered Stanton in my presence to review the analysis with me and if the news has not been balanced to see that the situation is immediately corrected. (Paley is in complete control of CBS -- Stanton is almost obsequious in Paley's presence.)

6. CBS does not defend the O'Brien appearance. Paley wanted to make it very clear that it would not happen again and that they would not permit partisan attacks on the President. They are doggedly determined to win their FCC case, however; as a matter of principle, even though they recognize that they made a mistake,

they don't want the FCC in the business of correcting
their mistakes.

7. ABC and NBC believe that the whole controversy over
    "answers" to the President can be handled by giving
    some time regularly to presentations by the Congress
    -- either debates or the State-of-The-Congress-type
    presentations with both parties in the Congress repre-
    sented. In this regard ABC will do anything we want.
    NBC proposes to provide a very limited Congressional
    coverage once or twice a year and additionally once a
    year "loyal opposition" type answers to the President's
    State of the Union address (which has been the practice
    since 1966). CBS takes quite a different position.
    Paley's policy is that the Congress cannot be the sole
    balancing mechanism and that the Democratic leadership
    in Congress should have time to present Democratic
    viewpoints on legislation. (On this point, which may
    become the most critical of all, we can split the net-
    works in a way that will be very much to our advantage.)

Conclusion:

I had to break every meeting. The networks badly want to
have these kinds of discussions which they said they had
had with other Administrations but never with ours. They
told me anytime we had a complaint about slanted coverage
for me to call them directly. Paley said that he would
like to come down to Washington and spend time with me
anytime that I wanted. In short, they are very much
afraid of us and are trying hard to prove they are "good
guys."

These meetings had a very salutary effect in letting them
know that we are determined to protect the President's
position, that we know precisely what is going on from
the standpoint of both law and policy and that we are not
going to permit them to get away with anything that inter-
feres with the President's ability to communicate.

Paley made the point that he was amazed at how many people
agree with the Vice President's criticism of the networks.
He also went out of his way to say how much he supports
the President, and how popular the President is. When
Stanton said twice as many people had seen President Nixon
on TV than any other President in a comparable period,
Paley said it was because this President is more popular.

The only ornament on Goodman's desk was the Nixon Inaugural
Medal. Hagerty said in Goldenson's presence that ABC is
"with us." This all adds up to the fact that they are
damned nervous and scared and we should continue to take
a very tough line, face to face, and in other ways.

As to follow-up, I believe the following is in order:

1. I will review with Stanton and Goodman the substantia-
tion of my assertion to them that their news coverage has
been slanted. We will go over it point by point. This
will, perhaps, make them even more cautious.

2. There should be a mechanism (through Herb, Ron or me)
every time we believe coverage is slanted whereby we point
it out either to the chief executive or to whomever he
designates. Each of them invited this and we should do it
so they know we are not bluffing.

3. I will pursue with ABC and NBC the possibility of
their issuing declarations of policy (one that we find
generally favorable as to the President's use of TV). If
I can get them to issue such a policy statement, CBS will
be backed into an untenable position.

4. I will pursue with Dean Burch the possibility of an
interpretive ruling by the FCC on the role of the President
when he uses TV, as soon as we have a majority. I think
that this point could be very favorably clarified and it
would, of course, have an inhibiting impact on the networks
and their professed concern with achieving balance.

5. I would like to continue a friendly but very firm relationship whenever they or we want to talk. I am realistic enough to realize that we probably won't see any obvious improvement in the news coverage but I think we can
dampen their ardor for putting on "loyal opposition" type
programs.

I have detailed notes on each meeting if you'd like a more
complete report.

                         Charles W. Colson

June 29, 1972
Excerpts from the Decision of the United States Supreme Court
in *Paul M. Branzburg, Petitioner,* v. *John P. Hayes, Judge, etc.
et al; In the Matter of Paul Pappas, Petitioner; United States,
Petitioner,* v. *Earl Caldwell* (408 US 665, 33 L Ed 2d 626, 92 S
Ct 2646)

*The following extract represents only a small part of the total
text of this decision. It sets out the essential lines of argument
through portions of the majority decision, written by Justice
White, and what seems to be the most eloquent dissent, that of
Justice Douglas. All the case citations have been omitted—not
only for brevity, but because of their obfuscatory quality for
the uninitiated—which is perhaps seriously misleading in what it
implies about the argument of the majority opinion. White cites
a wide range of precedent in both cases and past practice; he
does not accept any responsibility for any curtailment of traditional freedom of the press, but rather contends that, in effect,
the majority is simply bringing to bear in a particular problem
long-established practice. The full opinion is heavily scholarly;
in this version, it may appear to be largely rhetorical. For the
full text, the reader should see* U. S. Supreme Court Reports, *33
L Ed 2d.*

    *One other point should be noted: there is an uncon-
ventional element in the majority decision in that it casts doubt
upon the possibility of framing so-called shield laws which
this Court would find acceptable. Some of the bones of that
argument are included here but, again, the full presentation is
much more thorough. It is not unknown for the Court to try to
warn away legislative bodies from new legislation, but it is
uncommon, and it clearly represents a strong conviction on the
part of the majority.*

II

    Petitioners Branzburg and Pappas and respondent Caldwell press
First Amendment claims that may be simply put: that to gather news it is
often necessary to agree either not to identify the source of information

published or to publish only part of the facts revealed, or both; that if the reporter is nevertheless forced to reveal these confidences to a grand jury, the source so identified and other confidential sources of other reporters will be measurably deterred from furnishing publishable information, all to the detriment of the free flow of information protected by the First Amendment. Although the newsmen in these cases do not claim an absolute privilege against official interrogation in all circumstances, they assert that the reporter should not be forced either to appear or to testify before a grand jury or at trial until and unless sufficient grounds are shown for believing that the reporter possesses information relevant to a crime the grand jury is investigating, that the information the reporter has is unavailable from other sources, and that the need for the information is sufficiently compelling to override the claimed invasion of First Amendment interests occasioned by the disclosure. Principally relied upon are prior cases emphasizing the importance of the First Amendment guarantees to individual development and to our system of representative government, decisions requiring that official action with adverse impact on First Amendment rights be justified by a public interest that is "compelling" or "paramount," and those precedents establishing the principle that justifiable government goals may not be achieved by unduly broad means having an unnecessary impact on protected rights of speech, press, or association. . . .

We do not question the significance of free speech, press, or assembly to the country's welfare. Nor is it suggested that news gathering does not qualify for First Amendment protection; without some protection for seeking out the news, freedom of the press could be eviscerated. But these cases involve no intrusions upon speech or assembly, no prior restraint or restriction on what the press may publish, and no express or implied command that the press publish what it prefers to withhold. No exaction or tax for the privilege of publishing, and no penalty, civil or criminal, related to the content of published material is at issue here. The use of confidential sources by the press is not forbidden or restricted; reporters remain free to seek news from any source by means within the law. No attempt is made to require the press to publish its sources of information or indiscriminately to disclose them on request.

The sole issue before us is the obligation of reporters to respond to grand jury subpoenas as other citizens do and to answer questions relevant to an investigation into the commission of crime. Citizens generally are not constitutionally immune from grand jury subpoenas; and neither the First Amendment nor any other constitution provision protects the average citizen from disclosing to a grand jury information that he has received in confidence. The claim is, however, that reporters are exempt from these obligations because if forced to respond to subpoenas and identify their sources or disclose other confidences, their informants will refuse or be reluctant to furnish newsworthy information in the future. This asserted burden on news gathering is said to make compelled testimony from newsmen constitutionally suspect and to require a privileged position for them.

It is clear that the First Amendment does not invalidate every incidental burdening of the press that may result from the enforcement of civil or criminal statutes of general applicability. . . .

The prevailing view is that the press is not free to publish with impunity everything and anything it desires to publish. Although it may deter or regulate what is said or published, the press may not circulate knowing or reckless falsehoods damaging to private reputation without subjecting itself to liability for damages, including punitive damages, or even criminal prosecution. . . . A newspaper or a journalist may also be punished for contempt of court, in appropriate circumstances. . . .

It has generally been held that the First Amendment does not guarantee the press a constitutional right of special access to information not available to the public generally. . . . In Zemel v Rusk, . . . for example, the Court sustained the Government's refusal to validate passports to Cuba even though that restriction "render[ed] less than wholly free the flow of information concerning that country." . . . The ban on travel was held constitutional, for "[t]he right to speak and publish does not carry with it the unrestrained right to gather information." . . .

Despite the fact that news gathering may be hampered, the press is regularly excluded from grand jury proceedings, our own conferences, the meetings of other official bodies gathered in executive session, and the meetings of private organizations. Newsmen have no constitutional right of access to the scenes of crime or disaster when the general public is excluded, and they may be prohibited from attending or publishing information about trials if such restrictions are necessary to assure a defendant a fair trial before an impartial tribunal. . . .

It is thus not surprising that the great weight of authority is that newsmen are not exempt from the normal duty of appearing before a grand jury and answering questions relevant to a criminal investigation. At common law, courts consistently refused to recognize the existence of any privilege authorizing a newsman to refuse to reveal confidential information to a grand jury. . . . In 1958, a news gatherer asserted for the first time that the First Amendment exempted confidential information from public disclosure pursuant to a subpoena issued in a civil suit, Garland v Torre, . . . but the claim was denied, and this argument has been almost uniformly rejected since then, although there are occasional dicta that, in circumstances not presented here, a newsman might be excused. . . . These courts have applied the presumption against the existence of an asserted testimonial privilege, . . . and have concluded that the First Amendment interest asserted by the newsman was outweighed by the general obligation of a citizen to appear before a grand jury or at trial, pursuant to a subpoena, and give what information he possesses. The opinions of the state courts in

Branzburg and Pappas are typical of the prevailing view, although a few recent cases, such as Caldwell, have recognized and given effect to some form of constitutional newsman's privilege. . . .

The prevailing constitutional view of the newsman's privilege is very much rooted in the ancient role of the grand jury that has the dual function of determining if there is probable cause to believe that a crime has been committed and of protecting citizens against unfounded criminal prosecutions. Grand jury proceedings are constitutionally mandated for the institution of federal criminal prosecutions for capital or other serious crimes, and "its constitutional prerogatives are rooted in long centuries of Anglo-American history." . . . The Fifth Amendment provides that "[n]o person shall be held to answer for a capital, or otherwise infamous crime, unless on a presentment or indictment of a Grand Jury." The adoption of the grand jury "in our Constitution as the sole method for preferring charges in serious criminal cases shows the high place it held as an instrument of justice." . . .

A number of States have provided newsmen a statutory privilege of varying breadth, but the majority have not done so, and none has been provided by federal statute. Until now the only testimonial privilege for unofficial witnesses that is rooted in the Federal Constitution is the Fifth Amendment privilege against compelled self-incrimination. We are asked to create another by interpreting the First Amendment to grant newsmen a testimonial privilege that other citizens do not enjoy. This we decline to do. Fair and effective law enforcement aimed at providing security for the person and property of the individual is a fundamental function of government, and the grand jury plays an important, constitutionally mandated role in this process. On the records now before us, we perceive no basis for holding that the public interest in law enforcement and in ensuring effective grand jury proceedings is insufficient to override the consequential, but uncertain, burden on news gathering that is said to result from insisting that reporters, like other citizens, respond to relevant questions put to them in the course of a valid grand jury investigation or criminal trial. . . .

The preference for anonymity of those confidential informants involved in actual criminal conduct is presumably a product of their desire to escape criminal prosecution, and this preference, while understandable, is hardly deserving of constitutional protection. It would be frivolous to assert—and no one does in these cases—that the First Amendment, in the interest of securing news or otherwise, confers a license on either the reporter or his news sources to violate valid criminal laws. Although stealing documents or private wiretapping could provide newsworthy information, neither reporter nor source is immune from conviction for such conduct, whatever the impact on the flow of news. Neither is immune, on First Amendment grounds, from testifying against the other, before the grand jury or at a criminal trial. The Amendment does not reach so far as to override the interest of the public in ensuring that neither reporter nor source is invading the rights of other citizens through reprehensible conduct forbidden to all other persons. . . .

Thus, we cannot seriously entertain the notion that the First Amendment protects a newsman's agreement to conceal the criminal conduct of his source, or evidence thereof, on the theory that it is better to write about crime than to do something about it. Insofar as any reporter in these cases undertook not to reveal or testify about the crime he witnessed, his claim of privilege under the First Amendment presents no substantial question. The crimes of news sources are no less reprehensible and threatening to the public interest when witnessed by a reporter than when they are not. There remain those situations where a source is not engaged in criminal conduct but has information suggesting illegal conduct by others. Newsmen frequently receive information from such sources pursuant to a tacit or express agreement to withhold the source's name and suppress any information that the source wishes not published. Such informants presumably desire anonymity in order to avoid being entangled as a witness in a criminal trial or grand jury investigation. They may fear that disclosure will threaten their job security or personal safety or that it will simply result in dishonor or embarrassment.

The argument that the flow of news will be diminished by compelling reporters to aid the grand jury in a criminal investigation is not irrational, nor are the records before us silent on the matter. But we remain unclear how often and to what extent informers are actually deterred from furnishing information when newsmen are forced to testify before a grand jury. The available data indicate that some newsmen rely a great deal on confidential sources and that some informants are particularly sensitive to the threat of exposure and may be silenced if it is held by this Court that, ordinarily, newsmen must testify pursuant to subpoenas, but the evidence fails to demonstrate that there would be a significant constriction of the flow of news to the public if this Court reaffirms the prior common-law and constitutional rule regarding the testimonial obligations of newsmen. Estimates of the inhibiting effect of such subpoenas on the willingness of informants to make disclosures to newsmen are widely divergent and to a great extent speculative. It would be difficult to canvass the views of the informants themselves; surveys of reporters on this topic are chiefly opinions of predicted informant behavior and must be viewed in the light of the professional self-interest of the interviewees. Reliance by the press on confidential informants does not mean that all such sources will in fact dry up because of the later possible appearance of the newsman before a grand jury. The reporter may never be called and if he objects to testifying, the prosecution may not insist. Also, the relationship of many informants to the press is a symbiotic one which is unlikely to be greatly inhibited by the threat of subpoena: quite often, such informants are members of a minority political or cultural group that relies heavily on the media to propagate its views, publicize its aims, and magnify its exposure to the public. Moreover, grand juries characteristically conduct secret proceedings, and law enforcement officers are themselves experienced in dealing with informers, and have their own methods for protecting them without interference with the effective administration of justice. There is little before us indicating that informants whose interest in avoiding exposure is that it may threaten job security, personal safety, or peace of mind, would in fact be in a worse position, or would think they would be, if they risked placing their trust in public officials as well as reporters. We doubt if the informer who prefers anonymity but is sincerely interested in furnishing evidence of crime will always or very often be deterred by the prospect of dealing with those public authorities characteristically charged with the duty to protect the public interest as well as his.

Accepting the fact, however, that an undetermined number of informants not themselves implicated in crime will nevertheless, for whatever reason, refuse to talk to newsmen if they fear identification by a reporter in an official investigation, we cannot accept the argument that the public interest in possible future news about crime from undisclosed, unverified sources must take precedence over the public interest in pursuing and prosecuting those crimes reported to the press by informants and in thus deterring the commission of such crimes in the future. . . .

Neither are we now convinced that a virtually impenetrable constitutional shield, beyond legislative or judicial control, should be forged to protect a private system of informers operated by the press to report on criminal conduct, a system that would be unaccountable to the public, would pose a threat to the citizen's justifiable expectations of privacy, and would equally protect well-intentioned informants and those who for pay or otherwise betray their trust to their employer or associates. The public through its elected and appointed law enforcement officers regularly utilizes informers, and in proper circumstances may assert a privilege against disclosing the identity of these informers. But

"[t]he purpose of the privilege is the furtherance and protection of the public interest in effective law enforcement. The privilege recognizes the obligation of citizens to communicate their knowledge of the commission of crimes to law-enforcement officials and, by preserving their anonymity, encourages them to perform that obligation." . . .

Such informers enjoy no constitutional protection. Their testimony is available to the public when desired by grand juries or at criminal trials; their identity cannot be concealed from the defendant when it is critical to his case.

We are admonished that refusal to provide a First Amendment reporter's privilege will undermine the freedom of the press to collect and disseminate news. But this is not the lesson history teaches us. As noted previously, the common law recognized no such privilege, and the constitutional argument was not even asserted until 1958. From the beginning of our country the press has operated without constitutional protection for press informants, and the press has flourished. The existing constitutional rules have not been a serious obstacle to either the development or retention of confidential news sources by the press.

It is said that currently press subpoenas have multiplied, that mutual distrust and tension between press and officialdom have increased, that reporting styles have changed, and that there is now more need for confidential sources, particularly where the press seeks news about minority cultural and political groups or dissident organizations suspicious of the law and public officials. These developments, even if true, are treacherous grounds for a far-reaching interpretation of the First Amendment fastening a nationwide rule on courts, grand juries, and prosecuting officials everywhere. The obligation to testify in response to grand jury subpoenas will not threaten these sources not involved with criminal conduct and without information relevant to grand jury investigations, and we cannot hold that the Constitution places the sources in these two categories either above the law or beyond its reach. . . .

At the federal level, Congress has freedom to determine whether a statutory newsman's privilege is necessary and desirable and to fashion standards and rules as narrow or broad as deemed necessary to deal with the evil discerned and, equally important, to refashion those rules as experience from time to time may dictate. There is also merit in leaving state legislatures free, within First Amendment limits, to fashion their own standards in light of the conditions and problems with respect to the relations between law enforcement officials and press in their own areas. It goes without saying, of course, that we are powerless to bar state courts from responding in their own way and construing their own constitutions so as to recognize a newsman's privilege, either qualified or absolute.

In addition, there is much force in the pragmatic view that the press has at its disposal powerful mechanisms of communication and is far from helpless to protect itself from harassment or substantial harm. Furthermore, if what the newsmen urged in these cases is true—that law enforcement cannot hope to gain and may suffer from subpoenaing newsmen before grand juries—prosecutors will be loath to risk so much for so little. Thus, at the federal level the Attorney General has already fashioned a set of rules for federal officials in connection with subpoenaing members of the press to testify before grand juries or at criminal trials. These rules are a major step in the direction the reporters herein desire to move. They may prove wholly sufficient to resolve the bulk of disagreements and controversies between press and federal officials.

Finally, as we have earlier indicated, news gathering is not without its First Amendment protections, and grand jury investigations if instituted or conducted other than in good faith, would pose wholly different issues for resolution under the First Amendment. Official harassment of the press undertaken not for purposes of law enforcement but to disrupt a reporter's relationship with his news sources would have no justification. Grand juries are subject to judicial control and subpoenas to motions to quash. We do not expect courts will forget that grand juries must operate within the limits of the First Amendment as well as the fifth. . . .

Mr. Justice Douglas, dissenting in No. 70-57, United States v Caldwell. . . .

It is my view that there is no "compelling need" that can be shown which qualifies the reporter's immunity from appearing or testifying before a grand jury, unless the reporter himself is implicated in a crime. His immunity in my view is therefore quite complete, for, absent his involvement in a crime, the First Amendment, protects him against an appearance before a grand jury and if he is involved in a crime, the Fifth Amendment stands as a barrier. Since in my view there is no area of inquiry not protected by a privilege, the reporter need not appear for the futile purpose of invoking one to each question. And, since in my view a newsman has an absolute right not to appear before a grand jury, it follows for me that a journalist who voluntarily appears before that body may invoke his First Amendment privilege to specific questions. The basic issue is the extent to which the First Amendment (which is applicable to investigating committees . . .) must yield to the Government's asserted need to know a reporter's unprinted information.

The starting point for decision pretty well marks the range within which the end result lies. The New York Times, whose reporting functions are at issue here, takes the amazing position that First Amendment rights are to be balanced against other needs or conveniences of government. My belief is that all of the "balancing" was done by those who wrote the Bill of Rights. By casting the First Amendment in absolute terms, they repudiated the timid, watered-down, emasculated versions of the First Amendment which both the Government and the New York Times advance in the case.

My view is close to that of the late Alexander Meiklejohn:

"For the understanding of these principles it is essential to keep clear the crucial difference between 'the rights' of the governed and 'the powers' of the governors. And at this point, the title 'Bill of Rights' is lamentably inaccurate as a designation of the first ten amendments. They are not a 'Bill of Rights' but a 'Bill of Powers and Rights.' The Second through the Ninth Amendments limit the powers of the subordinate agencies in order that due regard shall be paid to the private 'rights of the governed.' The First and Tenth Amendments protect the governing 'powers' of the people from abridgment by the agencies which are established as their servants. In the field of our 'rights,' each one of us can claim 'due process of law.' In the field of our governing 'powers,' the notion of 'due process' is irrelevant."

He also believed that "[s] elf-government can exist only insofar as the voters acquire the intelligence, integrity, sensitivity, and generous devotion to the general welfare that, in theory, casting a ballot is assumed to express," and that "[p] ublic discussions of public issues, together with the spreading of information and opinion bearing on those issues, must have a freedom unabridged by our agents. Though they govern us, we, in a deeper sense, govern them. Over our governing, they have no power. Over their governing we have sovereign power."

Two principles which follow from this understanding of the First Amendment are at stake here. One is that the people, the ultimate governors, must have absolute freedom of, and therefore privacy of, their individual opinions and beliefs regardless of how suspect or strange they may appear to others. Ancillary to that principle is the conclusion that an individual must also have absolute privacy over whatever information he may generate in the course of testing his opinions and beliefs. In this regard, Caldwell's status as a reporter is less relevant than is his status as a student who affirmatively pursued empirical research to enlarge his own intellectual viewpoint. The second principle is that effective self-government cannot succeed unless the people are immersed in a steady, robust, unimpeded, and uncensored flow of opinion and reporting which are continuously subjected to critique, rebuttal, and re-examination. In this respect, Caldwell's status as a news gatherer and an integral part of that process becomes critical.

I

Government has many interests that compete with the First Amendment. Congressional investigations determine how existing laws actually operate or whether new laws are needed. While congressional committees have broad powers, they are subject to the restraints of the First Amendment. As we said in Watkins v United States, . . . "Clearly, an investigation is subject to the command that the Congress shall make no law abridging freedom of speech or press or assembly. While it is true that there is no statute to be reviewed, and that an investigation is not a law, nevertheless an investigation is part of lawmaking. It is justified solely as an adjunct to the legislative process. The First Amendment may be invoked against infringement of the protected freedoms by law or by lawmaking."

Hence, matters of belief, ideology, religious practices, social philosophy, and the like are beyond the pale and of no rightful concern of government, unless the belief or the speech, or other expression has been translated into action. . . .

Also at stake here is Caldwell's privacy of association. We have held that "[i] nviolability of privacy in group association may in many circumstances be indispensable to preservation of freedom of association, particularly where a group espouses dissident beliefs." . . .

The Court has not always been consistent in its protection of these First Amendment rights and has sometimes allowed a government interest to override the absolutes of the First Amendment. For example, under the banner of the "clear and present danger" test, and later under the influence of the "balancing" formula, the Court has permitted men to be penalized not for any harmful conduct but solely for holding unpopular beliefs.

In recent years we have said over and over again that where First Amendment rights are concerned any regulation "narrowly drawn," must be "compelling" and not merely "rational" as is the case where other activities are concerned. But the "compelling" interest in regulation neither includes paring down or diluting the right, nor embraces penalizing one solely for his intellectual viewpoint; it concerns the State's interest, for example, in regulating the time and place or perhaps manner of exercising First Amendment rights. Thus, one has an undoubted right to read and proclaim the First Amendment in the classroom or in a park. But he would not have the right to blare it forth from a sound truck rolling through the village or city at 2 a.m. The distinction drawn in Cantwell v Connecticut, . . . should still stand: "[T]he Amendment embraces two concepts,—freedom to believe and freedom to act. The first is absolute but, in the nature of things, the second cannot be."

Under these precedents there is no doubt that Caldwell could not be brought before the grand jury for the sole purpose of exposing his political beliefs. Yet today the Court effectively permits that result under the guise of allowing an attempt to elicit from him "factual information." To be sure, the inquiry will be couched only in terms of extracting Caldwell's recollection of what was said to him during the interviews, but the fact remains that his questions to the Panthers and therefore the respective answers were guided by Caldwell's own preconceptions and views about the Black Panthers. His entire experience was shaped by his intellectual viewpoint. Unlike the random bystander, those who affirmatively set out to test a hypothesis, as here, have no tidy means of segregating subjective opinion from objective facts.

Sooner or later, any test which provides less than blanket protection to beliefs and associations will be twisted and relaxed so as to provide virtually no protection at all. As Justice Holmes noted in Abrams v United States, . . . such was the fate of the "clear and present danger" test which he had coined in Schenck v United States, . . . Eventually, that formula was so watered down that the danger had to be neither clear nor present but merely "not improbable." . . . A compelling-interest test may prove as pliable as did the clear-and-present-danger test. Perceptions of the worth of state objectives will change with the composition of the Court and with the intensity of the politics of the times. . . .

II

Today's decision will impede the wide-open and robust dissemination of ideas and counterthought which a free press both fosters and protects and which is essential to the success of intelligent self-government. Forcing a reporter before a grand jury will have two retarding effects upon the ear and the pen of the press. Fear of exposure will cause dissidents to communicate less openly to trusted reporters. And, fear of accountability will cause editors and critics to write with more restrained pens.

I see no way of making mandatory the disclosure of a reporter's confidential source of the information on which he bases his news story.

The press has a preferred position in our constitutional scheme not to enable it to make money, not to set newsmen apart as a favored class, but to bring fulfillment to the public's right to know The right to know is crucial to the governing powers of the people, to paraphrase Alexander Meiklejohn. Knowledge is essential to informed decisions. . . .

Government has an interest in law and order; and history shows that the trend of rulers—the bureaucracy and the police—is to suppress the radical and his ideas and to arrest him rather than the hostile audience. . . .

The people who govern are often far removed from the cabals that threaten the regime; the people are often remote from the sources of truth even though they live in the city where the forces that would undermine society operate. The function of the press is to explore and investigate events, inform the people what is going on, and to expose the harmful as well as the good influences at work. There is no higher function performed under our constitutional regime. Its performance means that the press is often engaged in projects that bring anxiety or even fear to the bureaucracies, departments, or officials of government. The whole weight of government is therefore often brought to bear against a paper or a reporter.

A reporter is no better than his source of information. Unless he has a privilege to withhold the identity of his source, he will be the victim of governmental intrigue or aggression. If he can be summoned to testify in secret before a grand jury, his sources will dry up and the attempted exposure, the effort to enlighten the public, will be ended. If what the Court sanctions today becomes settled law, then the reporter's main function in American society will be to pass on to the public the press releases which the various departments of government issue.

It is no answer to reply that the risk that a newman will divulge one's secrets to the grand jury is no greater than the threat that he will in any event inform to the police. Even the most trustworthy reporter may not be able to withstand relentless badgering before a grand jury.

The record in this case is replete with weighty affidavits from responsible newsmen, telling how important is the sanctity of their sources of information. When we deny newsmen that protection, we deprive the people of the information needed to run the affairs of the Nation in an intelligent way.

Madison said:

"A popular Government, without popular information, or the means of acquiring it, is but a Prologue to a Farce or a Tragedy; or, perhaps both. Knowledge will forever govern ignorance: And a people who mean to be their own Governors, must arm themselves with the power which knowledge gives." . . .

Today decision is more than a clog upon news gathering. It is a signal to publishers and editors that they should exercise caution in how they use whatever information they can obtain. Without immunity they may be summoned to account for their criticism. Entrenched officers have been quick to crash their powers down upon unfriendly commentators. . . .

The intrusion of government into this domain is symptomatic of the disease of this society. As the years pass the power of government becomes more and more pervasive. It is a power to suffocate both people and causes. Those in power, whatever their politics, want only to perpetuate it. Now that the fences of the law and the tradition that has protected the press are broken down, the people are the victims. The First Amendment, as I read it, was designed precisely to prevent that tragedy. . . .

June 30, 1971
Excerpts from the Decision of the United States Supreme Court in *New York Times Company, Petitioner,* v. *United States; United States, Petitioner,* v. *The Washington Post Company* et al. (403 US 713, 29 L Ed 2d 822, 91 S Ct 2140)

THE PENTAGON PAPERS DECISION

These excerpts begin with the summary from U. S. Supreme Court Reports, 29 L Ed 2d, which includes a condensation of each justice's opinion. The formal decision is not included; it is brief and unsigned.

The Black concurring opinion represents the defense of the "absolutist" position, along with a "restatement" of the government's case. This was one of the last major opinions written by

Black. Brennan's opinion, brief excerpts from which follow, is to First Amendment libertarians an exercise in frustration. He fiercely opposes the use of the injunction as a device for instant prior restraint, but concedes that there may be circumstances in which the government would be justified in a permanent restriction. White speaks primarily to problems of application. Finally, a part of the dissent by Chief Justice Burger sets out the case for government's authority.

Cross-referencing and footnoting have been omitted. The reversal of order in petitioners in the formal heading of the case reflects the fact that the decisions in New York and Washington were different; see the account in chapter 4 of this study.

SUMMARY

In an action in the United States District Court for the Southern District of New York, the United States government sought an injunction against the publication by the New York Times of the contents of a classified study entitled "History of U. S. Decision-Making Process on Viet Nam Policy," and in an action in the United States District Court for the District of Columbia, the government sought a similar injunction against the Washington Post. Each District Court denied injunctive relief. The Court of Appeals for the District of Columbia affirmed the judgment of the District Court for the District of Columbia, but the Court of Appeals for the Second Circuit remanded the case to the District Court for the Southern District of New York for further hearings. . . .

On certiorari, the United States Supreme Court affirmed the judgment of the Court of Appeals for the District of Columbia, but reversed the judgment of the Court of Appeals for the Second Circuit and remanded the case with directions to enter a judgment affirming the judgment of the District Court for the Southern District of New York. In a per curiam opinion expressing the view of six members of the court, it was held that the government did not meet its burden of showing justification for the imposition of a prior restraint of expression.

Black, J., joined by Douglas, J., concurring, stated that under the First Amendment, the press must be left free to publish news, whatever the source, without censorship, injunctions, or prior restraints, and that the guarding of military and diplomatic secrets at the expense of informed representative government was not justified.

Douglas, J., joined by Black, J., concurring, stated that the First Amendment left no room for governmental restraint on the press, and that the dominant purpose of the First Amendment was to prohibit govern-mental suppression of embarassing information.

Brennan, J., concurring, stated that the First Amendment stood as an absolute bar to the imposition of judicial restraints in circumstances of the kind presented by the present cases.

Stewart, J., joined by White, J., concurring, stated that the court was asked to perform a function which the Constitution gave to the Executive, not to the Judiciary, and that it could not be said that disclosure of the documents involved in the present cases would surely result in direct, immediate, and irreparable damage to the nation or its people.

White, J., joined by Stewart, J., concurring, stated that although the government mistakenly chose to proceed by injunction, the court's deci-sion did not mean that the law invited newspapers or others to publish sensitive documents or that they would be immune from criminal action if they did so.

Marshall, J., concurring, stated that under the concept of separation of power, the court did not have authority to grant the requested relief, and that the court should not take on itself the burden of enacting law, especially law which Congress had refused to pass.

Burger, Ch. J., dissenting, stated that the First Amendment right was not an absolute, and that the present cases had been decided in unseemly haste and without an adequate record.

Harlan, J., joined by Burger, Ch. J., and Blackmun, J., dissenting, stated that the court had been almost irresponsibly feverish in dealing with the present cases, that the scope of the judicial function in passing upon the activities of the Executive in the field of foreign affairs was very narrowly restricted, and that the doctrine prohibiting prior restraints did not prevent courts from maintaining the status quo long enough to act responsibly.

Blackmun, J., dissenting, stated that the present litigation had main-tained a frenetic pace and character, that he could not subscribe to a doctrine of unlimited absolutism for the First Amendment at the cost of downgrading other provisions of the Constitution, and that there was a danger that publication of the critical documents involved in the present cases would result in the death of soldiers, the destruction of alliances, the greatly increased difficulty of negotiation with our enemies, the inability of our diplomats to negotiate, the prolongation of the war, and further delay in the freeing of United States prisoners.

SEPARATE OPINIONS

Mr. Justice Black, with whom Mr. Justice Douglas joins, concurring.

I adhere to the view that the Government's case against the Washington Post should have been dismissed and that the injunction against the New York Times should have been vacated without oral argument when the cases were first presented to this Court. I believe that every moment's continuance of the injunctions against these newspapers amounts to a flagrant, indefensible, and continuing violation of the First Amendment. Furthermore, after oral argument, I agree completely that we must affirm the judgment of the Court of Appeals for the District of Columbia Circuit and reverse the judgment of the Court of Appeals for the Second Circuit for the reasons stated by my Brothers Douglas and Brennan. In my view it is unfortunate that some of my Brethren are apparently willing to hold that the publication of news may sometimes be enjoined. Such a holding would make a shambles of the First Amendment.

Our Government was launched in 1789 with the adoption of the Constitution. The Bill of Rights, including the First Amendment, followed in 1791. Now, for the first time in the 182 years since the founding of the Republic, the federal courts are asked to hold that the First Amendment does not mean what it says, but rather means that the Government can halt the publication of current news of vital importance to the people of this country.

In seeking injunctions against these newspapers and in its presentation to the Court, the Executive Branch seems to have forgotten the essential purpose and history of the First Amendment. When the Constitution was adopted, many people strongly opposed it because the document contained no Bill of Rights to safeguard certain basic freedoms. They especially feared that the new powers granted to a central government might be interpreted to permit the government to curtail freedom of religion, press, assembly, and speech. In response to an overwhelming public clamor, James Madison offered a series of amendments to satisfy citizens that these great liberties would remain safe and beyond the power of government to abridge. Madison proposed what later became the First Amendment in three parts, two of which are set out below, and one of which proclaimed: "The people shall not be deprived or abridged of their right to speak, to write, or to publish their sentiments; *and the freedom of the press, as one of the great bulwarks of liberty, shall be inviolable.*" The amendments were offered to *curtail* and *restrict* the general powers granted to the Executive, Legislative, and Judicial Branches two years before in the original Constitution. The Bill of Rights changed the original Constitution into a new charter under which no branch of government could abridge the people's freedoms of press, speech, religion, and assembly. Yet the Solicitor General argues and some members of the Court appear to agree that the general powers of the Government adopted in the original Constitution should be interpreted to limit and restrict the specific and emphatic guarantees of the Bill of Rights adopted later. I can imagine no greater perversion of history. Madison and the other Framers of the First Amendment, able men that they were, wrote in language they earnestly believed could never be misunderstood: "Congress shall make no law . . . abridging the freedom . . . of the press. . . ." Both the history and language of the First Amendment support the view that the press must be left free to publish news, whatever the source, without censorship, injunctions, or prior restraints.

In the First Amendment the Founding Fathers gave the free press the protection it must have to fulfill its essential role in our democracy. The press was to serve the governed, not the governors. The Government's power to censor the press was abolished so that the press would remain forever free to censure the Government. The press was protected so that it could bare the secrets of government and inform the people. Only a free and unrestrained press can effectively expose deception in government. And paramount among the responsibilities of a free press is the duty to prevent any part of the government from deceiving the people and sending them off to distant lands to die of foreign fevers and foreign shot and shell. In my view, far from deserving condemnation for their courageous reporting, the New York Times, the Washington Post, and other newspapers should be commended for serving the purpose that the Founding Fathers saw so clearly. In revealing the workings of government that led to the Vietnam war, the newspapers nobly did precisely that which the Founders hoped and trusted they would do.

The Government's case here is based on premises entirely different from those that guided the Framers of the First Amendment. The Solicitor General has carefully and emphatically stated:

"Now, Mr. Justice [Black], your construction of . . . [the First Amendment] is well known, and I certainly respect it. You say that no law means no law, and that should be obvious. I can only say, Mr. Justice, that to me it is equally obvious that 'no law' does not mean 'no law', and I would seek to persuade the Court that that is true. . . . [T] here are other parts of the Constitution that grant powers and responsibilities to the Executive, and . . . the First Amendment was not intended to make it impossible for the Executive to function or to protect the security of the United States."

And the Government argues in its brief that in spite of the First Amendment, "[t] he authority of the Executive Department to protect the nation against publication of information whose disclosure would endanger the national security stems from two interrelated sources: the constitutional power of the President over the conduct of foreign affairs and his authority as Commander-in-Chief."

In other words, we are asked to hold that despite the First Amendment's emphatic command, the Executive Branch, the Congress, and the Judiciary can make laws enjoining publication of current news and abridging freedom of the press in the name of "national security." The Government does not even attempt to rely on any act of Congress. Instead it makes the bold and dangerously far-reaching contention that the courts should take it upon themselves to "make" a law abridging freedom of the press in the name of equity, presidential power, and national security, even when the representatives of the people in Congress have adhered to the command of the First Amendment and refused to make such a law. . . . To find that the President has "inherent power" to halt the publication of news by resort to the courts would wipe out the First Amendment and destroy the fundamental liberty and security of the very people the Government hopes to make "secure." No one can read the history of the adoption of the First Amendment without being convinced beyond any doubt that it was injunctions like those sought here that Madison and his collaborators intended to outlaw in this Nation for all time.

The word "security" is a broad, vague generality whose contours should not be invoked to abrogate the fundamental law embodied in the First Amendment. The guarding of military and diplomatic secrets at the expense of informed representative government provides no real security for our Republic. The Framers of the First Amendment, fully aware of both the need to defend a new nation and the abuses of the English and Colonial Governments, sought to give this new society strength and security by providing that freedom of speech, press, religion, and assembly should not be abridged. This thought was eloquently expressed in 1937 by Mr. Chief Justice Hughes—great man and great Chief Justice that he was—when the Court held a man could not be punished for attending a meeting run by Communists.

"The greater the importance of safeguarding the community from incitements to the overthrow of our institutions by force and violence, the more imperative is the need to preserve inviolate the constitutional rights of free speech, free press and free assembly in order to maintain the opportunity for free political discussion, to the end that government may be responsive to the will of the people and that changes, if desired, may be obtained by peaceful means. Therein lies the security of the Republic, the very foundation of constitutional government." . . .

Mr. Justice Brennan, concurring.

I

I write separately in these cases only to emphasize what should be apparent: that our judgments in the present cases may not be taken to indicate the propriety, in the future, of issuing temporary stays and restraining orders to block the publication of material sought to be suppressed by the Government. So far as I can determine, never before has the United States sought to enjoin a newspaper from publishing information in its possession. The relative novelty of the questions presented, the necessary haste with which decisions were reached, the magnitude of the interests asserted, and the fact that all the parties have concentrated their arguments upon the question whether permanent restraints were proper may have justified at least some of the restraints heretofore imposed in these cases. Certainly it is difficult to fault the several courts below for seeking to assure that the issues here involved were preserved for ultimate review by this Court. But even if it be assumed that some of the interim restraints were proper in the two cases before us, that assumption has no bearing upon the propriety of similar judicial action in the future. To begin with, there has now been ample time for reflection and judgment; whatever values there may be in the preservation of novel questions for appellate review may not support any restraints in the future. More important, the First Amendment stands as an absolute bar to the imposition of judicial restraints in circumstances of the kind presented by these cases.

II

The error that has pervaded these cases from the outset was the granting of any injunctive relief whatsoever, interim or otherwise. The entire thrust of the Government's claim throughout these cases has been that publication of the material sought to be enjoined "could," or "might," or "may" prejudice the national interest in various ways. But the First Amendment tolerates absolutely no prior judicial restraints of the press predicated upon surmise or conjecture that untoward consequences may result. Our cases, it is true, have indicated that there is a single, extremely narrow class of cases in which the First Amendment's ban on prior judicial restraint may be overridden. Our cases have thus far indicated that such cases may arise only when the Nation "is at war," . . . during which times "[n] o one would question but that a government might prevent actual obstruction to its recruiting service or the publication of the sailing dates of transports or the number and location of troops." . . . Even if the present world situation were assumed to be tantamount to a time of war, or if the power of presently available armaments would justify even in peacetime the suppression of information that would set in motion a nuclear holocaust, in neither of these actions has the Government presented or even alleged that publication of items from or based upon the material at issue would cause the happening of an event of that nature. "[T] he chief purpose of [the First Amendment's] guaranty [is] to prevent previous restraints upon publication." . . . Thus, only governmental allegation and proof that publication must inevitably, directly, and immediately cause the occurrence of an event kindred to imperiling the safety of a transport already at sea can support even the issuance of an interim restraining order. In no event may mere conclusions be sufficient: for if the Executive Branch seeks judicial aid in preventing publication, it must inevitably submit the basis upon which that aid is sought to scrutiny by the judiciary. And therefore, every restraint issued in this case, whatever its form, has violated the First Amendment—and not less so because that restraint was justified as necessary to afford the courts an opportunity to examine the claim more thoroughly. Unless and until the Government has clearly made out its case, the First Amendment commands that no injunction may issue. . . .

Mr. Justice White, with whom Mr. Justice Stewart joins, concurring.

I concur in today's judgments, but only because of the concededly extraordinary protection against prior restraints enjoyed by the press under our constitutional system. I do not say that in no circumstances would the First Amendment permit an injunction against publishing information about government plans or operations. Nor, after examining the materials the Government characterizes as the most sensitive and destructive, can I deny that revelation of these documents will do substantial damage to public interests. Indeed, I am confident that their disclosure will have that result. But I nevertheless agree that the United States has not satisfied the very heavy burden that it must meet to warrant an injunction against publication in these cases, at least in the absence of express and appropriately limited congressional authorization for prior restraints in circumstances such as these.

The Government's position is simply stated: The responsibility of the Executive for the conduct of the foreign affairs and for the security of the Nation is so basic that the President is entitled to an injunction against publication of a newspaper story whenever he can convince a court that the information to be revealed threatens "grave and irreparable" injury to the public interest; and the injunction should issue whether or not the material to be published is classified, whether or not publication would be lawful under relevant criminal statutes enacted by Congress, and regardless of the circumstances by which the newspaper came into possession of the information.

At least in the absence of legislation by Congress, based on its own investigations and findings, I am quite unable to agree that the inherent powers of the Executive and the courts reach so far as to authorize remedies having such sweeping potential for inhibiting publications by the press. Much of the difficulty inheres in the "grave and irreparable danger" standard suggested by the United States. If the United States were to have judgment under such a standard in these cases, our decision would be of little guidance to other courts in other cases, for the material at issue here would not be available from the Court's opinion or from public records, nor would it be published by the press. Indeed, even today where we hold that the United States has not met its burden, the material remains sealed in court records and it is properly not discussed in today's opinions. Moreover, because the material poses substantial dangers to national interests and because of the hazards of criminal sanctions, a responsible press may choose never to publish the more sensitive materials. To sustain the Government in these cases would start the courts down a long and hazardous road that I am not willing to travel, at least without congressional guidance and direction.

It is not easy to reject the proposition urged by the United States and to deny relief on its good-faith claims in these cases that publication will work serious damage to the country. But that discomfiture is considerably dispelled by the infrequency of prior-restraint cases. Normally, publication will occur and the damage be done before the Government has either opportunity or grounds for suppression. So here, publication has already begun and a substantial part of the threatened damage has already occurred. The fact of a massive breakdown in security is known, access to the documents by many unauthorized people is undeniable, and the efficacy of equitable relief against these or other newspapers to avert anticipated damage is doubtful at best.

What is more, terminating the ban on publication of the relatively few sensitive documents the Government now seeks to suppress does not mean that the law either requires or invites newspapers or others to publish them or that they will be immune from criminal action if they do. Prior restraints require an unusually heavy justification under the First Amendment; but failure by the Government to justify prior restraints does not measure its constitutional entitlement to a conviction for criminal publication. That the Government mistakenly chose to proceed by injunction does not mean that it could not successfully proceed in another way. . . .

Mr. Chief Justice Burger, dissenting.

So clear are the constitutional limitations on prior restraint against expression, that from the time of Near v Minnesota, . . . until recently in Organization for a Better Austin v Keefe, . . . we have had little occasion to be concerned with cases involving prior restraints against news reporting on matters of public interest. There is, therefore, little variation among the members of the Court in terms of resistance to prior restraints against publication. Adherence to this basic constitutional principle, however, does not make these cases simple. In these cases, the imperative of a free and unfettered press comes into collision with another imperative, the effective functioning of a complex modern government and specifically the effective exercise of certain constitutional powers of the Executive. Only those who view the First Amendment as an absolute in all circumstances—a view I respect, but reject—can find such cases as these to be simple or easy.

These cases are not simple for another and more immediate reason. We do not know the facts of the cases. No District Judge knew all the facts. No Court of Appeals judge knew all the facts. No member of this Court knows all the facts.

Why are we in this posture, in which only those judges to whom the First Amendment is absolute and permits of no restraint in any circumstances or for any reason, are really in a position to act?

I suggest we are in this posture because these cases have been conducted in unseemly haste. Mr. Justice Harlan covers the chronology of events demonstrating the hectic pressures under which these cases have been processed and I need not restate them. The prompt setting of these cases reflects our universal abhorrence of prior restraint. But prompt judicial action does not mean unjudicial haste.

Here, moreover, the frenetic haste is due in large part to the manner in which the Times proceeded from the date it obtained the purloined documents. It seems reasonably clear now that the haste precluded reasonable and deliberate judicial treatment of these cases and was not warranted. The precipitate action of this Court aborting trials not yet completed is not the kind of judicial conduct that ought to attend the disposition of a great issue.

The newspapers make a derivative claim under the First Amendment; they denominate this right as the public "right to know"; by implication, the Times asserts a sole trusteeship of that right by virtue of its journalistic "scoop." The right is asserted as an absolute. Of course, the First Amendment right itself is not an absolute, as Justice Holmes so long ago pointed out in his aphorism concerning the right to shout "fire" in a crowded theater if there was no fire. There are other exceptions, some of which Chief Justice Hughes mentioned by way of example in Near v Minnesota. There are no doubt other exceptions no one has had occasion to describe or discuss. Conceivably such exceptions may be lurking in these cases and would have been flushed had they been properly considered in the trial courts, free from unwarranted deadlines and frenetic pressures. An issue of this importance should be tried and heard in a judicial atmosphere conducive to thoughtful, reflective deliberation, especially when haste, in terms of hours, is unwarranted in light of the long period the Times, by its own choice, deferred publication.

It is not disputed that the Times has had unauthorized possession of the documents for three to four months, during which it has had its expert analysts studying them, presumably digesting them and preparing the material for publication. During all of this time, the Times, presumably in its capacity as trustee of the public's "right to know," has held up publication for purposes it considered proper and thus public knowledge was delayed. No doubt this was for a good reason; the analysis of 7,000 pages of complex material drawn from a vastly greater volume of material would inevitably take time and the writing of good news stories takes time. But why should the United States Government, from whom this information was illegally acquired by someone, along with all the counsel, trial judges, and appellate judges be placed under needless pressure? After these months of deferral, the alleged "right to know" has somehow and suddenly become a right that must be vindicated instanter.

Would it have been unreasonable, since the newspaper could anticipate the Government's objections to release of secret material, to give the Government an opportunity to review the entire collection and determine whether agreement could be reached on publication? Stolen or not, if security was not in fact jeopardized, much of the material could no doubt have been declassified, since it spans a period ending in 1968. With such an approach—one that great newspapers have in the past practiced and stated editorially to be the duty of an honorable press—the newspapers and Government might well have narrowed the area of disagreement as to what was and was not publishable, leaving the remainder to be resolved in orderly litigation, if necessary. To me it is hardly believable that a newspaper long regarded as a great institution in American life would fail to perform one of the basic and simple duties of every citizen with respect to the discovery or possession of stolen property or secret government documents. That duty, I had thought—perhaps naively—was to report forthwith, to responsible public officers. This duty rests on taxi drivers, Justices, and the New York Times. The course followed by the Times, whether so calculated or not, removed any possibility of orderly litigation of the issues. If the action of the judges up to now has been correct, that result is sheer happenstance.

Our grant of the writ of certiorari before final judgment in the Times case aborted the trial in the District Court before it had made a complete record pursuant to the mandate of the Court of Appeals for the Second Circuit.

The consequence of all this melancholy series of events is that we literally do not know what we are acting on. As I see it we have been forced to deal with litigation concerning rights of great magnitude without an adequate record, and surely without time for adequate treatment either in the prior proceedings or in this Court. It is interesting to note that counsel on both sides, in oral argument before this Court, were frequently unable to respond to questions on factual points. Not surprisingly they pointed out that they had been working literally "around the clock" and simply were unable to review the documents that give rise to these cases and were not familiar with them. This Court is in no better posture. . . .

December 18, 1972
Speech by Clay T. Whitehead, Director of the Office of Telecommunications Policy, Executive Office of the President

*The background, context, and import of this expression of the
carrot-and-stick approach to commercial broadcasters are set
out in detail in chapter 5. The text, from Whitehead's office, is
unedited.*

*At the time of this publication, a variety of adaptations of
the legislation Whitehead describes were current as proposals in
the Congress.*

In this calm during the holidays, we in Washington are thinking
ahead to 1973; among other things, planning our testimony before Congressional committees. For my part, I am particularly concerned about
testimony on broadcast license renewal legislation. Broadcasters are making a determined push for some reasonable measure of license renewal
security. Right now they are living over a trap door the FCC can spring at
the drop of a competing application or other renewal challenge. That is a
tough position to be in, and, considering all the fuss about so-called
"intimidation," you would think that there wouldn't be much opposition
to giving broadcasters a little more insulation from government's hand on
that trap door.

But there *is* opposition. Some tough questions will be asked—even
by those who are sympathetic to broadcasters. Questions about minority
groups' needs and interests. Questions about violence. Questions about
children's programming; about reruns; about commercials; about objectivity in news and public affairs programming—in short, all questions about
broadcasters' performance in fulfilling their public trust. These are questions the public is asking. Congress is asking the questions, too; Senator
Pastore on violence; Senator Moss on drug ads; Representative Staggers on
news misrepresentations. Despite this barrage of questioning, the Congress
is being urged to grant longer license terms and renewal protection to
broadcasters. Before voting it up, down, or around, the Congress will have
to judge the broadcasters' record of performance.

And where do we see that performance? It leaps out at you every
time you turn on a TV set, and it's definitely not all that it could be. How
many times do you see the rich variety, diversity, and creativity of
America represented on the TV screen? Where is the evidence of broadcasters doing their best to serve their audiences, rather than serving those
audiences up to sell to advertisers? And, most disturbing of all, how do
broadcasters demonstrate that they are living up to the obligation—as the
FCC puts it—to "assume and discharge responsibility for planning, select-

ing, and supervising all matter broadcast by the stations, whether such matter is produced by them or provided by networks or others."

It's been easy for broadcasters to give lip service to the uniquely American principle of placing broadcasting power and responsibility at the local level. But it has also been easy—too easy—for broadcasters to turn around and sell their responsibility along with their audiences to a network at the going rate for affiliate compensation.

The ease of passing the buck to make a buck is reflected in the steady increase in the amount of network programs carried by affiliates between 1960 and 1970. It took the FCC's prime time rule to reverse this trend, but even so, the average affiliate still devotes over 61% of his schedule to network programs. This wouldn't be so bad if the stations really exercised some responsibility for the programs and commercials that come down the network pipe. But all that many affiliates do is flip the switch in the control room to "network," throw the "switch" in the mailroom to forward viewer complaints to the network, sit back, and enjoy the fruits of a very profitable business.

Please don't misunderstand me when I stress the need for more local responsibility. I'm not talking about locally-produced programs, important though they are. I'm talking now about licensee responsibility for *all* programming, including the programs that come from the network.

This kind of local responsibility is the keystone of our private enterprise broadcast system operating under the First Amendment protections. But excessive concentration of control over broadcasting is as bad when exercised from New York as when exercised from Washington. When affiliates consistently pass the buck, to the networks, they're frustrating the fundamental purposes of the First Amendment's free press provision.

The press isn't guaranteed protection because it's guaranteed to be balanced and objective—to the contrary, the Constitution recognizes that balance and objectivity exist only in the eye of the beholder. The press *is* protected because a free flow of information and giving each "beholder" the opportunity to inform himself is central to our system of government. In essence, it's the right to learn instead of the right to be taught. The broadcast press has an obligation to serve this free flow of information goal by giving the audience the chance to pick and choose among a wide range of diverse and competing views on public issues.

This may all seem rather philosophical. Cynics may argue that all television, even the news, is entertainment programming. But in this age when television is the most relied upon and, surprisingly, the most credible of our media, we must accept this harsh truth: the First Amendment is meaningless if it does not apply fully to broadcasting. For too long we have been interpreting the First Amendment to fit the 1934 Communications Act. As many of you know, a little over a year ago I suggested ways to correct this inversion of values. One way is to eliminate the FCC's Fairness Doctrine as a means of enforcing the broadcasters' fairness obligation to provide reasonable opportunity for discussion of contrasting views on public issues.

Virtually everyone agrees that the Fairness Doctrine enforcement is a mess. Detailed and frequent court decisions and FCC supervision of broadcasters' journalistic judgment are unsatisfactory means of achieving the First Amendment goal for a free press. The FCC has shown signs of making improvements in what has become a chaotic scheme of Fairness Doctrine enforcement. These improvements are needed. But the basic Fairness Doctrine approach for all its problems, was, is and for the time being will remain a necessity; albeit an unfortunate necessity. So, while our long range goal should be a broadcast media structure just as free of government intrusion, just as competitive just as diverse as the print media, there are three harsh realities that make it impossible to do away with the Fairness Doctrine in the short run.

First, there is a scarcity of broadcasting outlets. *Second*, there is a substantial concentration of economic and social power in the networks and their affiliated TV stations. *Third*, there is a tendency for broadcasters and the networks to be self-indulgent and myopic in viewing the First Amendment as protecting only their rights as speakers. They forget that its primary purpose is to assure a free flow and wide range of information to the public. So we have license renewal requirements and the Fairness Doctrine as added requirements—to make sure that the networks and stations don't ignore the needs of those 200 million people sitting out there dependant on TV.

But this doesn't mean that we can forget about the broader mandates of the First Amendment, as it applies to broadcasting. We ought to begin where we can to change the Communications Act to fit the First Amendment. That has always been and continues to be the aim and intent of this Administration. We've got to make a start and we've got to do it now.

This brings me to an important first step the Administration is taking to increase freedom and responsibility in broadcasting.

OTP has submitted a license renewal bill for clearance through the Executive Branch, so the bill can be introduced in the Congress early next year. Our bill doesn't simply add a couple of years to the license term and guarantee profits as long as broadcasters follow the FCC's rules to the letter. Following rules isn't an *exercise* of responsibility; it's an *abdication* of responsibility. The Administration bill requires broadcasters to exercise their responsibility without the convenient crutch of FCC program categories or percentages.

The way we've done this is to establish two criteria the station must meet before the FCC will grant renewal. First, the broadcaster must demonstrate he has been substantially attuned to the needs and interests of the communities he serves. He must also make a good faith effort to respond to those needs and interests in all his programs, irrespective of whether those programs are created by the station, purchased from program suppliers, or obtained from a network. The idea is to have the broadcaster's performance evaluated from the perspective of the people in his community and not the bureaucrat in Washington.

Second, the broadcaster must show that he has afforded reasonable, realistic, and practical opportunities for the presentation and discussion of conflicting views on controversial issues.

I should add that these requirements have teeth. If a station can't demonstrate meaningful service to all elements of his community, the license should be taken away by the FCC. The standard should be applied with particular force to the large TV stations in our major cities, including the 15 stations owned by the TV networks and the stations that are owned by other large broadcast groups. These broadcasters, especially, have the resources to devote to community development, community service, and programs that reflect a commitment to excellence.

The community accountability standard will have special meaning for all network affiliates. They should be held accountable to their local audiences for the 61% of their schedules that are network programs, as well as for the programs they purchase or create for local origination.

For four years, broadcasters have been telling this Administration that, if they had more freedom and stability, they would use it to carry out their responsibilities. We have to believe this, for if broadcasters were simply masking their greed and actually seeking a so-called "license to steal," the country would have to give up on the idea of private enterprise broadcasting. Some are urging just that; but this Administration remains unshaken in its support of the principles of freedom and responsibility in a private enterprise broadcasting system.

But we are equally unshaken in our belief that broadcasters must do more to exercise the responsibility of private enterprise that is the prerequisite of freedom. Since broadcasters' success in meeting their responsibility will be measured at license renewal time, they must demonstrate it across the board. They can no longer accept network standards of taste, violence, and decency in programming. If the programs or commercials glorify the use of drugs; if the programs are violent or sadistic; if the commercials are false or misleading, or simply intrusive and obnoxious; the stations must jump on the networks rather than wince as the Congress and the FCC are forced to do so.

There is no area where management responsibility is more important than news. The station owners and managers cannot abdicate responsibility for news judgments. When a reporter or disc jockey slips in or passes over information in order to line his pocket, that's plugola, and management would take quick corrective action. But men also stress or suppress information in accordance with their beliefs. Will station licensees or network executives also take action against this ideological plugola?

Just as a newspaper publisher has responsibility for the wire service copy that appears in his newspaper—so television station owners and managers must have full responsibility for what goes out over the public's airwaves—no matter what the origin of the program. There should be no place in broadcasting for the "rip and read" ethic of journalism

Just as publishers and editors have professional responsibility for the news they print, station licensees have final responsibility for news balance—whether the information comes from their own newsroom or from a distant network. The old refrain that, quote, "We had nothing to do with that report, and could do nothing about it," is an evasion of responsibility and unacceptable as a defense.

Broadcasters and networks took decisive action to insulate their news departments from the sales departments, when charges were made that news coverage was biased by commercial considerations. But insulating station and network news departments from management oversight and supervision has *never* been responsible and *never* will be. The First Amendment's guarantee of a free press was not supposed to create a privileged class of men called journalists, who are immune from criticism by government or restraint by publishers and editors. To the contrary, the working journalist, if he follows a professional code of ethics, gives up the right to present his personal point of view when he is on the job. He takes on a higher responsibility to the institution of a free press, and he cannot be insulated from the management of that institution.

The truly professional journalist recognizes his responsibility to the institution of a free press. He realizes that he has no monopoly on the truth; that a pet view of reality can't be insinuated into the news. Who else but management, however, can assure that the audience is being served by journalists dedicated to the highest professional standards? Who else but management can or should correct so-called professionals who confuse sensationalism with sense and who dispense elitist gossip in the guise of news analysis?

Where there are only a few sources of national news on television, as we now have, editorial responsibility must be exercised more effectively by local broadcasters and by network management. If they do not provide the checks and balances in the system, who will?

Station managers and network officials who fail to act to correct imbalance or consistent bias from the networks—or who acquiesce by silence—can only be considered willing participants, to be held fully accountable by the broadcaster's community at license renewal time.

Over a year ago, I concluded a speech to an audience of broadcasters and network officials by stating that: "There is a world of difference between the *professional* responsibility of a free press and the *legal* responsibility of a regulated press. . . . Which will you be—private business or government agent?—a responsible free press or a regulated press? You cannot have it both ways—neither can government nor your critics." I think that my remarks today leave no doubt that this Administration comes out on the side of a responsible free press.

Notes

Chapter One

1. *Washington Post*, April 1, 1973.
2. One of two handwritten notes to Kennedy now in the Kennedy Library, Cambridge, Mass., dated August 11, 1962.
3. Ralph de Toledano, *Nixon* (New York: Henry Holt, 1956).
4. Earl Mazo and Stephen Hess, *Nixon: A Political Portrait* (New York: Harper and Row, 1967), p. 47.
5. These data are from an unpublished seminar study by Marianne Rzepka.
6. *Washington Post*, December 4, 1948.
7. Richard Nixon, *Six Crises* (Garden City: Doubleday & Company, 1962), p. 86.
8. *Washington Post*, July 12, 1952.
9. Nixon, *Six Crises*, pp. 80–81.
10. There are many accounts of this episode in addition to Nixon's, of course. The most provocative is that of Garry Wills, *Nixon Agonistes* (New York: Houghton Mifflin, 1970). Wills takes the unique position that Eisenhower was a knowing and expert politician, and sees his handling of this Nixon crisis as masterful.
11. *Washington Post*, September 20, 1952.
12. Nixon, *Six Crises*, p. 103.
13. Theodore H. White, *The Making of the President 1960* (New York: Atheneum, 1971).
14. William J. Small, *Political Power and the Press* (New York: W. W. Norton and Company, 1972), pp. 120–21.
15. Ralph de Toledano, *Nixon*, p. 49.
16. James Keogh, *President Nixon and the Press* (New York: Funk & Wagnalls, 1972), pp. 2–3.
17. Daniel Moynihan, "The Presidency and the Press," *Commentary*, March 1971.

18. For details of Hoover's fascinating (and disastrous) press relations see Elmer E. Cornwell, Jr., *Presidential Leadership of Public Opinion* (Bloomington: Indiana University Press, 1965). This is a fine historical analysis of presidential media relations up to the early Kennedy days.
19. See Bernard Cohen, *The Press and Foreign Policy* (Princeton: Princeton University Press, 1963).
20. *Wall Street Journal*, March 18, 1969.
21. *New York Times*, December 20, 1969.
22. Ibid.
23. *Washington Post*, June 27, 1973.
24. Arthur Krock, "Mr. Kennedy's Management of the News," *Fortune*, March 1963.
25. Richard Nixon to Saul Pett, February 14, 1973; carried in most Associated Press member papers.

Chapter Two

1. Herbert Klein told the story with obvious enjoyment to this writer in the interview of March 15, 1972.
2. *New York Times*, September 24, 1969.
3. Magruder to Haldeman, White House memorandum, October 17, 1969 (see Documents of Significance).
4. *Newsweek*, November 17, 1969, p. 38.
5. Ibid.
6. *Newsweek*, November 17, 1969, p. 39.
7. Stanton's deposition of April 26, 1974, submitted as part of CBS's reply to an antitrust action.
8. William J. Small, *Political Power and the Press* (New York: W. W. Norton and Company, 1972), p. 127. Small has the name wrong and calls the lady Rosenthal.
9. William Safire, *Before the Fall* (Garden City: Doubleday & Company, Inc., 1975), p. 352.
10. Small, *Political Power and the Press*, p. 130.

Chapter Three

1. William J. Small, *Political Power and the Press*, (New York: W. W. Norton and Company, 1972), p. 123.
2. Julius Duscha, "The White House Watch over TV and the Press," *New York Times Sunday Magazine*, August 20, 1972, p. 96.
3. Ibid.
4. *New York Times*, October 29, 1973.
5. Chet Huntley, *Life*, July 17, 1970, p. 36.

6. David Wise, *The Politics of Lying* (New York: Randon House, Inc., 1973), p. 343.
7. *New York Times*, August 7, 1970.
8. *United States Government Manual 1973/74* (Washington, D.C.: Office of the Federal Register, 1973), p. 86.
9. U. S., Congress, Senate, Subcommittee on Communications, Committee on Commerce, *Overview of the Office of Telecommunications Policy*, 93rd Cong., 1st session, 20 February 1973, p. 2.
10. *New York Times*, January 21, 1974.
11. *New York Times*, August 26, 1974.

Chapter Four

1. The most complete account is in Sanford J. Unger, *The Papers and the Papers* (New York: E. P. Dutton and Co., Inc., 1972). Two chapters of William J. Small, *Political Power and the Press* (New York: W. W. Norton and Company, 1972), also provide an account; there are interesting detailed references throughout David Wise, *The Politics of Lying* (New York: Random House, Inc., 1973). There is an excellent summary of legal aspects in Harold L. Nelson and Dwight L. Teeter, Jr., *Law of Mass Communications* (New York: Foundation Press, 1973).
2. Unger, *Papers and the Papers*, p. 109.
3. Ibid., p. 110.
4. John Ehrlichman, affidavit, April 26, 1974, *United States* v. *Ehrlichman*.
5. See U.S., Congress, House, Committee on the Judiciary, *White House Surveillance Activities and Campaign Activities:* Hearing on H.Res. 803, 93rd Cong., 2d sess., May-June 1974, bk. VII, pt. 2.
6. Unger, *Papers and the Papers*, p. 128.
7. Associated Press dispatch, April 4, 1974.
8. Don R. Pember, "The Pentagon Papers Decision: More Questions than Answers," *Journalism Quarterly* 48, no. 3 (1972): 405.
9. Unger, *Papers and the Papers*, p. 172. The British journalist Henry Fairlie, after extensive research, concluded that there was nothing of consequence at all in the Papers, as a matter of fact, that was not already a matter of public record.
10. Pember, "The Pentagon Papers Decision."
11. Unger, *Papers and the Papers*, p. 197.
12. Quoted in Unger, *Papers and the Papers*, p. 198.
13. There are many accounts of the arguments before the Supreme Court. In addition to Unger and Pember, there is an account in Hillier Kreighbaum, *Pressures on the Press* (New York: Coward McCann, 1973), pp. 50 ff., and a special issue of the *Columbia*

Journalism Review, "The First Amendment on Trial," 10, no. 3 (1971). Both the *Times* and the *Post,* of course, carried elaborate accounts, including much that was verbatim. Excerpts from the Court's opinion are reprinted in the section Documents of Significance.

14. Unger, *Papers and the Papers,* p. 236.
15. Nelson and Teeter, *Law of Mass Communications,* p. 55.
16. Salant to William E. Porter, April 11, 1974.
17. A transcript of the program was widely circulated by CBS as part of "From Subpoena to Recommittal—an indexed collection of materials and reprints dealing with the case of the subpoenaing of outtakes of the CBS News broadcast The Selling of the Pentagon." The fat packet represents a high point of documentation in the media-government struggle; there is nothing like it for other controversies, alas.
18. Klein interview with station KNX, April 22, 1971.
19. Transcript from the *New York Times,* May 2, 1971.
20. *Christian Science Monitor,* April 20, 1971.
21. Associated Press dispatch, June 24, 1971.
22. From Jack Caulfield to John Dean, October 14, 1971.
23. Quoted in the *New York Times,* December 17, 1971.
24. Ibid.

Chapter Five

1. Carl Bernstein and Bob Woodward, *All the President's Men* (New York: Simon and Schuster, 1974), p. 316.
2. The first column was issued from Anderson's office dated December 30, 1971; individual papers often schedule such material at their convenience, however.
3. There is a lively, detailed account of the whole Schorr episode in David Wise, *The Politics of Lying* (New York: Random House, Inc., 1973), p. 382 ff.
4. Quoted in Wise, *The Politics of Lying,* p. 392n.
5. Martin Mayer, *About Television* (New York: Harper & Row, 1972), p. 321.
6. Mayer, *About Television,* p. 327.
7. *Newsweek,* January 1, 1973.
8. *Detroit Free Press,* April 28, 1973.
9. For a graphic and fascinating account of this process, see Lee M. Rich, "Sheriff Who?" *Advertising Age,* November 6, 1967.
10. *New York Times,* April 18, 1972.
11. *White House* memorandum, "Memorandum for CBS and ABC in Opposition to the Government's Motion to Strike Defenses and Bar,"

p. 4. This document and the accompanying 350 page appendix of supporting material is the source of most of the information in this section.

12. *New York Times,* June 15, 1972.
13. *New York Times,* June 18, 1972.
14. *Washington Post,* June 21, 1973.
15. *New York Times,* July 23, 1972.
16. *New York Times,* August 9, 1972.
17. See Joe McGinnis, *The Selling of the President 1968* (New York: Trident Press, 1969), especially the staff memoranda in the appendix.
18. *Washington Post,* May 16, 1974.
19. Barry Sussman, *The Great Coverup: Nixon and the Scandal of Watergate* (New York: New American Library, 1974), p. 128.
20. *Detroit News,* November 2, 1972.
21. *New York Times,* November 13, 1972.
22. The organization recently has changed its name to something a bit less collegiate—Society of Professional Journalists, Sigma Delta Chi.
23. This account of the meeting is drawn from a letter to the writer from Christo Nizamoff, editor of the weekly *Macedonia Tribune,* then president of the Indianapolis chapter of Sigma Delta Chi.
24. *Washington Post,* May 26, 1970.
25. Judith Martin to William E. Porter, June 24, 1974.

Chapter Six

1. *New York Times,* August 2, 1972.
2. *Newsweek,* November 5, 1973, p. 71.
3. Feders in a memo to his superior, William Small of CBS; quoted in the *New York Times,* November 13, 1973.
4. As published in the *Washington Post,* August 9, 1974.
5. Transcript published by the *New York Times,* August 10, 1974.
6. Personal communication from Thomas Winship, editor, *Boston Globe.*
7. William Safire, *Before the Fall* (Garden City: Doubleday & Company, Inc., 1975), p. 352 and several mentions.

Chapter Seven

1. *Rolling Stone,* April 26, 1973.
2. *New York Times,* June 7, 1973.
3. Fred W. Friendly, *Due to Circumstances Beyond Our Control* (New York: Random House, 1967), p. 92.
4. *New York Times,* December 17, 1973.

5. Christopher Porterfield to William E. Porter, January 28, 1975.
6. Dick Cavett and Christopher Porterfield, *Cavett* (New York: Harcourt Brace Jovanovich, 1974), p. 344.
7. From the original script; letter to this writer from Porterfield.
8. Jules Witcover, "Two Weeks that Shook the Press," *Columbia Journalism Review* 10, no. 3 (1971): 15.
9. Thomas Emerson, "Where We Stand: A Legal View," *Columbia Journalism Review* 10, no. 3 (1971): 34–39.
10. Roger Hilsman, *To Move a Nation* (Garden City: Doubleday & Co., Inc., 1967), p. 447.
11. Norman Isaacs, "There Will Be Worse to Come from This Court," *Columbia Journalism Review* 10, no. 3 (1971): 18.
12. See Vincent Blasi, *Press Subpoenas: An Empirical and Legal Analysis*, Reporters Committee for Freedom of the Press Legal Defense and Research Fund (Washington, D. C., 1971).
13. Personal communication from Edward Barrett.
14. *Los Angeles Times*, January 14, 1973.
15. *New York Times*, November 24, 1973.
16. Robert L. Bishop, "The Rush to Chain Ownership," *Columbia Journalism Review* 11, no. 4 (1972): 10.

Index